"Let's play twenty questions."

"Okay. But I ask the questions this time."

"Fine."

"If I guess it before five, I'll be really disappointed."

The corners of his lips twisted up in a smile and he said, "Don't insult me."

"Are you alive?"

"Yes."

"Do you live here?"

"Yes."

"Do I know you?"

"Yes."

"Did I make you up?"

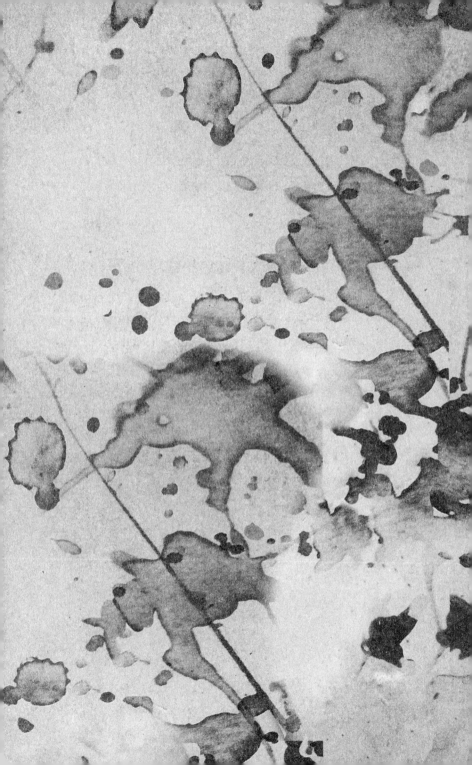

MADE YOU UP

by Francesca Zappia

Greenwillow Books
An Imprint of
HarperCollins *Publishers*

For my parents
(Told you so.)

Made You Up
Copyright © 2015 by Francesca Zappia. First published in hardcover in 2015; first paperback edition, 2017. All rights reserved. No part of this book may be used or reproduced in any manner whatsoever without written permission except in the case of brief quotations embodied in critical articles and reviews. Printed in the United States of America. For information address HarperCollins Children's Books, a division of HarperCollins Publishers, 195 Broadway, New York, NY 10007.
www.epicreads.com

Excerpt from "Mad Girl's Love Song" from *The Bell Jar* by Sylvia Plath. Copyright © 1971 by Harper & Row, Publishers, Inc. Reprinted by permission of HarperCollins Publishers.

The text of this book is set in Sabon.
Book design by Sylvie Le Floc'h

Library of Congress Cataloging-in-Publication Data
Zappia, Francesca.
Made you up / by Francesca Zappia.
pages cm
"Greenwillow Books."
Summary: "Armed with her camera and a Magic 8 Ball and her only ally (her little sister), Alex wages a war against her schizophrenia, determined to stay sane long enough to get into college"—Provided by publisher.
ISBN 978-0-06-229010-6 (hardback)—ISBN 978-0-06-229011-3 (paperback)
[1. Schizophrenia—Fiction. 2. Mental illness—Fiction.] I. Title.
PZ7.1.Z36Mad 2015
[Fic]—dc23   2014045003

17 18 19 20 21 PC/LSCH 10 9 8 7 6 5 4 3 2 1

Greenwillow Books

I shut my eyes and all the world drops dead;
I lift my lids and all is born again.
(I think I made you up inside my head.)

You really are not helpful at all.

It is decidedly so

I'm glad we're on the same page.

Prologue

The Freeing of the Lobsters

If I was good at the grocery store, I got a Yoo-hoo. If I was *really* good, I got to see the lobsters.

Today, I was really good.

My mother left me at the lobster tank in the middle of the main aisle while she went to get Dad's pork chops from the deli counter. Lobsters fascinated me. Everything from their name to their claws to their magnificent red had me hooked.

My hair was that red, the kind of red that looks okay on everything but people, because a person's hair is not supposed to be red. Orange, yes. Auburn, sure.

But not lobster red.

I took my pigtails, pressed them against the glass, and stared the nearest lobster straight in the eye.

Dad said my hair was lobster red. My mother said it was Communist red. I didn't know what a Communist was, but it didn't sound good. Even pressing my hair flat against the glass, I couldn't tell if my dad was right. Part of me didn't want either of them to be right.

"Let me out," said the lobster.

He always said that. I rubbed my hair against the glass like the tank was a genie's lamp and the action would stir up some magic. Maybe, somehow, I could get those lobsters out. They looked so sad, all huddled on top of one another, antennae twitching, claws rubber-banded together.

"Are you buying one?"

I saw Blue Eyes's reflection in the glass of the lobster tank before he spoke. Big blue eyes. Blueberry blue. No, that was too dark. Ocean blue. Too green. Blue like all the blue crayons I had, all melted into one.

The straw I'd jammed down the neck of my Yoo-hoo bottle dangled from my lips.

"Are you buying one?" he said again. I shook my head. He pushed his glasses up his nose, back into place on his golden-freckled cheeks. The dirty collar of his shirt slipped down to reveal a freckled shoulder. The stench of fish and pond scum clung to him.

"Did you know fossils of the clawed lobster date back to the Cretaceous?" he asked. I shook my head—I would have to ask Dad what a "Cretaceous" was—and took a long, slurping drink of Yoo-hoo.

He was staring at me and not the lobster. *"Animalia Arthropoda Malacostraca Decapoda Nephropidae,"* he said.

He tripped up a little on the last word, but it didn't matter since I hadn't understood anything that had come out of his mouth.

"I like scientific classification," he said.

"I don't know what that means," I said.

He pushed his glasses up again. *"Plantae Sapindales Rutaceae Citrus."*

"I don't know what that means, either."

"You smell like lemons."

I felt a flurry of delirious joy because he'd said, "You smell like lemons" instead of "Your hair is red."

I knew my hair was red. Everyone could see my hair was red. I did not, however, know that I smelled like fruit.

"You smell like fish," I told him.

He wilted, his freckled cheeks burning. "I know."

I looked around for my mother. She was still standing in line at the deli counter and didn't seem to have any plans to collect me soon. I grabbed his hand. He jumped and stared at the connection like something both magical and dangerous had happened.

"Do you wanna be friends?" I asked. He looked up and reset his glasses once again.

"Okay."

"Yoo-hoo?" I offered the drink.

"What's a Yoo-hoo?"

I pushed the drink a little closer to his face, in case he hadn't seen it. He took the bottle and inspected the straw.

"Mom said I shouldn't drink after someone else. It's unsanitary."

"But it's chocolate," I replied.

He looked uncertainly at the Yoo-hoo bottle before taking a wimpy sort of sip and shoving the bottle back my way. He didn't move for a second, didn't speak, but, eventually, he leaned over for another drink.

As it turned out, Blue Eyes knew a lot more than the scientific classifications of plants and animals. He knew everything. He knew the prices of everything in the store. He knew how much it would cost to buy all the lobsters in the lobster tank ($101.68, sales tax not included). He knew the names of presidents and what order they served in. He knew the Roman emperors, which impressed me even more. He knew that the circumference of the Earth was forty thousand kilometers, and that only the male cardinal was bright red.

But he really knew words.

Blue Eyes had a word for everything.

Words like *dactylion* and *brontide* and *petrichor*. Words whose meanings slipped from my grasp like water.

I didn't understand most of what he said, but I didn't mind. He was the first friend I'd ever had. The first real friend.

Also, I really liked holding his hand.

"Why do you smell like fish?" I asked him. We walked slowly as we talked, making long circles in the main aisle.

"I was in a pond," he said.

"Why?"

"I got thrown in."

"Why?"

He shrugged and reached down to scratch at his legs, which were covered in Band-Aids.

"Why are you hurt?" I asked.

"Animalia Annelida Hirudinea."

The words left his mouth like a curse. His cheeks flared red as he scratched more fervently. His eyes had gone all watery. We stopped at the tank.

One of the store employees came out from behind the seafood counter and, ignoring us, opened a hatch on top of the lobster tank. With one gloved hand, he reached in and pulled out Mr. Lobster. He closed the hatch and carried the lobster off.

And I got an idea.

"Come here." I pulled Blue Eyes to the back of the tank. He wiped his eyes. I stared at him until he stared back. "Will you help me get the lobsters out?"

He sniffed. Then he nodded.

I set my Yoo-hoo bottle on the floor and held my arms up. "Can you lift me?"

He wrapped his arms around my waist and lifted me. My head shot above the top of the lobster tank, my shoulders level with the hatch. I was a chubby kid and Blue Eyes probably should've snapped in half, but he only wobbled a bit, grunting.

"Just hold still," I told him.

The hatch had a handle near the edge. I grabbed it and pulled it open, shivering at the chilly blast of air that whooshed out.

"What are you doing?" Blue Eyes asked, his voice muffled by his strain and my shirt.

"Be quiet!" I said, looking around. No one had noticed us yet.

The lobsters were piled up just below the hatch. I plunged my hand in. Shock raced up my spine from the cold. My fingers closed around the nearest lobster.

I expected it to thrash its claws and curl and uncurl its tail. But it didn't. I felt like I was holding a heavy shell. I pulled it out of the water.

"Thank you," the lobster said.

"You're welcome," I replied. I dropped it on the ground.

Blue Eyes stumbled, but didn't lose his grip on me. The lobster sat there for a moment, then started crawling along the tile.

I reached in for another. And another. And another. And pretty soon the entire tank of lobsters was crawling across the tile floor of the Meijer supermarket. I didn't know where they were going, but they seemed to have a pretty good idea. Blue Eyes dropped me with a huff and we both landed in a puddle of cold water. He stared at me, his glasses clinging to the tip of his nose.

"Do you do this all the time?" he asked.

"No," I said. "Just today."

He smiled.

Then the yelling started. Hands grabbed my arms and jerked me to my feet. My mother was shouting at me, pulling me away from the tank. I looked past her. The lobsters were already gone. Freezing water dripped from my arm.

Blue Eyes still stood in the puddle. He picked up my abandoned Yoo-hoo bottle and waved good-bye. I tried to get my mother to stop, to go back so I could ask him his name.

She just walked faster.

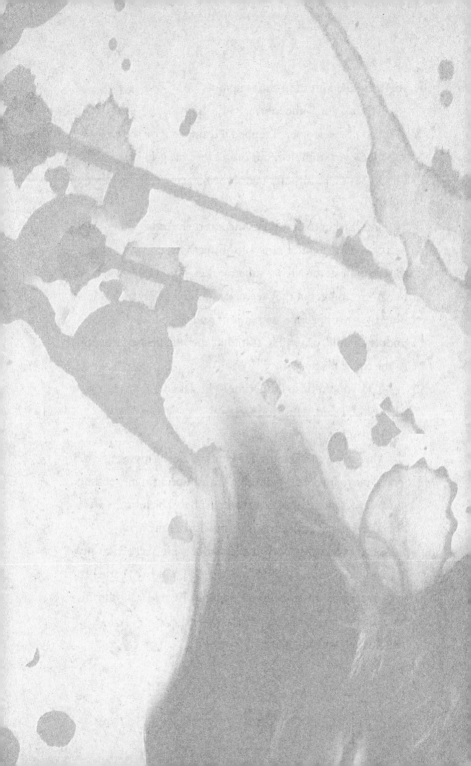

Part One | The Tank

Chapter
One

Sometimes I think people take reality for granted.

I mean like how you can tell the difference between a dream and real life. When you're in the dream you may not know it, but as soon as you wake up, you know that your dream was a dream and whatever happened in it, good or bad, wasn't real. Unless we're in the Matrix, this world is real, and what you do in it is real, and that's pretty much all you ever need to know.

People take that for granted.

For two years after that fateful day in the supermarket, I thought I'd really set the lobsters free. I thought they'd crawled away and found the sea and lived happily ever after. When I turned ten, my mother found out that I thought that I was some kind of lobster savior.

She also found out all lobsters looked bright red to me.

First she told me that I hadn't set any lobsters free. I'd gotten my arm into the tank before she'd appeared to pull me away, embarrassed. Then she explained that lobsters only turn bright red after they're boiled. I didn't believe her, because to me they had never been any other color. She never mentioned Blue Eyes, and I didn't need to ask. My first-ever friend was a hallucination: a sparkling entry on my new resume as a crazy person.

Then my mother had taken me to see a child therapist, and I'd gotten my first real introduction to the word *insane*.

Schizophrenia isn't supposed to manifest until a person's late teens, at the earliest, but I'd gotten a shot of it at just seven years old. I was diagnosed at thirteen. *Paranoid* got tacked on about a year later, after I verbally attacked a librarian for trying to hand me propaganda pamphlets for an underground Communist force operating out of the basement of the public library. (She'd always been a very suspect type of librarian—I refuse to believe donning rubber gloves to handle books is a normal and accepted practice, and I don't care what anyone says.)

My medication helped sometimes. I knew it was working when the world wasn't as colorful and interesting as it normally was. Like when I could tell the lobsters in the tank were not bright red. Or when I realized that checking my food for tracers was ridiculous (but did it anyway because it calmed the prickle of paranoia on the back of my neck). I also knew it was working when I couldn't remember things clearly, felt like I hadn't slept in days, and tried to put my shoes on backward.

Half the time, the doctors weren't even sure what the medicine would do. "Well, it should lessen the paranoia, delusions, and hallucinations, but we'll have to wait and see. Oh, and you'll probably feel tired sometimes. Drink a lot of fluids, too—you can get dehydrated easily. Also, it could cause a lot of fluctuation in your weight. Really, it's up in the air."

The doctors were oodles of help, but I developed my own system for figuring out what was real and what wasn't. I took pictures. Over time, the real remained in the photo while the hallucinations faded away. I discovered what sorts of things my mind liked to make up. Like billboards whose occupants wore gas masks and reminded passersby that poison gas from Hitler's Nazi Germany was still a very real threat.

I didn't have the luxury of taking reality for granted. And I wouldn't say I hated people who did, because that's just about everyone. I didn't hate them. They didn't live in my world.

But that never stopped me from wishing I lived in theirs.

Chapter
Two

The night before my first day of senior year at East Shoal High School, I sat behind the counter at Finnegan's diner, my eyes scanning the dark windows for signs of suspicious movement. Normally the paranoia wasn't so bad. I blamed it on the first-day thing. Getting chased out of the last school was one thing—starting at a new one was something completely different. I'd spent all summer at Finnegan's trying not to think about it.

"You know, if Finnegan was here, he'd call you crazy and tell you to get back to work."

I spun around. Tucker leaned against the door to the kitchen, hands jammed in the pockets of his apron, grinning at me. I would've snapped at him if he weren't my only informant about East Shoal—and my only friend. Gangly, bespectacled, hair black as an oil slick and always perfectly combed forward, Tucker was a busboy, waiter, and cashier here at Finnegan's, not to mention the smartest person I'd ever met.

He didn't know about me. So his saying that Finnegan would call me crazy was pure coincidence. Finnegan knew, of course; his sister was my latest therapist, the one who'd gotten me this job. But none of the other employees—like Gus, our mute, chain-smoking cook—had any idea, and I planned on keeping it that way.

"Har har," I replied, trying to act cool. *Beat down the crazy,* said the little voice in the back of my head. *Don't let it out, you idiot.*

The only reason I'd taken the job here was because I needed to appear normal. And maybe a little bit because my mother forced me to take it.

"Any other questions?" Tucker asked, walking over to lean against the counter next to me. "Or is the crusade over?"

"You mean the inquisition. And yes, it is." I kept my gaze from wandering back to the windows. "I've been in high school for three years already—East Shoal can't be that much different than Hillpark."

Tucker snorted. "East Shoal is different than *everywhere*. But I guess you'll find out tomorrow."

Tucker was the only person who seemed to think East Shoal wasn't the perfect place to be. My mother thought a new school was a great idea. My therapist insisted I'd do better there. Dad said it'd be okay, but he sounded like my mother had threatened him, and if he'd been here and not somewhere in Africa he would've told me what he really thought.

"Anyway," Tucker said, "weeknights aren't nearly as bad as weekends."

I could tell. It was ten-thirty, and the place was dead. And by dead, I mean it was like the entire possum population of suburban Indiana. Tucker was supposed to be training me to work nights. I'd only worked the day shift during summer, a plan concocted by my therapist that my mother had quickly blessed. But now that school was starting, we'd agreed I could work at night.

I grabbed Finnegan's Magic 8 Ball from behind the cash register. My thumb went for the red scuff mark on the back of the ball, trying to rub it out like I always did whenever I got bored. Tucker was now preoccupied with lining up a pepper shaker cavalry across from a hostile regiment of saltshaker footmen.

"We'll still get a few stragglers," he said. "Creepy late nighters. We got this really drunk guy one time—you remember him, Gus?"

A thin line of cigarette smoke trailed through the short-order window and up to the ceiling. In response to Tucker's question, several large puffs clouded the air. I was pretty sure Gus's cigarette wasn't real. If it was, we were breaking about a hundred health codes.

Tucker's expression went dark. His eyebrows drew together, his voice flattening out. "Oh. And there's Miles."

"Miles who?"

"He should be here soon." Tucker squinted at his condiment skirmish. "He comes on his way home from work. He's *all* yours."

I narrowed my eyes. "And why, exactly, is he *all* mine?"

"You'll see." He glanced up when a pair of headlights illuminated the parking lot. "He's here. Rule one: don't make eye contact."

"What, is he a gorilla? Is this Jurassic Park? Am I going to get attacked?"

Tucker shot me a serious look. "It's a definite possibility."

A kid our age walked through the door. He was wearing a white T-shirt and black jeans. A Meijer polo dangled from one hand. If this was Miles, he didn't give me much of a chance to make eye contact; he went straight to the corner table in my section and sat with his back to the wall. From experience, I knew that seat was the best vantage point in the room. But not everyone was as paranoid as I was.

Tucker leaned through the short-order window. "Hey, Gus. You have Miles's usual?"

Gus's cigarette smoke curled in the air as he handed over a cheeseburger and fries. Tucker took the plate, filled a glass with water, and plunked everything on the counter beside me.

I jumped when I realized Miles was staring at us over the rims of his glasses. A wad of cash had already been placed on the edge of the table.

"Is there something wrong with him?" I whispered. "You know . . . mentally?"

"He's definitely not like the rest of us." Tucker huffed and went back to building his armies.

He's not a Communist. He's not wired. Don't check under the table, idiot. He's just a kid who wants some food.

Miles lowered his eyes as I walked up.

"Hi!" I said, cringing even as the word left my mouth. Too perky. I coughed, scanned the windows on either side of the table. "Um, I'm Alex." I lowered my voice. "I'll be your waitress." I set the food and water down. "Can I get you anything else?"

"No, thank you." He finally looked up.

Several synapses imploded inside my brain. His *eyes.*

Those eyes.

His glare peeled away the layers of my skin and

pinned me to the spot. Blood rushed to my face, my neck, my ears. He had the bluest eyes I'd ever seen. And they were completely impossible.

My palms itched for my camera. I needed to take a picture of him. I needed to document this. Because the Freeing of the Lobsters hadn't been real, and neither was Blue Eyes. My mother had never mentioned him. Not to the therapists, or to Dad, or to anyone. He couldn't be real.

I screamed curses at Finnegan in my head. He'd forbidden me from bringing my camera to work after I'd photographed an irate man with an eye patch and a peg leg.

Miles nudged the wad of cash toward me with an index finger. "Keep the change," he muttered.

I grabbed it and raced back to the counter.

"*Hi!*" Tucker mimicked in a high falsetto.

"Shut up. I didn't sound like that."

"I can't believe he didn't bite your head off."

I shoved the wad of cash into the register and brushed my hair back with shaking hands. "Yeah," I said. "Me either."

While Tucker stepped out back for his break, I commandeered his condiment armies. Gus's cigarette smoke wafted toward the ceiling, pulled into the vent. The oscillating fan on the wall made the papers on the employee bulletin board flutter.

Halfway through my recreation of the Battle of the Bulge, I shook Finnegan's Magic 8 Ball to find out if the German saltshaker would be successful in his offensive.

Ask again later.

Useless thing. If the Allies had taken that advice, the Axis would have won the war. I kept myself from looking at Miles for as long as I could. But eventually my eyes wandered back to him, and I couldn't look away. He ate with stiff movements, like he was barely keeping himself from stuffing everything into his mouth. And every few seconds, his glasses slid down his nose and he pushed them back up.

He didn't move when I refilled his water. I stared at the top of his sandy-haired head as I poured, mentally urging him to look up.

I was so busy focusing that I didn't notice the cup was full until the water ran over the top. I dropped it in shock. The water splashed all over him—across his arm, down his shirt, into his lap. He stood up so fast his head smashed into the overhead light and the entire table tipped.

"I—oh, crap, I'm sorry—" I ran back to the counter where Tucker stood, a hand clamped over his mouth, his face turning red, and grabbed a towel.

Miles used his Meijer polo to absorb some of the water, but he was soaked.

"I am *so* sorry." I reached out to dry his arm, very aware

that my hands were still shaking.

He recoiled before I could touch him, glaring at me, the towel, back at me. Then he grabbed his polo, shoved his glasses up his nose, and escaped.

"It's fine," he muttered as he passed me. He was out the door before I could say another word.

I finished cleaning up the table, then trudged back to the counter.

Tucker, composed, took the dishes from me. "Bravo. Brilliant job."

"Tucker."

"Yes?"

"Shut up."

He laughed and disappeared into the kitchen.

Was that Blue Eyes?

I grabbed the Magic 8 Ball and rubbed the scuff mark as I looked down into its round window.

Better not tell you now.

Evasive little bitch.

Chapter
Three

The first thing I noticed about East Shoal High School was that it didn't have a bike rack. You know a school is run by stuck-up sons of bitches when it doesn't even have a bike rack.

I shoved Erwin behind the blocky green shrubs lining the school's front walk and stepped back to make sure the tires and handlebars were hidden. I didn't expect anyone to steal, touch, or notice him, since his rusty diarrhea color made people subconsciously avert their eyes, but I felt better knowing he was out of harm's way.

I checked my bag. Books, folders, notebooks, pens, and pencils. My cheap digital camera—one of the first things I'd bought when I'd gotten the job at Finnegan's—dangled from its strap around my wrist. I'd already taken a picture of four suspicious-looking squirrels lined up on the red brick wall outside my neighbor's house this morning, but other than that, the memory card was empty.

Then I did my perimeter check. Perimeter checks entailed three things: getting a 360-degree view of my surroundings, noting anything that seemed out of place—like the huge scorched spiral design covering the surface of the parking lot—and filing those things away in case they tried to sneak up on me later.

Kids funneled from their cars to the school, ignoring the men in black suits and red ties who stood at even intervals along the school's roof. I should've known public school would have some weird security. We just had normal security officers at The Hillpark School, my (former) private school.

I joined the procession of students—keeping an arm's-length distance between myself and the rest of them, because God knows who was bringing weapons to school these days—all the way to the guidance office, where I stood in line for four minutes to get my schedule. While I was there, I took a bunch of college brochures out of the stand in the corner and stuffed them in my backpack, ignoring the weird stares I got from the kid in front of me. I didn't take crap when it came to college—I had to get in, no matter how early I had to start or how many applications I had to send. If I was lucky, I could guilt-trip some scholarships out of a school or two, the way my parents had done with Hillpark.

It didn't matter how I did it; either I got in or I worked at Finnegan's for the rest of my life.

I realized everyone around me was wearing a uniform. Black pants, white button-down shirts, green ties. Gotta love the smell of institutional equality in the morning.

My locker was near the cafeteria. Only one other person was there, his locker right next to mine.

Miles.

Memories of Blue Eyes hit me rapid-fire, and I had to turn in a full circle to make sure my surroundings were normal. As I inched closer, I peered into his locker. Nothing unusual. I took a deep breath.

Be polite, Alex. Be polite. He won't kill you because of some water. He's not a hallucination. Be polite.

"Um, hi," I said, stepping up to my locker.

Miles turned, saw me, and jumped so badly his locker door banged against the one next to it and he almost tripped over his backpack on the floor. His glare burned a hole through my head.

"Sorry," I said. "Didn't mean to scare you."

When he didn't reply, I focused on my locker combination. I glanced at him as I tossed books into my locker. His expression hadn't changed.

"I, uh, I'm really sorry about the water." I held out my hand against my better judgment. My mother always said to be polite, no matter what. Even if the other person might have a knife concealed up his sleeve. "I'm Alex."

He quirked an eyebrow. The expression was so sudden, so perfect, and so obviously right that I almost laughed.

Slowly, so it looked like he thought he might burn himself by touching me, Miles reached out to shake my hand. His fingers were long and thin. Spidery, but strong.

"Miles," he replied.

"Okay, cool." We released our grips at the same time, hands shooting down to our sides. "Glad we got that out of the way. I'll see you later, then."

Go go go get away get away.

I walked away as quickly as I could. Had I just come into contact with Blue Eyes again after ten years? Oh God. Okay.

It wouldn't be that bad if he was real, would it? Just because my mother never mentioned him didn't mean he wasn't real. But what if he was an asshole?

Screw you, brain.

It wasn't until I got to the stairs that I realized I was being followed. The hairs on the back of my neck prickled, and I grabbed for my camera as I spun around.

Miles stood behind me.

"Are you doing that on purpose?" I asked.

"Doing what on purpose?" he replied.

"Walking a few steps behind me, close enough so I realize you're there but not so close you look creepy doing it. And staring."

He blinked. "No."

"It sure feels like you are."

"Maybe you're paranoid."

I stiffened.

He rolled his eyes. "Gunthrie?" he asked.

Mr. Gunthrie, AP English, first period. "Yes," I said.

Miles pulled a paper from his pocket, unfolded it, and held it out. His schedule. There, at the top of the page, was his name: *Richter, Miles J.* His first period was AP English 12, Gunthrie.

"Fine," I said. "But you don't have to be such a creeper about it." I turned and stalked the rest of the way up the stairs.

"Sucks being new, doesn't it?" Miles appeared beside me, a weird edge lacing his voice. Shivers worked their way up my arms.

"It's not so bad," I said through a clenched jaw.

"Either way," he said, "I think you have an inalienable right to know that dyeing your hair is against the dress code."

"It's not dyed," I snapped.

"Sure." Miles quirked the eyebrow again. "Sure it's not."

Chapter Four

When I walked into first period, all I could see of Mr. Gunthrie was a pair of thick-soled black boots propped on a class roster. The rest of him hid behind this morning's paper. I did a quick scan of the room, then twisted my way through tight rows of desks and stood in front of him, hoping he'd notice me.

He didn't.

"Excuse me."

A pair of eyes topped by a heavy line of eyebrow appeared over the paper. He was a stout guy, probably in his fifties, with close-cut, steel-gray hair. I took a step back from the desk, my books in front of my chest like a shield.

He lowered the paper. "Yes?"

"I'm new. I need a uniform."

"The bookstore sells them for about seventy."

"*Dollars?*"

"You can get a spare for free from the janitor, but it won't have the school crest. And don't expect it to fit. Or have been washed." He looked over my head at the clock on the wall. "If you could please take a seat."

I sat down with my back to the wall. The PA system crackled to life.

"Students of East Shoal, welcome back for another year of school." I recognized the weedy voice of Mr. McCoy, the principal. My mother and I had talked to him before. She loved him. I was unimpressed. "I hope you all had a great summer vacation, but now it's time to get back in the swing of things. If you don't have a school uniform, one can be purchased from the bookstore for a minimum fee."

I snorted. No bike rack, seventy-dollar uniforms, oblivious principal—this place was just rainbows and unicorns.

"Also," McCoy continued, "this is the yearly reminder that our beloved scoreboard's birthday, the anniversary of its donation to the school, is coming up in just a few short weeks. So everyone get ready, prepare your offerings, and be ready to celebrate this great occasion!"

The PA system went quiet. I stared at the ceiling. Did he say "offerings"?

For a *scoreboard*?

"ROLL CALL!"

Mr. Gunthrie's voice jerked me back to Earth. The talking of the other students in the room ceased. I got the sinking feeling that Gunnery Sergeant Hartman would be teaching us this year. I slipped my camera over the lip of the desk and began taking pictures.

"WHEN I CALL YOUR NAME, I WILL POINT TO A DESK. THAT IS YOUR DESK. THERE WILL BE NO SWITCHING, TRADING, OR COMPLAINING. IS THAT UNDERSTOOD?"

"YES, SIR!" came the united reply.

"GOOD. CLIFFORD ACKERLEY." Mr. Gunthrie pointed to the first desk of the first row.

"Here, sir!" A burly kid stood up and moved to his new seat.

"GOOD TO SEE YOU IN AP, ACKERLEY." Mr. Gunthrie moved down his list. "TUCKER BEAUMONT."

Tucker stood from somewhere on the side and went to sit behind Clifford. He saw me in the back and smiled. To my dismay, he looked even more hopelessly nerdy here—his school uniform starched straight, his arms full of textbooks and already-scribbled-on papers—the sort of nerdy that gets picked on by guys like Clifford Ackerley.

But I couldn't help giggling a little. It happened every

time I heard Tucker's last name. It always reminded me of Chevalier d'Eon, full name Charles-Geneviève-Louis-Auguste-André-Timothée d'Éon de Beaumont, a French spy who lived the second half of his life as a woman.

Mr. Gunthrie called a few more people before getting to Claude Gunthrie, who gave no indication that his father, barking orders at him, bothered him in the least.

I took pictures of everyone. I could analyze details later—I didn't plan on getting close enough to anyone to do it in person.

"CELIA HENDRICKS!"

Celia Hendricks had been assaulted by a cosmetics store. No hair was naturally that shade of yellow (and that was me talking, ha ha ha), and her real skin was locked inside a makeup shell. She wore a black skirt instead of pants, and it rode dangerously up her thigh.

Mr. Gunthrie didn't miss this.

"HENDRICKS, THAT SKIRT VIOLATES THE DRESS CODE ON SEVERAL LEVELS."

"But it's the first day of school, and I didn't know—"

"BULLSHIT."

I stared, wide-eyed, at Mr. Gunthrie, praying nothing about him was a figment of my imagination. Either he was badass, or I was dreaming.

"GO CHANGE, NOW."

With a huff, Celia stomped out of the room. Mr. Gunthrie sighed and returned to his list. A few more people shifted places.

"MILES RICHTER."

Miles yawned as he dragged his tall self across the room. He fell into his new seat. There were only two people left—me and a girl who'd been talking to Clifford before class had started. Maybe, just maybe, her last name would be between Ric- and Rid-.

"ALEXANDRA RIDGEMONT."

Damn.

Everyone turned to look at me as I sat down behind Miles. If they hadn't noticed me before, they did now—and the hair. Oh, the *hair* . . .

Stop it, idiot! It's fine, they're not looking at you. Okay, they are *looking at you. But they're not coming after you. You're okay. Everything's okay.*

"Alex is fine," I said weakly.

"MARIA WOLF."

"Ria!" the last girl said, almost skipping to her spot behind me. Her strawberry blond ponytail jumped happily as she went.

Mr. Gunthrie tossed the class list back onto his desk and stood at the front of the room, hands clasped behind his back, square jaw high.

"TODAY WE WILL HAVE PAIR DISCUSSIONS OF YOUR SUMMER READING. I WILL PICK THE PAIRS. THERE WILL BE NO SWITCHING, TRADING, OR COMPLAINING. IS THAT UNDERSTOOD?"

"YES, SIR!"

"GOOD."

As if he remembered all of our names after only seeing them once, Mr. Gunthrie pulled pairs out of thin air.

Being stuck in the seat behind Miles was my payment for getting to be partners with Tucker, I guess.

"I didn't know you'd be in my class!" I said when I raced out of my seat and slid into the chair behind his. He was the one person in this room who didn't give me the creeps. "And you weren't lying about this place."

"People around these parts don't lie about a thing like that." Tucker tipped an imaginary ten-gallon hat. "And you didn't tell me you were going to be in AP English. I could've told you. Mr. Gunthrie teaches the only one in the school." He held up the papers he'd scribbled on. "I already finished the discussion. He does the same first assignment every year. Hope you don't mind." He paused, frowning over my shoulder. "God. Hendricks is doing that thing again. I don't even see why she likes him."

Celia Hendricks, who'd returned wearing a baggy pair of black sweatpants, was leaning over her chair and doing some weird flips with her hair and whisper-calling Miles, who had his back to her. When he ignored her, she began launching balled-up pieces of notebook paper at his head.

"Why do you hate him so much?" I asked Tucker.

"I don't know if 'hate' is the right word," he replied. "'Am afraid of him,' 'wish he'd stop staring,' and 'think he's a lunatic' are more accurate."

"Afraid of him?"

"The whole school is."

"Why?"

"Because it's impossible to know what's going on in his head." Tucker looked back to me. "Have you ever seen a person completely change? Like, *completely* completely? So much that they don't even have the same facial expressions they used to? That's what happened to him."

I hesitated at Tucker's sudden seriousness. "Sounds creepy."

"It *was* creepy." Tucker concentrated on a design someone had etched into his desktop. "And then, he, you know. Had to be the *best* . . ."

"You . . . wait a minute . . . he's the valedictorian?"

I knew Tucker didn't like the valedictorian, but during his rants at work he'd never said who it was. Just that the kid didn't deserve it.

"It's not even that he's beating me!" Tucker hissed, casting a quick look back at Miles. "It's that he doesn't *try*. He doesn't even have to read the book! He just *knows* everything! I mean, he was sort of like that in middle school, but he was never the best. Half the time he didn't do his work because he thought it was pointless."

I looked back at Miles. He and Claude had apparently finished their discussion, and he'd fallen asleep on his desk. Someone had taped a paper sign to his back that said "Nazi" in black marker.

I shivered. I liked researching Nazis as much as the next war historian, but I would never use the term as a nickname. Nazis scared the daylights out of me. Either everyone at this school was an idiot, or Miles Richter really was as bad as Tucker was making him out to be.

"He has this ridiculous club, too," Tucker said. "The East Shoal Recreational Athletics Support Club. It's just the sort of obnoxious name he'd pick."

I swallowed the sudden unease in my throat. I knew the club name, but I hadn't known it was *his* club. The sign on Miles's back rose and fell with his breathing.

"Um. Hey." Tucker nudged me. "Don't let him try to pull anything on you, okay?"

"Pull anything? Like what?"

"Like unscrewing your chair from your desk, or tearing a hole in the bottom of your backpack."

"Ohhhkay," I said, frowning. "You know, now I'm

pretty sure he's either a gorilla, a T-Rex, or a poltergeist. Anything else I should know about him?"

"Yeah," Tucker said. "If he ever starts talking with a German accent, call me."

Chapter Five

My next three classes of the day were like the first. I walked into the classrooms and spun in a circle, checking everything. If I found something strange—like a World War II–era propaganda poster on the wall—I took a picture of it. I was asked four times if my hair was dyed. My AP Macro teacher let me know it was against the rules. I told him it was natural. He didn't believe me. I showed him the picture of my mother and my little sister, Charlie, that I always carried with me, because their hair was the same. He sort of believed me. I sat in the chair closest to the door and kept a watchful eye on him for the rest of the period.

The cafeteria was huge, so there were plenty of open spots. That was a good thing, because no one paid attention to me in the seat against the wall, picking through my food for Communist tracers. Mr. McCoy came over the PA to make another announcement about the scoreboard. People stopped talking and eating to snicker about it, but no one seemed surprised.

Miles Richter was in all of my AP classes.

My fifth period, study hall, was the only class he wasn't in. I still wasn't sure what Tucker had meant when he'd told me not to let Miles pull anything on me. He hadn't done anything Tucker had warned me about, but he certainly hadn't ignored me.

Pre-lunch, when I dropped my pencil in AP U.S. History, he kicked it to the far side of the room before I could pick it up. Because he leaned back and looked at me like, *What are you going to do about it?* I shoved his backpack off his desk.

In AP Government that afternoon, he "accidentally" stepped on my shoelace and I nearly fell on my face. When the teacher passed our first homework assignments down the rows, I gave Miles one that had "accidentally" been ripped in half.

In AP Chemistry, Ms. Dalton seated us in alphabetical order and handed out lab notebooks, which look like notebooks on the outside but are filled with graph paper and make you want to kill yourself. She dropped mine onto my desk with a loud *THWUMP*.

I kept a careful eye on the back of Miles's neck as I wrote my name on the cover. It turned out lopsided and scratchy, but still legible. Good enough.

"I figured we'd start off the school year with a little icebreaker lab," Mrs. Dalton said with a certain lazy cheerfulness as she returned to her desk, popped open a Diet Coke, and chugged half of it down in one go. "Nothing hard, of course. I'm going to assign lab partners and you can get to know each other."

I suspected bad karma sneaking up on me with a nine iron. Probably because of the time I flushed Charlie's entire line of black pawns down the toilet and told her Santa didn't exist.

Drawing slips of paper from a beaker filled with names, Mrs. Dalton called out pairs, and I watched the desks slowly empty and partners migrate to lab tables stationed around the edge of the room.

"Alexandra Ridgemont," Ms. Dalton said.

Karma prepared to swing.

"And Miles Richter."

Direct hit. Results: minor concussion. May have trouble walking, seeing. Should not engage in any strenuous activity or operate heavy machinery.

I got to the lab table before Miles even left his seat. A survey paper waited for us. I checked the kids on the other

side of the table—they didn't look remotely threa\
but the worst ones were always the least threatening-
cabinets above my head, and the drain in the sink.

"Well, let's get this over with," I said when Miles
arrived. He didn't answer, just pulled his pen from behind
his ear and flipped open his notebook. I braced my feet
farther apart when it felt like the ground was skewing to
the left.

I waited until he was done writing. "Ready?"

"You can go first." He pushed his glasses up. I wanted
to grab them off his face and pulverize them.

I grabbed the paper instead. "First question: 'What's
your full name?'"

"Wow. This is going to be stupid." It was the first
reasonable thing he'd said all day. "Miles James Richter."

I wrote it down. "Alexandra Victoria Ridgemont."

"Well, we both have middle names that don't fit." Out
came the Magnificent Quirked Eyebrow. "Next."

"Birthday?"

"May twenty-ninth, 1993."

"April fifteenth, same year," I said. "Siblings?"

"None."

No wonder he was such a brat. Only child. He was
probably rich, too.

"I have a sister, Charlie. Any pets?"

"A dog." Miles wrinkled his nose when he said it, which didn't surprise me—I imagined that Miles was sort of like an overgrown house cat. Slept a lot. Always looked bored. Liked to play with his food before he ate it.

I watched a ladybug crawl along the edge of the sink. I was pretty sure it wasn't real—its spots were shaped like stars. I'd left my camera in my backpack. "None. My dad's allergic."

Miles grabbed the paper from me and looked it over. "You'd think they could bother to make the questions a little more interesting. 'Favorite Color'? What can that possibly tell you about a person? Your favorite color could be chartreuse, and it wouldn't make a damn bit of difference."

Then, without waiting for me to answer the question, he wrote "chartreuse" under "Favorite Color."

It was the most animated I'd seen him all day. Listening to him rant relaxed me, in a weird kind of way. If he was an angry ranting asshole, he wasn't Blue Eyes.

"Then yours is mauve," I said, writing it in the blank.

"And look—'Favorite Food'? What's that going to tell me?"

"Agreed. What do you like to eat? Pickled frog hearts?" I pressed my pen to my bottom lip and mulled it over. "Yeah. You love pickled frog hearts."

We got through a few more questions. I knew I wasn't

imagining the awed looks of our comrades across the table. When we got to "Pet Peeves," Miles said, "When people say 'catsup' instead of 'ketchup.' It's a condiment, not animal vomit." He paused a moment and said, "And that one's true."

"I can't stand it when people get history wrong," I said. "Like saying that Columbus was the first explorer to land on North America, when he didn't even land on North America, and the first explorer was Leif Ericson. And that one is also true."

We answered a few more, and by the time we got near the end, something strange started happening to his voice.

It was rougher, somehow. Less fluent. His *th*'s slurred together, and his *w*'s started sounding like *v*'s. The group across the table stared at him like it was the advent of the apocalypse.

I moved down to the last question. "Thank God, we're almost done. What's one thing you remember from your childhood?"

"*Animalia Annelida Hirudinea.*" Miles bit the end of his pen like he wished he hadn't said it. He didn't look at me, but stared at the two silver faucets arching over the sink basin.

Those words . . . the bandages. The pain I hadn't understood. The Yoo-hoo. The smell of fish.

A chill seeped from my head to my feet, freezing me to the spot. I stared at him. Sandy brown hair that stuck up all over the place. Metal-frame glasses. Golden freckles sprinkled over nose and cheekbones. Blue eyes.

Stop looking at him, idiot! He'll think you like him, or something!

I didn't like him. He wasn't even that cute. Was he? Maybe another look would help. *No, dammit!* Oh hell.

I scratched awkwardly at my notebook, ignoring my pounding heart. Was I supposed to write down what he said? Why was he speaking in scientific classifications? Blue Eyes wasn't real. There had been no one to help me free the lobsters. He hadn't just said that. This was my mind screwing with me. Again.

I coughed delicately, pulling on a piece of my hair. "Well. You can write down 'Yoo-hoos' for mine."

"Yoo-hoos," he said slowly.

"Yoo-hoos—you know, the best drink ever?"

Now he was the one staring at me. I rolled my eyes. "Y-O-O-H—"

"I can spell, thanks." His voice had snapped back to normal. Fluent and clear. As he began writing, I glanced up at the clock. Class was almost over. My hands shook.

When the bell rang, I sprang to collect my bag and join the others moving into the hallway. I felt better when I got away from Miles, like the revelation I'd had in the chemistry classroom had been nothing but a dream, and I'd woken up from it. I didn't understand him—he'd come right out of my delusions, but here he was. He straddled the line between my world and everyone else's, and I didn't like it.

We arrived at our lockers at the same time. I ignored him, opened my locker, and reached for my textbooks.

They fell right out of their covers like guts out of a fish.

"Looks like someone destroyed the binding in your books," said Miles.

No shit, asshat. Screw him—Blue Eyes or not, I wasn't putting up with this.

I picked up my ruined books, stuffed them into my bag, and slammed my locker shut. "Guess I'll have to fix them." And then I stomped off toward the gym, knowing I wouldn't be able to get away from him now.

Chapter Six

Tucker was wrong about the East Shoal Recreational Athletics Support Club. Miles hadn't chosen that name. Principal McCoy had, and he'd told me so when he explained my mandatory community service to me and my mother.

I walked to the main gym now with Miles on my heels. His cat stare burned into my shoulder blades. I stopped inside the gym doors and looked around, trying to be inconspicuous about spinning in circles.

The gym was older than the one at Hillpark; I'd expected it to be newer, remodeled, like East Shoal's disgustingly expensive football stadium. The bleacher row adjacent to the main doors housed the table with the scoreboard controls. The basketball goals were raised to the ceiling, giving me a straight view across the gym to the scoreboard hanging on the far wall. "East Shoal High School" was spelled along its top in green letters.

Miles tapped me on the shoulder. Just the tip of his index finger, just a jolt; I jumped.

"Don't keep them waiting," he said, slipping past me.

At the scorer's table stood five kids laughing together. One of them was a girl I recognized from English; she had a pair of pencils spiking out of her messy blond bun. The two boys standing next to her were so identical I couldn't tell them apart. I'd never seen the other two, but every one of them stood at attention when Miles walked up. I hovered awkwardly behind him.

"This is Alex," he said without any sort of greeting. "Alex, this is Theo*philia*." He motioned to the girl from English class.

"Just Theo," the girl replied, glaring at him.

"—and these are her brothers, Evan and Ian." He motioned to the two identical boys, who grinned in unison.

"To reduce confusion, we're triplets." Theo thrust out a hand, very businesslike. "And please don't call me Theophilia."

"No worries," I said, staring at her hand—guilt had made me shake Miles's, but I had no good reason to go near hers. "My parents wanted two boys—they named me after Alexander the Great and my sister after Charlemagne."

Theo put her hand down, apparently not at all offended by my refusal to shake it, and laughed. "Yeah, my parents wanted boys, too. Instead they got two idiots and a girl."

"Hey!" Theo's brothers cried in unison. She dropped the clipboard and faked a punch toward their crotches. Both boys recoiled. I knew how genetics worked—even normal identical twins didn't look as identical as Theo's brothers. My fingers tightened around my camera.

Miles rolled his eyes and went on. "And this is Jetta Lorenc and Art Babrow."

Jetta shot Miles a dimpled smile, shoveling her mass of curly hair back over her shoulder. "Eet is nice to meet you," she said, holding out a hand like she'd wait as long as it took for me to shake it.

I didn't. "Are you French?" I asked instead.

"*Oui!*"

Foreign. Foreign spy. French Communist Party acted on Stalin's instructions during part of World War II. French Communist spy.

Stop it stop it stop it

I turned to Art, a black kid who was a foot and a half taller than me and whose pecs were about to burst out of his shirt and eat someone. I gave him a two on the delusion detector. I didn't trust those pecs.

"Hi," he rumbled.

I waved weakly.

"This is the rest of the club," Miles said, gesturing around to all of them. "Theo, concession stand. Evan and Ian, bleacher duty."

"Aye aye, Boss!" The triplets saluted and left for their posts.

"Jetta, net and ball carts. Art, get the poles."

The other two departed as well. I relaxed once they were all gone, even though I still had Miles to deal with. Miles, who turned to the scoreboard controls and forgot about me.

"So what do I do?" I asked.

He ignored me.

"MILES."

He turned, sporting the Magnificent Quirked Eyebrow.

"What do I do?"

"You're going to go up there"—he pointed at the empty bleachers—"and shut up."

Was there some kind of law about drop-kicking assholes in the face? Probably. They always had laws against things that really needed to be done.

"No," I replied. "I think I'll go sit over *there*." I pointed to a spot a few feet from where he had, then marched off to sit there. I crossed my arms and glared at him until he and his eyebrow looked away. Then I yanked all the ruined books out of my bag, piled them beside me, and started my homework.

When the volleyball team entered the gym, I paused homework to snap pictures: Jetta and Art setting up the volleyball net like pros; Theo manning the concession stand; Evan and Ian scouring the bleachers for trash; the volleyball team looking perky and athletic in their spandex.

The only thing missing was Miles. But he was probably circling somewhere, destroying villages and hoarding gold in his mountain lair.

I cracked my neck and returned to calculus. Homework was a bitch, especially since this year I'd be doing it in the free time I had between school, work, and community service. Not to mention I still had to look for scholarships and fill out college applications. And visit my damned therapist twice a week.

But I had to do it. Had to get it right this time. No screwups with my medicine, however much I hated the stuff. No distractions. I didn't have time to worry about what other people thought of me, yet I had to—if I seemed too on edge, too paranoid, it wouldn't matter what my grades were. If anyone decided I was crazy or dangerous, I could say good-bye to a future and hello to the Happy House.

Miles walked back into the gym and settled himself at the scorer's table. For half a second he turned, stared up at me, and quirked that eyebrow, before facing the Spandex Squad again. The base of my skull tingled. I hadn't thought about it before—why hadn't I thought about it before? Miles. Miles was a genius. Miles liked to screw with people.

Miles didn't seem to particularly like me, and I'd been antagonizing him all day. It would be easy for him to figure me out. Especially if I kept staring at him like I had in chemistry. Maybe I could head him off. Tell him about it before he found out, then beg for his silence or something.

Or you could grow some balls, said the little voice. That was probably the best option.

I turned my attention to the scoreboard. McCoy had made at least five different announcements about it today, and during each one somebody would mimic him and everyone would laugh.

"There's an urban legend about that scoreboard, you know." Tucker appeared next to me, holding a Coke. I looked around. The bleachers were already full. *How did that happen?* I glanced over my shoulder, expecting someone to be standing there with a knife.

"Really?" I asked absentmindedly, doing a belated perimeter check. "Somehow I don't find that surprising."

Cliff Ackerley and a few other football player types stood at the foot of the bleachers, holding up signs for Ria Wolf, who I gathered was the starting setter. I spotted Celia

Hendricks on the edge of a bigger group of students who didn't look like they were putting any effort toward actually watching the game. Parents filed into the gym from the rotunda, holding popcorn and hot dogs and wearing shirts that read "Go Sabres!"

"What a ridiculous sport," said a woman near me, her voice laced with acid. "Volleyball. They should call it 'sluts in spandex.'"

I searched for the disgruntled parent, but teenagers surrounded me. I squeezed myself into a smaller space.

"Did you hear that woman?" I asked Tucker.

"What woman?"

"The one who said the thing about volleyball players being sluts."

Tucker looked around. "Are you sure that's what you heard?"

I shook my head. "Must've been nothing." I'd learned a long time ago that asking someone else if they heard something was much safer than asking them if they saw it. Most people didn't trust their ears as much as they trusted their eyes. Of course, auditory hallucinations were also the most common kind of hallucinations. Not good for me.

"Now *cheerleading*, that's a sport. A sport with dignity. You make it or you don't. There's no gray area, not like with *volleyball*."

Her voice mingled with the crowd and the squeak of shoes on the court, then faded out.

Tucker shifted beside me. "The legend says that some chick who went to East Shoal years ago was so obsessed with high school that she refused to leave it, and, in a weird suicide stunt, made the scoreboard fall on herself. Now her soul inhabits the scoreboard, influencing matches to help East Shoal win. Or lose. Depends on how she feels that day, I guess."

"Why didn't you tell me that before? Geez, I thought everyone was obsessed with it for no reason."

"Well. I don't know if everyone's obsessed with it because of the legend or if the legend grew because everyone's obsessed with it. Anyway, McCoy says we're not supposed to talk about it. But if you *really* want creepy, you should watch him take care of it. Cleans every lightbulb by hand. *Caresses* it."

I laughed.

Tucker paused, his neck and ears turning red. He fidgeted. "There's also the myth about a python in the ceiling tiles, being fed by the lunch ladies. But that one's not too interesting. Do you know about Red Witch Bridge?"

I shot him a look out of the corner of my eye. "I've heard of it."

"Never drive through the covered bridge by Hannibal's

Rest at night. You hear the witch scream right before she rips you to shreds and leaves your car empty by the side of the road." A gleam of excitement lit his eyes as he waited for my reaction. Normally he only got that look when he was telling me about one of his conspiracy theories.

"Have you ever done it?" I asked.

"Me? Drive through Red Witch Bridge? No, I'm brave as soggy potato salad."

"You? Soggy potato salad? *No*."

Tucker laughed and puffed out his skinny chest in mock bravado. "I know I don't look it, but I'd run the other direction before I got anywhere near that bridge." He dropped the act and offered me the Coke. "Thirsty?"

"You don't want it?"

"Nah. Bought it and then remembered that I hate soda."

I took it hesitantly. "You didn't put anything in it, did you?"

"Do I look like that type of person?"

"I don't know, Mr. Soggy Potato Salad. You're a wild card."

I technically wasn't supposed to have caffeine—my mother said it made me too excitable and screwed with my medicine, which made her a liar because I felt perfectly fine whenever I broke the rules—but I drank it anyway.

"I see your textbooks have had a rough day." Tucker

prodded the binding of my calculus book.

"Mm," I said. "Stray cat found its way into my locker."

"Superglue will fix that right up."

Superglue? Now there was an idea. I glanced down at Miles. He was staring over his shoulder at us, eyes narrowed. The enormity of this balancing act hit me all at once, made my stomach lurch. I couldn't let him walk all over me, but I couldn't make him angry, either.

Tucker gave him the finger. Miles turned back to the court.

"I'll regret that later," Tucker said, "when my steering column is gone."

Either Tucker would regret it, or I would.

"Are you okay?" Tucker asked. "You look like you're going to vomit."

"Yes." No. "I'm okay." This was the least okay thing that had happened to me since the Hillpark Gym Graffiti Incident.

I realized too late that I'd snapped at him. I didn't mean to be harsh, but I hated worry, and pity, and that look people got when they knew something wasn't okay with you and they also knew that you were in denial about it.

I wasn't in denial. I just couldn't let it slip this time.

Chapter
Seven

I spent the rest of the game flipping my focus back and forth between my homework and Miles. He didn't look back up at us, but I knew he knew I was watching him.

I distracted myself by trying to think of ways to pay Tucker back for the Coke. He ignored me when I brought it up and changed the subject to conspiracy theories— Roswell, the Illuminati, Elvis faking his own death, and when Miles glared up at us again, a nice little story about a Nazi moon base.

Tucker was the sort of intelligent, history-savvy person I could throw at my mother and watch him stick, but also the sort of person I'd never do that to, because I had a soul.

Then I thought, *Hey, I could hug him. I'm sure he wouldn't mind if I hugged him.* But I knew that physical contact meant certain things in the world of normal social conduct, and while I trusted Tucker more than most of the other people I knew, I didn't want to mean those certain things toward him.

Tucker left with the crowd when the game ended. I stayed behind to help the club, but they were so quick and efficient that the net was down and the ball carts stowed before I'd stepped off the bleachers.

Miles and Jetta stood at the scorer's table. When I walked up to them, they fell silent; I was pretty sure they hadn't been speaking English.

"What?" Miles snapped.

"Do you need me for anything or can I go home?"

"Yeah, go." He turned back to Jetta.

"*Bis später*, Alex!" Jetta smiled and waved as I walked away. Apparently any feelings I'd hurt by not shaking her hand had been forgotten.

"Um. See you," I replied.

Outside the school was pandemonium. I expected big crowds after football games, but this looked like the entire school had formed one huge tailgating party. At eight at night. After a volleyball game. On the first day of school.

There was no way I could do a sufficient perimeter check here, so I went for plan B: Get out. I wheeled Erwin out of the bushes where I'd hidden him, and hoped to God no one noticed me. The people closest to the school entrance were the men still standing on the roof, the few football players probably waiting for their girlfriends, and Celia Hendricks and two other girls, doing who the hell knows what.

"Nice bike!" Celia called over her shoulder, flipping her bleached hair out of the way. Her two friends stifled laughs. "Where'd you get it?"

"Egypt," I said, trying to figure out if she was serious.

Celia laughed. "Remind me never to go to Egypt."

I ignored her and continued past the football players. I didn't get far; all 230 pounds of Cliff Ackerley fell into step beside me. "Hey, you're the new girl, right?"

"Yes." His closeness sent shivers crawling up my spine. I veered away to put some distance between us.

He planted himself in front of me, pointed at my hair, and yelled, "HILLPARK FAN!"

A thunderous, rolling *BOO* instantly rose from the crowd. Most of them probably had no clue I'd actually gone to Hillpark, but brandishing any kind of red around here was asking for trouble.

I tried to move around Cliff, but he stuck his foot on Erwin's front tire and pushed. "What the hell?" I stumbled backward to keep Erwin upright.

"What the hell?" one of the other guys mocked in a high falsetto, a million times more sinister than when Tucker had done it at work the night before. The rest of Cliff's friends circled around me. I squeezed tighter against Erwin. Either these guys were all drunk or they were all douche bags. If they were drunk, they were less likely to see reason but also less likely to catch me if I ran for it. But I couldn't run with Erwin. Maybe I could use him as a shield. That meant leaving him behind, and the last thing I wanted to do was leave Erwin behind. No matter how I played this situation, *Outlook not so good.*

"Why don't you stop being a dick and get out of my way?"

"Ooh, harsh words." Cliff grinned. "Here's the deal— I'll let you by if you agree to let us dye your hair green."

"My hair isn't dyed; it's naturally this red. And *no.*"

"Fine, then we'll shave it off. Jones has a razor in his car, don't you, Jones?"

I backed away, tugging on a lock of hair. I'd seen documentaries about stuff like this. Bullying, student brutality. They wouldn't really shave my head, would they? But there were so many people, all watching, waiting. The men in suits on the roof weren't doing a thing—so much for school security.

The ring of people drew in tighter. There was no . . . I

wouldn't be able to get out . . . Maybe I could kick Ackerley in the balls and call it a day . . . .

Then everyone went quiet. Cliff's gaze roamed to a spot above my shoulder.

Miles stood there, staring Cliff down. The Light triplets at his side.

Cliff scoffed. "Need something, Richter?"

"Not at all." Miles shrugged. "Please, continue."

Cliff narrowed his eyes and took a step back, looking me over. He leaned to the side and peered around me.

"Problem?" I asked.

Cliff scoffed again and stepped out of my way, his lips curling in distaste. Miles and the triplets moved to flank me, helping clear a path through the party. There were no more boos, no jeering, no search for razors. But when I looked back, Cliff and his friends had their heads together, and past them, Celia glared daggers at me.

"Thanks," I said.

"Didn't do it for you." Miles stopped beside a rusty sky-blue pickup on the far edge of the parking lot. He yanked the driver's door open and tossed his bag in. "I really hate that guy."

"Don't listen to anything Cliff says," Theo chimed in, pulling the pencils from her bun and shaking her hair out. "He's a moron—he thinks we planned to have you do something to make him look stupid. That's why he left you alone. Besides, I don't think he'd know how to use a razor if he had one."

"I'm pretty sure his mother shaves his facial hair," said Evan.

"I'm pretty sure a monkey shaves his facial hair," said Ian. "Did you see his face last track season? I thought he'd need a blood donation."

"Disregarding his faults in personal hygiene," Miles interrupted, "I still think he needs his head shoved into a wood chipper."

I took a long step away from Miles. "Right. Well, I'll see you all tomorrow."

The Light triplets said good-bye. Maybe they weren't so bad after all, even if Evan and Ian did look like the exact same person. I hopped on Erwin and rode out of the parking lot, trying to forget about Cliff, Celia, that weird-ass scoreboard, and everything else.

I marked Miles's parking spot so I could find his truck again tomorrow morning.

I wouldn't let East Shoal and its psychotic inhabitants get the best of me.

Chapter Eight

My delusions became more frequent in the dark. More than once when I was little, I heard voices coming from beneath my bed, claws reaching up around the mattress to get me. Riding home, the sunlight fading, an enormous red bird with long tail feathers sailed over me. I stopped to take a picture of it. On the camera screen, its feathers glowed like fire. Freaking phoenixes. I'd had an obsession with phoenixes when I was ten, and this one followed me home every night. The Phoenix of Hannibal's Rest.

Hannibal's Rest. Home.

Here's the thing about Hannibal's Rest, Indiana: It is astoundingly small. So small I'm sure it wouldn't show up on a GPS. You'd pass right through without realizing you were anywhere different. It's just like the rest of central

Indiana: hot in the summer, cold in the winter, and the only way to know the weather other times of the year is to walk outside. You drive west to get to Hillpark and east to get to East Shoal, but nobody from either school can tell you the name of a single person who goes to the other, and they all hate one another.

My parents didn't grow up here or anything. They chose to live in this nowhere town. Why? Because it was named after Hannibal of Carthage. Their basic train of thought was this: *Hannibal's Rest? And we're naming our child after Alexander the Great? MARVELOUS. Ah, the history, it tickles.*

Sometimes I wanted to beat my parents over the head with a frying pan.

If you could say one thing about them, it was that they loved history. Literally, both of them were *in love* with history. Sure, they were in love with each other, but history was like the be-all, end-all of intellectual stimulation to them. They were married to each other and to history.

So, naturally, they weren't going to give their kids any old *normal* names.

I was the lucky one. Alexander to Alexandra wasn't a huge leap. Charlie, on the other hand, got the entire blunt force of the namesake sledgehammer: Charlemagne. So from the day she was born, I called her Charlie.

I turned down my street and aimed for the one-story, dirt-colored house lit up like a Christmas tree. My mother had this thing about leaving all the lights on until I got home, as if I would forget which house was ours. The sounds of a furious violin poured from the living-room window. Tchaikovsky's *1812 Overture*, as usual.

I leaned Erwin up against the garage door and did a perimeter check. Street. Driveway. Garage. Front yard. Porch. House. The porch swing creaked and swayed like someone had just gotten out of it, but that could've been the wind. I did another check when I stepped in through the front door, but the house looked like it always did, cramped and barren at the same time. Charlie stood in the living room with her violin, playing her musical prodigy stuff. When my mother wasn't teaching online college classes, she homeschooled Charlie like she had me, so Charlie was always practicing.

My mother was in the kitchen. I braced myself, remembered not to do another perimeter check—my mother hated them—and went to find her. She stood at the sink, dishrag in hand.

"I'm home," I said.

She turned. "I left out a bowl of soup for you. It's mushroom, your favorite."

Minestrone was my favorite soup. Mushroom was Dad's. She always got them mixed up. "Thanks, but I'm not really hungry. I'm gonna go do my homework."

"Alexandra, you need to eat."

I hated that voice. *Alexandra, you need to eat. Alexandra, you need to take your pills. Alexandra, you need to put your shirt on right side out.*

I sat down at the table, dropping my bag next to me. My books made a pitiful *shunk* sound, reminding me that I couldn't let my mother look in my bag. She'd think I'd destroyed them, and that would definitely warrant a therapist call.

"So, how was it?"

"All right," I replied, swirling the cold soup in the bowl, checking for poison. I didn't *really* think my mother would poison me. Most of the time.

"That's it?"

I shrugged. "It was all right. It was a day of school."

"Meet anyone interesting?"

"Everyone's interesting if you stare at them long enough."

She put her hands on her hips. Tally one for Things Alex Shouldn't Say at the Dinner Table.

"How did it go with that club?"

"I really didn't have to do that much. I like them, though. They're nice." Most of them. Mom hmm'd in her very passive-aggressive way.

"What?" I shot.

"Nothing."

I sipped a bit of soup. "I'm on speaking terms with the valedictorian and the salutatorian, if that makes you feel any better," I said.

Okay, so the valedictorian was a bit of a stretch. Most of our conversations that day had ended with one of us pissed off. But I did, technically, speak to him.

Thoughts of Blue Eyes strutted forward once again, and I beat them back. The moment I mentioned a lobster tank, my mother would have a conniption. She'd spent years trying to forget the Freeing of the Lobsters.

"Oh really?" My mother perked up a bit. "And what are they like?"

"The salutatorian's really nice, but the valedictorian could work on his people skills."

"You should ask them for college advice, you know," she said. "I bet they're aiming for the Ivy League. Oh, they could help you with your essays! You've never really been good at writing."

Tally one for Mother Mentions College Future and Unlikeliness of Such at Dinner Table. It probably wouldn't help my case to tell her Tucker had applied to half a dozen Ivy League schools, and had already been accepted at twice as many less prestigious institutions. "I don't need help getting into college. I have good grades, and most people can't write to save their lives, but they get in. Besides, you have to be an idiot not to get into state college."

"You're saying that now," she said, waving a soapy knife at me. "But what are you going to do when you don't get in?"

I dropped my spoon. "The hell, Mom? Do you want me to get in or not?"

"Language!" she snapped, going back to the dishes. I rolled my eyes and hunched over my soup.

The violin music came to an abrupt halt. There was the patter of small feet in the hallway, and then Charlie's arms wrapped around me and her momentum nearly knocked me out of my chair. She was undersized for her age but hit like a wrecking ball.

"Hi, Charlie."

"Hi." My shirt muffled her voice.

I pried Charlie away from my side and stood up, pulling my bag with me. "I'm going to my room."

"I expect lights out by ten," my mother said.

"Oh, and apparently I need a school uniform."

She slapped a wet hand against her forehead. Water ran down the side of her face. "Oh, I completely forgot. Your principal mentioned a uniform to me when we went for that tour. How much are they?"

"Like, seventy dollars. It's ridiculous. All for a school crest on the breast pocket."

My mother turned to look at me again, her face creased with that damn *pity* look. We weren't so poor that we couldn't pay seventy dollars for something I had to have, but she would make me feel awful about it anyway.

"I'm getting a spare from the janitor tomorrow," I said quickly. "It shouldn't be a problem."

"Okay, good." She relaxed. "I already laid out your clothes for tomorrow, so you can wear those to school and bring them home with you."

"Fine."

I stalked out of the kitchen and down the back hallway, Charlie close on my heels. She jabbered incessantly about the song she'd been playing, what she thought of our mother's mushroom soup, how much she wanted to go to high school.

She hustled to get inside my bedroom door before I closed it. Even in the room I'd slept in for seventeen years, the place I knew better than anywhere else, I had to make sure nothing was out of the ordinary.

"What's it like?" Charlie flung herself on my bed and pulled the covers up over her head like a cloak. The resulting gust of air made the pictures tacked to the walls flutter. The artifacts on my shelves rattled ominously.

"Be careful, Charlie. You break anything, you're paying for it." I opened up the top dresser drawer and pushed pairs of striped socks out of the way until I found my stash of superglue, hidden so my mother didn't think I was huffing it. I tossed it onto the nightstand partly as a warning to Charlie and partly as a reminder to myself to pick it up for the morning. "I don't know. It was school." I grabbed the clothes my mother had left out on the end of the bed and tossed them on the floor. After seventeen years, she still picked out my clothes. I was a schizophrenic, not a damn invalid.

"But what was it *like*?"

This was understandable. Charlie had never set foot in a real school.

"It was like school. I went to class and listened to the teacher and did the work."

"And there were other kids there?"

"Yes, Charlie, there are lots of other kids there. It's a school."

"Did they discriminate against you because you're new?"

Discriminate. There it was. Charlie's Word of the Week. Every week, Charlie had a word that she used whenever she could fit it in. This week it was *discriminate*. Last week it was *usurp*. The week before that was *defenestrate*, compliments of me. Just thinking about Charlie whipping that one out of her vocabulary utility belt in front of our mother made me smile.

"Has Mom been letting you watch the Disney Channel again?" I opened my closet to look for my pajamas.

"So . . . they don't sing at lunch?"

"Nope."

"Oh." The blanket fell away from her head, revealing her straight, ketchup-red hair and big blue eyes. She pulled a black chess piece from her pocket and jammed it into her mouth. She'd been chewing on things since she was four years old. "Did you meet anyone cool?"

"Define *cool*."

"You know. *Cool*."

"Not really. I met nice people and stupid people and complete jerks, but I didn't really meet any cool people."

Charlie gasped, her eyes became the size of plates, and the chess piece fell out of her mouth. "Did you meet your *soul mate*? That always happens on the first day of school, right?"

"Oh God, Charlie, she's letting you read again! You went straight to the paranormal section, didn't you?"

Charlie huffed and crossed her arms. "No. But the TV doesn't do high school very well."

"The TV doesn't do anything very well, Charlie."

She looked glum after that, and I felt sorry that I'd crushed her hopes. She'd never go to high school. The only reason our mother had stopped homeschooling me was because my therapist said I'd do better around people my age. That led to my involvement in the Hillpark Gym Graffiti Incident and my senior year condemnation at East Shoal.

A familiar pang of guilt poked at my stomach whenever I looked at Charlie. I was the big sister. I was supposed to set an example and lead the way so people would say, *"Hey, you're Alex's sister, aren't you? You two look exactly alike!"* instead of *"Hey, you're Alex's sister, aren't you? Are you crazy, too?"*

The only example I was ever going to set for her was to always check her food before she ate it.

Relief washed over me. Relief that she wasn't old enough yet to understand why she should hate me.

"Get out of my room. I need to change."

Charlie whined and pouted but grabbed the chess piece, scrambled off the bed, and hurried out the door. I changed into my pajamas and slipped under the covers.

I looked around the room at all my pictures and artifacts.

The pictures had no rhyme or reason. I realized a few years back that sometimes I'd look at an old picture and something would be different in it. Something would be missing. I reached into my bag and pulled out my camera, then flipped through the pictures I'd taken today. The first one from this morning, the one of the squirrels—it was already different. It looked like I'd just taken a picture of the neighbor's lawn. The squirrels were gone.

It wasn't always so easy. Some things took longer to disappear than others. But this technique helped me figure out what was a hallucination and what wasn't. I had albums full of pictures, too, but the albums were for things I knew were real, like my parents. Charlie had a whole album to herself. More than once I'd caught her in my room, looking through it.

My artifacts came from my dad. First and foremost, Dad was an archaeologist. I didn't blame him. If I could do nothing but play in the dirt all day, I'd be an archaeologist, too. My mother used to travel with him, but then they had me and they took too long trying to decide if they wanted to take me to the digs. By that time, my mother had ended up homeschooling me and didn't want to take me anywhere, and then Charlie was born and they didn't have the money to take both of us. So my mother stayed home all the time and Dad was always gone.

Whenever he came home, he brought stuff: most of the things we owned, our furniture, and even some of our clothes. My mother crammed every available corner with

Dad's stuff, and the house didn't feel so empty.

I tried not to think about the fact that shipping things like that across the ocean must cost a lot of money.

I remembered a few times, before I was diagnosed, when I'd lay in bed and my artifacts would talk to me or to one another and I would listen to them until I fell asleep.

My artifacts didn't talk to me anymore. At least not when the medicine was working.

I turned off my light and rolled over onto my side, pulling my sheet with me. The little boy at the lobster tank was losing his definition—until I reminded myself that even if he was real, which he wasn't, he and Miles were not necessarily the same person.

That was *ten years ago*. Ten years, and I hadn't seen him since. It would take some ridiculous odds to bring us full circle like that.

I didn't fall asleep. I couldn't. I waited until I heard Mom walk down the hall and close her door (Charlie had shut herself in her room half an hour ago), then slipped out from under the covers, put on a jacket and an old pair of sneakers, and grabbed the aluminum baseball bat I kept under my bed. I popped the screen out of the window and set it carefully against the wall.

I didn't often ride my bike in the dark, but I walked. Baseball bat clinking against the heels of my Converse, nighttime breeze brushing against my legs, I trekked through my backyard and into the woods of Hannibal's Rest. The creek whispered up ahead. I took the last bend in the road and stood face-to-face with Red Witch Bridge.

I didn't feel the need to do a perimeter check, because this was where the worlds met. Everyone thought they saw or heard strange things here, and I didn't have to hide the fact that I really did.

I laughed when I remembered Tucker bringing up the bridge earlier. The Red Witch? The one who gutted travelers, coated herself in their blood, and screamed like a banshee? No, I wasn't scared of her. The nighttime might have made everything upside down, inside out, scary as hell, but not to me.

The baseball bat *clink-clink-clinked* as I walked toward Red Witch Bridge.

I was the scariest thing out here tonight.

Chapter Nine

Einstein's definition of insanity is doing the same thing over and over again and expecting different results. I kept taking pictures, hoping I'd look at one and know its subject was a hallucination. I did my perimeter checks, thinking I'd eventually be able to walk around paranoia-free. I spent every day hoping someone would tell me I smelled like lemons.

If I wasn't insane by anyone else's definition, I figured I was at least insane by Einstein's.

Chapter
Ten

The first thing I did the day after the parking-lot incident was look for Miles's truck at school. Rusty, sky blue, 1982 GMC. Looked like he'd saved it from a scrap heap. It wasn't there. Marvelous.

My second order of business was with his locker. I hurried into school, checked to make sure no one was around and the ceiling wasn't wired, then delved into my bag in search of superglue. Two tubes and seventeen Popsicle sticks later, Miles's locker was well and truly glued shut. I tossed the evidence into the nearest trash can, swapped out what books I needed from my own locker (most still severed from their covers), and left to find a uniform.

The janitors' closet was next to my chemistry room. When I knocked, there was a crash inside. The door cracked open and a familiar bespectacled eye looked out.

"Oh, hi, Alex." Tucker opened the door a little wider. His gaze flitted around the hallway behind me. "W-what are you doing here?"

"Uh, they said I could get a uniform from the janitor."

"Oh, yeah. There are some here . . . hold on a sec. . . ."

He disappeared and I heard some muted, angry cursing. When he returned, he held a uniform. "It might be a little big, but it's the only clean one. The others were yellow."

I took the uniform. "Thanks, Tucker. What are you doing in the janitors' closet?" I looked behind him, but I didn't see anyone else.

He gave me a weak smile. "Don't worry about it." And then he closed the door.

I forced myself not to take any pictures—it was Tucker; Tucker was not a hallucination, even if he was hanging out in a janitors' closet—and ducked into the nearest bathroom to change. Tucker had really been playing it down when he said the uniform might be "a little big." I needed swimming lessons to wear it.

I had to pass through the science hallway on my way to class, and that was when I saw the snake.

Its head hung down between ceiling tiles that had been shifted to the side for some reason. I jumped. I'd only ever seen pythons in the zoo, behind glass—but annoyance settled in when I got over the initial shock of seeing it.

Freaking snake. I didn't even bother getting my camera out. A snake hanging out of the ceiling was exactly the sort of thing my mind would cook up. I stuck out my tongue and hissed at the python as I walked underneath it.

I slunk to Mr. Gunthrie's room, hoping I wouldn't meet Cliff or Celia or, God forbid, Miles on my way. People still stared at me—this hair, this damn hair, why did it have to be so damn red—but I ignored them.

Theo was kneeling outside the classroom door, mixing condiments inside a Mason jar, while Miles stood next to her with his arms crossed. A shiver ran up my spine when I walked past him, but I forced my face to remain expressionless. He didn't notice me—if he did, he didn't say anything.

I got a glimpse of Theo's disgusting concoction. Pickle juice, mustard, what looked like pepper shavings, sour cream, horseradish—basically all the things you put together when you're thirteen and you want to trick a younger sibling into a vomit-induced coma (Charlie had never forgiven me for that one).

I slipped into my seat, keeping them in my peripheral vision while I did a perimeter check. Theo capped the Mason jar, shook it, and handed it to Miles. Miles watched the cloudy, swirling liquid for a second, then raised it to his lips, and chugged the whole thing in one fell swoop.

I gagged and yanked my collar up over my nose. Ironically, the collar smelled like barf already, so I lowered it. Miles sauntered into the room and dropped into the chair in front of me, his gaze fixed on the whiteboard.

Class started normally. As normally as it could, I suppose, when the first announcement of the day is about a scoreboard, and your drill sergeant of a teacher is yelling at everyone. I tried paying attention to Mr. Gunthrie's lecture on British literature, but the side of Miles's face had turned chalky white and was morphing into sickly green.

". . . THE FACT THAT BURGESS TAUGHT ALONGSIDE THE WOMAN WHO WOULD GIVE HIM IDEAS FOR *A CLOCKWORK ORANGE* IS VERY LITTLE-KNOWN. HE WAS IN THE ARMY AT THE TIME."

Mr. Gunthrie stopped in front of Cliff's desk, leaned over, and got right into Cliff's face. Cliff, who had been making hand signs across the room at Ria Wolf, jumped and faced forward.

"TELL ME, MR. ACKERLEY, DO YOU KNOW WHERE BURGESS WAS STATIONED?"

Cliff's mouth popped open like he was going to say something.

"NO? THAT'S A PITY, MR. ACKERLEY. PERHAPS

I SHOULD ASK SOMEONE ELSE. DO YOU THINK I
SHOULD ASK SOMEONE ELSE, MR. ACKERLEY?"

"Uh, yes?"

"WHO DO YOU THINK I SHOULD ASK,
ACKERLEY?"

"Uh . . . Richter?"

"UH, RICHTER. THAT SOUNDS LIKE A QUESTION,
ACKERLEY. DID I GIVE YOU PERMISSION TO ASK
ME A QUESTION?"

"No."

"NO WHAT?"

"No, sir!"

"NOW I'M GOING TO ASK YOU AGAIN,
MR. ACKERLEY. TO WHOM SHOULD I ASK THE
QUESTION YOUR INCOMPETENT ASS COULDN'T
ANSWER?"

"Ask Richter, sir!"

Mr. Gunthrie straightened up and marched across the
room to Miles's desk.

"RICHTER. COULD YOU PLEASE TELL ME WHERE
ANTHONY BURGESS WAS STATIONED WHEN HE
TAUGHT ALONGSIDE ANN MCGLINN AND TOOK
HER IDEAS ON COMMUNISM FOR *A CLOCKWORK
ORANGE?*"

Miles didn't answer at first. He was hunched in his

seat, swaying a little. Slowly, he looked up and met Mr. Gunthrie's gaze.

Please throw up on him, I thought. *Please, please throw up on Mr. Gunthrie.*

"Gibraltar," Miles said, then he lurched out of his seat and made it to the trash can in time to be violently ill. Several girls squealed. Tucker yanked his collar up over his nose.

"You all right, Richter?" Mr. Gunthrie dropped his book and walked over to clap Miles on the back. Miles spit one more time and put a hand on Mr. Gunthrie's shoulder.

"Yeah, I'm fine. Must have eaten something bad at breakfast." Miles wiped his mouth on his sleeve. "If I could go to the restroom . . . clean up . . ."

"Of course." Mr. Gunthrie gave Miles another sharp slap on the back. "Take as much time as you need. I'm sure you've got this all memorized anyway, haven't you?"

Miles gave him a wry smile and left.

Chapter Eleven

Tucker found me after lunch and reassured me that Miles had been running a job.

"A job? What, like the mafia?"

"Sort of." Tucker leaned back against the wall outside the cafeteria. "People pay him to do things. Usually revenge stuff. You know, steal someone's homework and paste it on the ceiling. Put dead fish in someone's glove compartment. Stuff like that."

"So what was he doing this morning?" I asked.

Tucker shrugged. "You usually don't know until it happens. One time he hid a hundred water balloons full of grape juice into Leslie Stapleford's locker. When she opened it, there were toothpicks or something that popped all the balloons and set off a chain reaction. Ruined everything she had."

Note to self: Stand to side of locker door when opening.

"Did you hear the announcement today?" Tucker asked, changing the subject.

"Oh, about McCoy hiring someone to fit the scoreboard with gold plating?"

"Yeah. I told you he was crazy, right? I heard he does some weird stuff at home, too." He said it with a conspiratorial stage whisper. "Like mowing his lawn, and trimming his peonies."

"Peonies?" I balked. "God, he really is a freak."

Tucker laughed. The cafeteria doors beside him swung open and Celia Hendricks walked out with Britney Carver and Stacey Burns. I stepped back, slightly behind Tucker.

"What's funny, Beaumont?" she asked with a sneer, as if he'd been laughing at her.

"None of your business, Celia." All humor left Tucker's face. "Don't you have a Makeup Addicts Anonymous meeting to get to?"

"Don't you have a Cult in a Closet to get to?" she shot back. "Oh, wait, I forgot, you have no friends. My bad."

The tips of Tucker's ears turned pink and he glared at her, but didn't say anything else.

"God, Beaumont, you're so weird. Maybe if you acted like a normal person once in a while—"

"I'm his friend," I cut in. "And I think he's perfectly normal."

Celia looked me up and down, her eyes lingering on my hair. And then she huffed and stomped away without another word.

"You didn't have to say that," Tucker mumbled.

"Yeah, I did," I replied.

There is no force in high school more powerful than one person's blunt disagreement.

The rest of the day passed without a hitch. Miles did not acknowledge my presence. I did not acknowledge his.

Miles's locker was still glued shut when I left for the gym.

The entire west side of the school was for extracurriculars. The gym, pool, and auditorium were all connected by hallways that ran behind them and a large rotunda at their center, linked to the rest of the school by a main hall. Lining the rotunda were huge glass cases filled with trophies the school had won over the years: athletics, music competitions, color guard. There were pictures in black and white of the winning teams alongside some of them.

The picture that caught my attention didn't have a trophy and wasn't from a competition. It was a framed newspaper clipping. Someone had taken a bright red marker to the girl in the picture, partially obscuring her face, but I could tell she was pretty, blonde, and wearing an old East Shoal cheerleader's uniform. She stood next to the scoreboard, which looked brand-new.

Beneath the picture was the caption: "Scarlet Fletcher, captain of the East Shoal cheerleading squad, helps introduce 'Scarlet's Scoreboard,' a commemoration of the charity and goodwill her father, Randall Fletcher, has shown toward the school."

The picture was framed in gold and set up on a tiny dais like it was sacred.

I spotted Miles on the other side of the rotunda. He was standing outside the concession stand, talking to a kid I'd never seen before. As I watched, they made a quick exchange. Miles gave the kid something thin and gold and got a handful of cash in return.

"What was that?" I asked, stomping up to Miles as soon as the kid had walked away. "It looked very much like Mr. Gunthrie's fountain pen. I'm not ruling out the possibility that you're an accomplished pickpocket."

Miles raised his eyebrow as if I was a very amusing puppy.

"So that's the only reason you drank that awful stuff this morning? So you could steal a teacher's pen? For money?"

Miles shoved his hands into his pockets. "Are you done now?"

"Lemme see." I tapped my chin. "Yep, all done. Asshat."

I started to walk away.

"Alex. Wait."

I turned back. It was the first time he'd said my name. He held a hand out. "Well played," he said.

Oh no. No, we were not doing this. I hadn't spent ten minutes gluing his locker shut just to admit it to him. So I arched my own eyebrow and said, "I don't know what you're talking about."

The corners of his lips twisted up right before I walked away.

It can't be him. It's not him, is it?

Cannot predict now

*I know I've asked you a dozen times already,
but . . . just . . . yes or no?*

Concentrate and ask again

*You only have twice as many positive answers
as negative and noncommittal—how does this
keep happening? It's not him, is it?*

Better not tell you now

*You said that one before. I'm going to ask one
more time: He's a jerk, so he can't be Blue Eyes, right?*

Reply hazy try again

Reply hazy my ass.

Chapter Twelve

The transition from Hillpark to East Shoal was significantly easier than I'd expected. It was the same basic high school garbage wrapped in a slightly different skin. The only difference was that everything at East Shoal was completely insane.

There were several things I learned that first month.

One: The scoreboard really was a school legend, and Mr. McCoy really was dearly, dearly in love with it. McCoy had his own brand of crazy: he continually reminded everyone of "Scoreboard Day," when we were all supposed to bring in an offering of flowers or lightbulbs for the scoreboard, as if it was a wrathful Mayan deity that would kill us if we disobeyed. Somehow, he managed to cover this insanity with a mask of good test scores and even better student conduct. It seemed like, as far as the parents and teachers were concerned, he was a perfect principal.

Two: There was a cult entirely dedicated to discussing preexisting conspiracy theories and determining if they were true. They met in a janitors' closet.

Three: The cult was run by Tucker Beaumont.

Four: Mr. Gunthrie, the most in-your-face teacher in the school (because of the yelling, see), was nicknamed "The General" because of his penchant for going on war-related rants and wielding his treasured golden fountain pen as a weapon. He'd done two tours in Vietnam, and he had a long family history of war-related deaths, which rendered me almost incapable of not calling him Lieutenant Dan.

Five: Twenty years ago, as the senior prank, someone had let the biology teacher's pet python loose. It had escaped behind the ceiling tiles, never to be seen again.

Six: Everyone—and when I say everyone, I mean absolutely, positively everyone, from the librarians to the students to the staff to the oldest, crustiest janitor—was piss-down-their-legs scared of Miles Richter.

Of all the crazy things I heard about East Shoal, that was the only thing I couldn't believe.

Chapter Thirteen

I must have set a record. With the backpack-pushing and the assignment-ripping and all the general childishness that occurred between me and Miles, it only took him a month to banish me to work in the concession stand with Theo.

I was fine with this because a) I liked Theo better than him, b) I was less paranoid when he wasn't around, and c) I didn't have to sit in a gym full of people I didn't know. It didn't take me long to get used to Theo—she was so good at getting things done that I figured if she wanted to hurt me, she would've done it by now.

I thought I had a lot of homework, but Theo's back should've broken from the size of her bag.

"Seven AP classes, plus I'm retaking the SATs and ACTs because I *know* I got cheated last time," she said. "I keep all the other stuff I need over here in this pocket, and then my first-aid kit is in this pocket. . . ."

"Why do you have a first-aid kit?" I asked.

"When you have two brothers like mine, someone's always getting hurt." She shoved her physics book onto the counter and opened it up.

"I don't know how you do that," I said. "Do you go home after club and do homework all night?"

She shrugged. "Not most of the time. I work graveyard shifts at the Showtime. You wouldn't believe how late people come in to watch movies." She paused, then said with a sigh, "My parents make me."

"Why?"

She shrugged again. "That's just the way it is. They've always been like that. They wanted me to take all these AP classes, too."

"They made you join the club, too?"

Theo grinned. "No. None of us voluntarily joined the club. Except Jetta. Evan and Ian and I got put here when we snuck laxatives into the chili at lunch two years ago." She laughed. "So worth it."

I snorted. Theo was okay. "How'd everyone else get here?"

"They found Art with some weed in the bathroom, but he's the best wrestler we've got, so instead of suspending him from the team, they sent him here."

"I didn't peg Art as a pot smoker."

"That's because he's not," said Theo. "He was trying to stop some of his teammates from smoking, and they let him take the fall."

"Does anyone actually get thrown out of this school, or are they all given to Miles for safekeeping?"

"I've only ever heard of people getting expelled for violent stuff, like fighting or bringing a weapon to school."

"What about Jetta?"

Theo stared at her physics textbook and sighed. "I think Jetta's here because of Boss."

"What do you mean?"

"Jetta came here last year, and she didn't speak English very well. Boss was the only one who bothered to talk to her."

"What about Miles?" I asked quickly, before Theo could turn to her homework. "What'd he do to get here?"

"Hmm?" Theo looked up. "Oh, Boss? I'm not sure. Me and Evan and Ian were the first people to join the club, but Boss has always been here. He used to do all this stuff by himself."

She suddenly stopped talking. Miles was at the big concession stand window. He dropped a worn black notebook on the counter and leaned in.

"How's the game?" Theo asked.

"Imagine a thousand starving orphans on a sinking ship in the middle of a shark-infested sea, and you're getting close to how much I don't want to be there," Miles said dryly. "I get to hear Clifford talk about how nice Ria's ass is every fifteen seconds. They've been dating since seventh grade; you'd think he'd be over it by now."

"Mm-hmm."

"I'm bored," said Miles.

"What's new?" asked Theo.

"Let's play Five Questions."

Theo snapped her book shut. "Why, may I ask? It's not going to make you any less bored. And we might as well start calling it Three Questions, because it doesn't take you five anymore."

"What's Five Questions?" I asked.

"It's like Twenty Questions, only not twenty because Boss can do it in five," said Theo. "I've got someone. Go."

"Are you a president?" asked Miles.

"Yes."

"Do your first and last names start with the same letter?"

"Yes."

"You're Ronald Reagan."

"See?" Theo threw her hands in the air. "Two! Two questions!"

I didn't mind not having many responsibilities with the club, as long as Miles kept reporting that I was doing what I was supposed to. It gave me more time to write out long-winded college essays about how my illness shaped me. My nightly mountains of homework made the Tower of Babel look like a toothpick, and it was only worsened by my late shifts at Finnegan's. Finnegan's wasn't too bad on its own, but as soon as Miles waltzed in, I had the sudden urge to both hide and put soap in his food.

Every time I walked past Miles, I got the distinct feeling that he'd stick his leg out and trip me. He didn't, of course, because that wouldn't be subtle at all, and not Miles Richter's style. Nail files, hedge trimmers, and homemade flamethrowers were more his speed.

I gave him his burger and retreated behind the counter, where I asked the Magic 8 Ball, *Will Miles Richter try to kill me?*

Most likely, it replied.

By late September, we had regular labs every week. I glanced at him a few times as he made tables in his lab notebook. He was bent over, his glasses slipping down his nose, his left hand curled around so he could write properly. His sleeves were rolled up, and I noticed for the first time that his forearms were freckled, too. Were they warm? They seemed like they'd be warm. Blue Eyes's hand had been warm. There were four inches between my hand and his arm—four inches and I'd know for sure.

Don't do it, idiot. Don't you dare do it.

I stifled the urge and asked a question instead.

"So. Can you really speak another language?"

I hadn't heard that weird accent from him since the first day, but I knew he and Jetta had been speaking German.

"Where'd you hear that?" Miles didn't look up.

"Is it true?"

"Maybe. Depends on who told you."

"I figured it out myself," I said. "It wasn't hard. Is it German?"

Miles slapped his pen on his lab notebook. "Why are you here, exactly?"

"Because they put me in this class. Don't look at me like it's my fault."

"Why are you here? In this school? In the club?" His voice was too low for our neighbors across the table to hear. "What did you do?"

"What did *you* do?" I shot back. "Because it must have been pretty weird if they made you run the whole club by yourself, without a teacher supervising."

"Nothing," he said.

"Seriously, though."

"Seriously, nothing. Now why don't you answer my question, since you seem so intent on getting information out of me, but refuse to give any up yourself."

I looked at the calcium carbonate. "I spray-painted the gym floor."

"Spray-painted what?"

"The gym floor, I just said."

"*What* did you spray paint *on* the gym floor?" The *w* in "what" came out hard like a *v*.

"Words."

I smiled brightly at the pissy expression on his face. Screwing with him was so unexplainably worth it. I turned back to the Bunsen burner and listened to him seethe.

Game nights in the concession stand hit occasional lulls, so Theo and I entertained ourselves making plastic cup pyramids and talking about English class.

I found out that Theo wrote for the school newspaper, which was why I always saw her talking to Claude Gunthrie, the editor. ("I know he looks kind of constipated all the time"—she knocked over a stack of cups in her excitement—"but you haven't seen his biceps. My God, they're beautiful.")

"I feel like I should constantly be watching my back in that class, you know?" I said. "I've had a weird feeling about Ria since school started." Ria sat near me in class, but all I'd ever seen her do was bat her eyelashes at Cliff and giggle like some kind of perky, latte-fueled automaton.

"Ria's really not all that bad," said Theo. "You'd think she would be. She's popular, but she doesn't go picking for food among us lower beings. Unless she's looking for a distraction from Cliff."

"Why would she need a distraction from Cliff?"

"They've been dating since seventh grade, but the real drama didn't start till freshman year. Biggest. Shitstorm. Ever. She always accuses him of cheating; he's always treating her like a trophy. So, like, once a year, she'll go find a guy to sleep with to make Cliff jealous. Cliff finds the guy, beats the crap out of him, and then Cliff and Ria make up and the whole cycle starts again." Theo reached over her head to place a cup on top of the pyramid. "No, the people you really want to watch out for are Celia and the Siamese Twins."

Celia's two cronies, Britney and Stacey, might as well have been joined at the hip. I could tell Theo's brothers apart better than I could those two. I reached around and added to the pyramid's edge. "Celia gives Miles these looks in English class. Like she wants to eat him."

Theo shivered. "Don't mention that while Boss is

around. She's obsessed with him. Has been since freshman year, since she started getting weird. Never came out and said it, but you can tell."

"Well, she's a bitch and he's a douche; they're perfect for each other," I said, smiling.

Theo gave me one of those looks, the ones parents give their kid when the kid is talking about something they don't understand. That look stung more than I thought it would; I shifted and hid behind the pyramid, my face burning. What had I said? What was there about this picture that I didn't get?

"Bored again?" Theo asked suddenly. Miles stood at the window, still holding that tattered black notebook.

"I hate volleyball," he said.

Theo smiled wickedly. "No, you hate Ria Wolf. Don't take your anger out on the poor sport."

Miles gave her the same pissy look he'd given me earlier and drummed his long fingers impatiently on the counter.

Theo rolled her eyes and kept stacking. "I've got someone," she said.

"Were you alive during the last century?"

"Yes."

Miles rested his chin on top of his notebook, looking (as I couldn't help noticing) very much like a mischievous little boy knowing he was about to win a game. A golden-freckled, blue-eyed little boy. "Were you an Allied leader in World War II?"

I heard Theo grinding her teeth. "Yes."

"You're Chiang Kai-shek."

Theo hurled her cup and the entire pyramid came tumbling down. "Why didn't you say Churchill? Dammit, you were supposed to say Churchill or Roosevelt or Stalin!"

Miles just stared at her. Theo grumbled loudly and turned to help me clean up.

It was in English a week later when possibly the strangest thing of all happened.

When I tried to sit down, I instead found myself on the floor in a very painful position. The bar connecting the desk and the seat had been partially severed at one end, so my weight broke it the rest of the way. For a second, I thought I was imagining it. People were staring at me. Cursing under my breath, I got up, shoved the ruined desk to the back of the room, and pulled over an unused whole one.

Mr. Gunthrie hadn't even looked up from his paper. Miles, always politely oblivious, pretended nothing had happened and continued writing in his black notebook.

That also meant that he wasn't paying attention when I got into his backpack and emptied a tube of fire ants from the colony I'd found in the woods. With six classes together, there was no way I wouldn't see the reaction.

This was not the strange part.

Celia Hendricks, always on the prowl, materialized next to Miles's desk. She did that weird hair flip-and-twirl routine, like she'd learned how to flirt from a tween magazine. Miles glared at her.

"What do you want, Hendricks?"

Celia gave him a winning smile. "Hey. I'm having my bonfire soon. We're going to have a fake scoreboard to graffiti and everything. You should come."

"Every year I say no. Why should I say yes now?"

"Because, it'll be fun!" she whined. She tried to put her hand on his arm, but he recoiled. I could have sworn he was about to snarl at her.

"Get off my desk, Celia."

"Pleeeease, Miles? What can I do to get you to come?" Her voice dropped low and she looked at him through her eyelashes. She leaned over the desk. He snapped the notebook closed before she could look inside. "Anything," she said. "Name it."

Miles paused for a long moment. Then he jabbed his thumb over his shoulder and said, "Invite Alex. Then I'll come."

Celia's expression shuffled so quickly I almost didn't catch it. One second she'd been trying to seduce Miles, the next she glared at me like I should be impaled on a pike, and finally she settled on a sort of confused surprise.

"Oh! Well . . . you promise?" She was right in Miles's face. Miles leaned back. I had the immediate image of an idiot backing an angry viper into a corner.

"Sure. Promise," he said venomously.

"Good!" Celia pulled a card from the pocket of her shirt and reached over Miles's shoulder to give it to me. She was clearly on a mission to get his face in her cleavage. I let him squirm for longer than necessary before I took the card. She hopped off his desk.

"Can't wait to see you there, Milesie!"

I snorted.

Miles glared at me.

"Milesie?" I said. "Can I call you that?"

"You had better show up," he said, his gaze flat and cold.

Celia's bonfire wasn't until mid-October, on Scoreboard Day. It took me a long time to decide to go, and only after consulting Finnegan's Magic 8 Ball (*Signs point to yes*) and much prodding from the rest of the club. Except Miles, of course, who only deemed it necessary to give me one prod. (Days later, he still had a wonderful array of bright red welts on the back of his right hand.)

The fact that the club wanted me to go made it feel like I wasn't so much using it as an excuse to make my mother and therapist happy, but more like I actually wanted to spend time with. . . .

With friends.

I'd be paranoid as hell while I was there, but my mother was so ecstatic about the idea that I knew there was no way I could back out. She might have even blown a few synapses when I asked her if I could go, because she stood there and stared blankly at me for a minute before asking if I was supposed to take food and how much. She called my therapist with the good news, and my therapist immediately wanted to talk to me and ask why I'd made the decision and how I felt about it.

My mother also said she'd drive me, but I headed her off; Theo had already offered a ride, and I'd accepted. Having my mother and her Firenza drop me off in front of a huge house in one of the richest neighborhoods in town, at a party that I hadn't really been invited to, was more than enough to make my stomach bottom out.

The Wednesday before the party, Theo put her homework aside to tell me what to expect at the bonfire.

"Don't eat any of the food," she said as she handed a customer his hot dog. "Not even joking. Eat before you go. And don't drink anything."

Well, that certainly wouldn't be a problem. I almost thanked Theo for giving me an excuse to be paranoid about the food.

"Why? Does she poison it?"

"There's no guaranteeing that someone won't try to slip you a roofie." Theo turned to refill the popcorn machine. "You'll be fine. Don't eat or drink; stay inconspicuous."

So my normal routine, then.

"Oh, and don't go upstairs," Theo added.

"Why would I go upstairs?"

"Just don't do it, okay?"

"All right, fine."

"Anyway, everyone only goes to these parties to deface the fake scoreboard and get stories about crazy stuff. Celia's parties make better stories than Celia does."

Crazy stuff happening at parties with roofies and questionable upstairs goings-on didn't make me feel very good about the whole thing, but if I tried to back out now, my mother and my therapist would be on me like hounds. There was pretty much no way I wasn't going.

"FUCK IT, I'M BORED."

"Here he comes." Theo didn't even look up when Miles rounded the corner and tossed his notebook onto the counter. "I don't think cursing is going to help," she told him.

"Maybe it fucking will." Miles seethed. "I hate everyone in that gym. Pick someone."

"No, I don't want to play."

"It won't take that long."

"That's why I don't want to play."

"Can I do one?" I raised my hand. "It might actually take you more than five questions, too."

Miles quirked his eyebrow. "Oh, you think so?"

"If you get this in five, I'll be thoroughly impressed."

He leaned over the counter, looking eager. Weirdly, weirdly eager. Not like he wanted to rub my face into the floor. Not like he knew he was going to beat me. Just . . . excited. "Okay," he said. "Are you fictional?"

Broad question. He didn't know me as well as he knew Theo, so it was to be expected.

"No," I said.

"Are you still alive?"

"No."

"Are you a leader?"

"Yes."

"Was your civilization conquered by a European nation?"

"Yes."

"Are you . . . a leader of the Olmec?"

"How'd you get *there*?" Theo blurted out, but Miles ignored her.

"No," I said, trying not to let him see how close he'd come. "And the Olmec weren't conquered by the Europeans. They died out."

Miles frowned. "Mayan?"

"No."

"Incan."

"No."

"Aztec."

"Yes."

The corners of his lips twisted up, but he said, "Shouldn't have taken so many guesses for that one." Then he said, "Did you found the Tlatocan?"

"No."

"Did you reign after 1500?"

"No."

Theo watched the conversation like a tennis match.

"Are you Ahuitzotl?"

"No." I smiled. This kid knew his history.

"Tizoc?"

"No."

"Axayacatl?"

"No."

"Moctezuma I?"

"Nope."

"Itzcoatl?"

"No."

"Chimalpopoca?"

"No."

"Huitzilihuitl?"

"What the hell are you saying?" Theo cried.

He'd cut off a chunk of the Aztec emperors and whittled them down until there was only one remaining. But now he had three questions left—two he didn't need.

Why hadn't he cut it down again? Surely he could have shortened his options and not guessed his way through all the emperors. Was this some kind of test? Or was . . . was he showing off?

"You're Acamapichtli."

There was a fanatical gleam in his eye, another smile playing on his lips. Both were gone as soon as I said, "Almost twenty. Not quite, but I almost had you."

"I'm never playing this game again," said Theo, sighing and returning to her homework.

The little boy from the lobster tank disappeared from Miles's face.

Why did he invite me?

Most likely

I wish you could say more than yes or no.

Chapter Fourteen

Charlie planted herself in my bedroom doorway with her hands on her hips, the head of a black bishop clenched between her teeth. "Can I come with you?"

"This isn't an eight-year-old sort of party."

"What's that supposed to mean?"

"It means *no*." I ducked back into my shallow closet in search of something different to wear. Old jeans littered the floor and shirts hung lopsided from hangers. A ratty pair of ginger cat-shaped house slippers curled up underneath a fraying sweatshirt. The slippers purred when my foot brushed against them.

"Why not?" Charlie stamped her foot. Her cheeks were round and red. With her expression and her tiny frame, she looked closer to four than eight.

"Why are you being so whiny tonight? Usually you give up after a while."

She wouldn't look at me.

"Are you crying?"

"No!" She sucked in snot.

"It's not like I'm leaving permanently. I'll be back later." I finally decided it would be easier not to change at all and yanked the Lacedaemon Spartans XXL sweatshirt away from the (hissing) cat slippers to pull it on.

My mother called from the living room. "Alex! Your friends are here!"

It might have been the first time she ever said those words in that order in her life. I picked Charlie up under her armpits and carried her down the hallway, setting her on the carpet in the living room. The triplets waited at the end of the driveway in Theo's Camry.

"Are you sure you don't have to take anything?" asked my mother.

"I'll be fine, Mom," I said. "But I've been dying for some Yoo-hoos lately." Had to get the requests in while she was still on this normality high. "See you later. If Dad calls, tell him he's got horrible timing."

"I wanna go!" Charlie tugged on my pant leg.

"You can't—it's a big-girl party," I said.

"I'm not *four*!" Charlie screeched, the black bishop dancing on her lip.

"No," I said, "you're eight. And you need to stop chewing on those things—you're going to choke."

My mother's eyebrows creased in worry right before I ducked out the door. Maybe she cared more about what happened at this party than she let on.

Being in a car with Theo and her brothers was like shutting myself in a bank vault with eighty pounds of TNT and a lit fuse. Theo let me sit in the front seat, but even then it felt like Evan and Ian were too close. The three of them sang earsplitting drinking songs the whole way and only stopped when Theo turned into Downing Heights.

Downing Heights was the richest neighborhood in town. All the houses here were huge and immaculate and eggshell white, but it didn't take long to figure out which one was Celia's. Cars lined up on both sides of the road nearly ten houses in either direction. Theo parked, and we walked to the two-story McMansion at the center of all the chaos.

A bad feeling roiled in my stomach. I'd never been to this neighborhood before, and eyes watched me from the dark spaces in the landscaping. I balled my fists in the hem of my sweatshirt.

Music beat a steady rhythm from a huge stereo on the back porch; the bonfire crackled a short distance away. Inside the house, lights flashed, and people came and went through all sorts of doors and windows like flies on a hot day.

"Keep calm," Evan said, grinning, as he led the way into the house.

"Don't go upstairs," said Theo.

"And don't. Ingest. Anything," Ian finished. And then the triplets were gone. Sucked into the crowd beyond the door. Unfamiliar bodies pressed in on me from every side.

My perimeter check wouldn't do any good in here. I could hardly see five feet in front of me. Checking each person for a weapon would be more than impossible. I had my camera, tucked in my sweatshirt pocket, but that wouldn't do me any good. I'd never remember what I'd seen and what I hadn't.

I slipped my way through the sweaty bodies and loud voices, looking for a familiar face. I thought I saw Tucker and headed toward him, but when I made it across the room, he'd vanished.

As I edged around the elaborate, china-cabinet-flanked dining room, I wondered where Celia's parents were and if they knew exactly how many cans of beer were stacked on their polished mahogany dining table. (Answer: seventy-six.)

The curving staircase was around the corner from the dining room; the upstairs seemed a lot quieter and less alcohol-filled than the downstairs. I knew what Theo had said, but unless someone was going to ambush me, I didn't see any reason not to go up.

At the top of the staircase was a gloriously quiet hallway lined on either side with doors. Most of them were closed. Probably bedrooms. About halfway down was a narrow table covered with framed pictures. I could see Celia in them, Celia *smiling*, but before I could get near them, a girl's voice floated out of a bedroom up ahead.

"Stop squirming! Shut up and sit still . . . I thought you were going to do what I said."

I tiptoed closer to the cracked-open door until I had a view of the room's occupants. There was a bed. And on the bed was a half-naked Ria Wolf on top of a half-naked guy who was definitely not Cliff Ackerley. Ria, her back to me, sat up and flipped her hair over her shoulder.

I pushed away from the door and sprinted for the stairs. Holy—*that* was what Theo had been talking about—Ria's revenge plot—wow, okay. My skin crawled as I cut a path through the thicket of bodies at the foot of the stairs. I rushed into the shiny white kitchen and escaped to the back porch.

Everyone was either clustered around the stereo or the seven-foot-tall piece of plyboard, propped up on the lawn, which had been painted to look like the scoreboard. Beer, candy wrappers, old movie ticket stubs, and one soiled pair of underwear had been left on the ground around it as offerings. A rainbow of fluorescent graffiti covered its face. Curse words, cartoon penises, obscene suggestions for what McCoy could do with his genitals. Nothing you wouldn't find carved into the desk of the average teenaged boy. Several people were busy spray-painting the words *Rich Dick McCoy Forever* along its bottom edge in bright pink.

I could only think of the Hillpark Gym Graffiti Incident. Not exactly my shining moment. I headed to the lawn. The nighttime silence and the crackle of the bonfire made a sort of wall against the blaring music on the porch. Three benches were arranged in a triangle around the fire: one had been smashed in the middle by a bowling ball that still rested between the halves; another was occupied by a couple so tightly wrapped around each other I'd need the Jaws of Life to pry them apart. Astronomical amounts of bird crap covered the benches, but the couple didn't seem to mind and bowling balls tend to be astoundingly unobservant.

The third bench had only one occupant, sitting with his back to me, watching the marshmallow on his skewer burn black in the fire.

When I realized who he was, my heart rose and fell and I considered going back inside before that flaming marshmallow could be weaponized. But then he turned and saw me and arched his eyebrow, *that freaking eyebrow can I rip it off already.*

"You can sit here, if you want." Miles scooted to one end of the bench. There was something weird, subdued, about his voice. He sounded normal. Calm. Like we were friends or something.

I sat down on the other end of the bench ("the other end" being five inches away), checked him from head to toe for sharp objects, and tugged on my hair. If he was my only point of normalcy in this party from hell, I'd take him. He'd ditched his school uniform for a worn pair of jeans, thick-soled work boots, a white-and-blue baseball shirt, and a heavy bomber jacket that looked like it'd come straight out of World War II.

"What brings you to the fireside?" he asked, lifting his skewer and watching the marshmallow burn without the slightest hint of interest.

"It's too crowded." I didn't know what he was playing at—if anything—or if he was going to snap back to regular old Miles. "And too noisy. Mob mentality is running rampant in there."

Miles grunted.

"So why'd you make Celia invite me?" I asked. "I can't believe you're that hard up for company."

Miles shrugged. "I don't know. Seemed like a good idea at the time. Consider it payback." The marshmallow dropped dead into the fiery depths. He started on a second.

"I asked off work for this. You'd think with all the alcohol consumption and the people groping each other"—he motioned to our Jaws of Life bench friends—"and the anonymous bedroom sex, it'd be a little more interesting."

I shivered. "I definitely kind of walked in on someone in a bedroom upstairs."

Miles made a weird coughing sound, like he was holding back a laugh. I'd never heard him laugh. "You walked in on them? What did they do?"

"I didn't actually walk in. The door was cracked open, and I heard someone talking—"

"Who was it?"

"Ria. I don't know who the guy was, but it wasn't Cliff."

Miles's eyebrows set in a hard line above his eyes. The second marshmallow fell. He grabbed a third. "Whoever he was, I hope he doesn't mind having his nose cartilage lodged in the back of his skull. Cliff can be territorial."

"You sound like you've experienced this. Does it have something to do with why you hate Ria? Ooh, were you one of those guys? The ones that she . . . y'know . . ."

"No." His look was deadly. "I hate Ria because there's nothing going on inside her head besides volleyball and sparkly things. I hate Cliff for the same reason, only football instead of volleyball and sex instead of sparkly things."

It certainly hadn't taken long for Evil Miles to show up

again. He didn't say anything else. We sat quietly for a few minutes, listening to the snap of the fire and the music from the deck and the sounds coming from the bench couple, who were really going at it. Even with them making out right there and the bowling ball being so conspicuous, I still wanted to take a picture of it all.

Miles burned his way through another three marshmallows. "I think Celia may hate you now," he said finally.

"No kidding? I wasn't sure—that viper glare she gave me when you made her invite me didn't quite get the message across, I guess." I grabbed a skewer and jammed the prongs into a burning log. "What's with her, anyway? She's all over you. Is she your ex-girlfriend or something?"

"No. I've never"—he switched gears in the blink of an eye—"she's always been like that. I don't know why."

"She likes you." I still stood by what I'd said to Theo, even if she thought it was weird.

"That's . . . stupid."

"Oh, so you think so, too?" I said.

Miles looked over at me. "Do you hate me?"

The question was so sudden, and his voice was so bland and devoid of emotion, that I wondered if he even wanted an answer. "Um. You're a bit of a jerk."

He seemed unconvinced.

"Okay, okay, you're a complete douche bag. You're the biggest asshat on the planet. Is that what you wanted to hear?"

"No, the truth'll do fine."

"Okay. You're a jerk." *And you have beautiful eyes.* "But no, I don't hate you." I became very intent on moving ashes into piles. I didn't want to look at him again, but I could feel his eyes on me. "I do think the gutting of the books was a step too far."

"And gluing my locker shut wasn't? Good job on not admitting that, by the way."

"Thanks. How's your hand?"

"Better," he said. "*Animalia Arthropoda Insecta Hymenoptera Formicidae Solenopsis.* Little bastards. Lucky I'm not allergic to the damn things. If I'd had a reaction, I would've sued."

"And what business would a rich kid like you have suing a poor kid like me?"

The end of Miles's skewer hit the ground next to the fire. He turned his full attention on me. "What makes you think I'm rich?"

I shrugged. "You're a brat? You're an only child? Your shoes are always polished?" It was true—his shirt was always wrinkle-free, his tie straight, his pants sharp and ironed, and his shoes were blacker and shinier than anyone else's. And his *hair*, let's not even get started on his hair, because he had hair that looked like he'd walked right out of the shower every morning and artfully styled it to dry in the most amazingly messy way. Like good-looking bed head, if that's even possible. Whatever he was, he certainly took pains to make himself look nice.

"My shoes are always polished?" he said incredulously. "*That's* why you think I'm rich? Because I like *shiny shoes?*"

I shrugged again, heat seeping into my face.

"And sometimes there's a good reason why someone's an only child, so don't even go there."

"Fine!" I held up my hands. "Sorry, okay? You're not rich."

Miles turned back to the fire. Another silence blanketed us, but this one wasn't awkward, either. Just really, really heavy. Like one of us should have kept talking until we ran out of things to say.

"Exactly how good are you with history?" Miles asked, his tone back to bland and unaffected.

"That depends. There's a lot of history—what do you want to know?"

"Everything," he said, but before I could ask what the hell that meant, he added, "Who was the fourteenth president of the US?"

"Franklin Pierce. The only president from New Hampshire."

"What was his second child's name and what did that child die from?"

"Ben—no, Frank—Robert Pierce. Frank Robert Pierce. Died of . . . typhus."

"At what age?"

"Uh . . . four? Five? I can't remember. Why are you so interested in an obscure president's second child?"

Miles shook his head and looked away. But he also smiled. Weird, lopsided, more of a smirk than a smile, really, but it got the point across. How smart was he? A genius, but in what? It seemed like he was good at everything— he helped Theo with calculus, he could destroy chemistry without blinking, he slept through his A+ in English, and everything else seemed to bore him. He knew the name Huitzilihuitl. (And, more importantly, how to pronounce it.) He knew *everything*.

Except the truth about me. And I needed to keep it that way.

I locked my eyes on the fire, but was quickly distracted by the Jaws of Life couple; clothes were being removed, and if Miles's expression was anything to go by, they were going to get skewered if it went any further.

A second later it didn't matter. The noise from the deck swelled toward us, and before I could consider running, Celia Hendricks slid onto the bench beside me and someone else slid in on Miles's other side, and the five inches between us disappeared. We were smashed together, my shoulder in his armpit, his arm braced behind us, my legs nearly on top of his. Seemingly everyone from the back deck made a ring around the fire.

I froze. I'd never been this close to so much of a person. Except Charlie. I didn't even let my mother get this close to me.

Miles's neck and ears had gone red. This must have been torture for him, too. Because of the people crowding us, I probably looked like I'd thrown myself at Miles, and he probably looked like he wanted it.

"Well. This is awkward," said Miles.

The triplets laughed somewhere behind us. Miles and I twisted to find them at the same time. His jaw smacked my forehead.

He groaned. "God, is your head made of steel?"

"Why, too hard to bite through, Jaws?" I sniped back, rubbing my forehead. The triplets were already on their way, blond blurs in the crowd.

A hand dug into my ribs.

"Hey guys!" Celia flashed two rows of white teeth. "How d'you like the party?"

"It's . . . um . . . great," I said as Miles grabbed my leg and pulled it over his, shifting my weight off his rib cage. I lost my balance, and he grabbed my leg again to steady me.

The leg in question had turned to jelly.

Kids crowded all along the back of the bench, barricading any escape. I barely kept myself from punching Celia. I didn't realize I was squeezing myself closer to Miles until he coughed and tilted his chin up to avoid my head.

The scent of tobacco and wood shavings filled my nose. His jacket. It was the kind of smell I'd only previously caught off my parents' pipe-smoking, dirt-digging history colleagues. I was close enough to him to get a clear whiff of something else . . . pastries. And one more. Mint soap. It was like someone had mixed together all the best-smelling things in the world and made Miles bathe in them.

"Get me out of here," he muttered. The arm he'd been holding out behind me dropped, and his hand brushed down along my side. Hairs shot up all over my body. Miles's face went red. "Sorry . . . arm was getting tired . . ."

We were nose to nose. Straight nose. Square jaw. Clear eyes. *Yes*, I thought, *yes, very cute. Cuteness confirmed.*

"I'm going to try to find a way out," I said breathlessly, twisting around. My task was made much harder by Celia, still trying to get Miles's attention.

And also by the flicker of light behind Celia, the pungent smell of burning hair, and someone yelling, "YOU'RE ON FIRE!"

Chapter
Fifteen

The two seconds between the realizations that I wasn't on fire and Celia was were a very blissful two seconds.

Celia screamed and batted at herself, making it hard to see if the fire had caught her hair or her clothes or both. Someone ran up behind her and dumped a bucket of water over her head, dousing her. She stood motionless for a moment, the ends of her hair curled and black, her makeup running in streaks down her face.

"WHO DID IT?"

Everyone stared at her. She'd been sitting too far from the fire for it to reach her, hadn't she? The back of her sweatshirt was as singed as her hair. She didn't seem hurt, though. She seethed, eyes roving through the crowd, until she zeroed in on me.

I had my camera pointed at her. I'd gotten it out before I realized that her burning hair was not a delusion.

"You were right next to me!" she screeched.

I shoved my camera into my pocket and tried to retreat, but the bench hit the backs of my knees. "You think *I* did it?"

"You were RIGHT. NEXT. TO. ME. Who else?"

I don't know. Only the ten or so people behind you.

I stood there looking stupid, because that's what I do when I'm accused of something I didn't do. Forget making a case or, you know, *denying* that I'd done it.

Denying hadn't helped me in the past.

"Oh my God, you *did* do it! What the hell is wrong with you?" Celia grabbed at the burnt tips of her hair, her face contorting in rage. She looked between Miles and me, then cranked her bitch level up to eleven. "You're *jealous*!"

I stared at Miles. Miles stared at me. We both stared at Celia.

"The fuck?" Miles said.

Then Celia lunged at me, and everything fell to pandemonium. Someone pulled me over the bench and through the sea of bodies as everyone converged, ready for a fight. People were going every direction, yelling, screaming, the music suddenly louder than ever.

As soon as we broke free, I saw it was Art dragging me

along, his mammoth muscles straining against his shirt. I would have been thankful if it wasn't for the fact that he usually showed up when Miles was pulling a job. If Art had been there waiting to yank me out of harm's way, then Miles must have been involved with the fire, right?

I set my jaw; as soon as we were back on the driveway, I yanked my arm out of Art's grip, grabbed his huge shoulder, and spun him to face me. "Did Miles do that?"

"No," he said immediately. He scrubbed at his short hair.

The brush of invisible fingers crawled up the back of my neck. I jabbed a finger at him. "You had better be telling me the truth, Art Babrow. Not just what Miles tells you to say."

"Scout's honor," Art said, holding up his hand.

I didn't believe him. I couldn't. It felt like I had cotton packed down my throat. I was suffocating. I tugged on my hair with both hands, turned in a full circle to make sure there were no cameras on the houses or the lampposts, and set off down the sidewalk.

"Where are you going?" Art called. "I know you didn't drive here yourself."

"I'm going home!" I yelled.

Home. Home was good.

"Isn't your house a few miles away?"

"Probably."

"The *fuck*," someone said. The privacy fence gate clacked closed. "Where are you going? I told you to keep her here."

I looked behind me; Miles had caught up to Art. I marched back, planting a finger in the middle of Miles's chest. "What the hell do you think you're doing? You torch someone's hair and let her blame me? Because apparently I'm jealous? What kind of retribution is that? The books were one thing, and the desk, and all that other stuff—but this is ridiculous."

Miles rolled his eyes. "Would you shut up and stop assuming you know everything?"

"Would you stop being such a jackass?"

It came out of my mouth too quickly, a reflex reaction to the guilt flooding my stomach. I had no proof, but I wanted him to stop talking. It worked—his mouth snapped shut, his hands balled into fists. A muscle worked in his jaw. I glared at him as he floundered, but I floundered, too; I couldn't think of what to do next.

Home. Had to get home.

I kept picturing a Celia-led mob chasing me down the street, screaming about my devilish crime like Puritans at a witch trial. I hadn't done anything wrong—I *never* did anything wrong—it wasn't my fault. . . .

"Alex, I can take you home," Art said.

Always be polite. "No, thank you."

I turned and started walking again. I didn't care where. Anywhere other than here. Art said something else. The words hit me and bounced off. I kept my eyes forward. The street went very quiet.

Ahead of me, Miles stepped out from behind a tree.

How had he gotten there so hellishly fast? He'd been standing behind me not ten seconds ago, and now he emerged at least three houses down the street. He ambled toward me with his clothes in tatters, like he'd gotten mauled by a bear. When he got close, the smell of alcohol and pond scum invaded the air.

Where his freckles had been, a hundred little holes pulsed blood down his pale cheeks.

"I don't want to talk to you." I tried to walk past him, but he loped backward, keeping his eyes on mine. His hands hung limp at his sides. His fingers looked longer than usual, like he had too many knuckles. My stomach knotted. I didn't know what he'd done to his freckles, but I couldn't let him see how much they creeped me out.

He wouldn't leave.

I wanted him to leave.

"Go away!" I yelled at him. He didn't blink. His eyes were bluer than ever, bluer than they should have been in the darkness. The sun glowed behind them, melting them from inside like candle wax. The color seeped from his skin.

"Alex!"

Someone grabbed my arm. Spun me around.

Miles was there, too. Except not bleeding. And his clothes weren't torn. And his eyes were the right shade of blue. I pulled my arm away and backed up. And ran into Miles.

"Who are you talking to?" Miles—regular Miles—asked. Art was right behind him.

"I . . . I don't . . ."

Oh no. There were two of him. I knew it was wrong, I knew there shouldn't be, but he reached up for my face, and I felt the cold roiling off his skin.

The roots of my hair screamed as I tugged on them.

"Both of you stay away from me." I pointed to both Mileses, backing up onto the nearest lawn. One Miles was bad enough. Two was unbearable.

Regular Miles frowned. "What are you talking about?"

Keep your mouth shut, idiot! the little voice in the back of my head screamed. It wasn't supposed to be this bad.

He's not real.

He is.

He's not he's not.

A cold finger brushed down my cheek.

Then how can he touch you?

Bloody Miles stared at me, his mouth curving into a wide grin. The blood stained his teeth, too. Miles never smiled. Not like that.

I dropped to the ground as Bloody Miles lunged at me. The world went dark. I heard footsteps. Art yelled something I couldn't understand.

Fingers grabbed my shoulders and tried to pull me up. I balled my hand into a fist and lashed out, connecting with something fleshy.

A groan.

The fingers released me.

"Damn. She clocked you, Boss."

"No shit. Can you carry her?"

"I can try."

I squirmed away, but Art's spicy aftershave drowned out the smell of alcohol and pond scum. One big arm snaked around my shoulders, the other behind my knees. He lifted me up. "She's shaking so bad—I can hardly hold on to her."

"This way. I'll take her home."

Warm air moved past my face. I didn't open my eyes, because he would be there.

The truck door creaked open. I cracked my eyes open to see Art buckling me into the passenger seat.

"Go back to the party." Miles climbed in the driver's side. "Don't tell anyone about this."

No, Art! Don't leave me alone with him!

But Art nodded and turned away. Miles started the truck.

"Alex."

I stared out the window. Where was he?

"Alex, *please* look at me."

I didn't.

"What's going on?" His voice rose and cracked. "What are you afraid of? Just look at me!"

I glanced at him out of the corner of my eye. I could smell pastries and mint soap, crisp and sharp in the cold air. Miles let out a quick breath, but didn't relax. His glasses slipped down his nose. A bruise already bloomed across his right cheekbone. His eyes flickered back to the road.

"What's wrong?" he asked again. "What did you see? There was no one out there besides you and me and Art."

I shook my head.

I couldn't tell him.

He could never know.

Chapter
Sixteen

My mother opened the door.

"She just . . ." was all Miles got out before she yanked me from his arms.

"What happened?" She pushed me into the house. "What did you do?"

"He didn't do anything, Mom." She pushed me onto the bench in the hall. The room spun, threatened to disappear. I realized she'd been talking to me, not Miles.

"We were at the bonfire, and she said . . . she started talking to someone else," said Miles. "She fell down screaming, and we got her up and I brought her here."

My mother stared at him. "What's that mark? Did she hit you?"

"Yes, but . . ."

She rounded on me, eyes flashing. "Thank you," she said over her shoulder to Miles. "I'm very sorry for your trouble. If there's anything I can do for you, please let me know."

"But wait—is she okay?"

My mother closed the door in his face.

"Mom!"

"Alexandra Victoria Ridgemont. You haven't been taking your medicine, have you?"

"Mom, I—I thought I was—"

She stormed into the bathroom and returned with my prescription bottle, thrusting it into my hands. "Take them. Now." She bent down and pulled my shoes off like I was four. "I *trusted* you to take those on time. I thought, after years of this, I could count on you to do it yourself." One of her nails scratched my heel. "I can't believe you hit him. What if his parents decide to press assault charges? I can't believe you were so irresponsible. Are you still seeing things?"

"How am I supposed to know, Mom?" I had to force the words through the knot in my throat. I wiped tears from my eyes. I clawed open the pill bottle and choked down the medicine.

"Go into the living room. I'm calling Leann."

Leann Graves, my therapist. The Gravedigger.

My stomach convulsed.

"I'm fine, Mom, really," I said, voice wavering. "I'm okay now. It snuck up on me."

But she already had the phone in her hand, her thumbs flying over the buttons. How did she not have the Gravedigger on speed dial? She smashed the phone against her ear.

"I'm calling your father after this," she said in her most severe, threatening tone.

"Good!" The strength of my voice surprised me. "He listens better than you do!"

She pressed her lips into a thin white line and disappeared into the kitchen.

I stood, hurled the pill bottle on the floor, and ran to my room. The pictures floated from the walls when I threw the door open. I tossed my camera onto the bed and ripped the nearest picture off. In it was a tree with bright red and orange leaves. The problem was, the other trees were all green. Because I'd taken the picture at the end of spring. I tore another snapshot down. This one was my first sighting of the Hannibal's Rest phoenix. It perched on top of Red Witch Bridge, staring straight into the camera. I took another picture down, and another.

All of them still had their subjects. Nothing had changed.

I sunk down on the rug. Pictures spilled across the

floor, leaving new gaps in my photograph-covered walls. The tears came on full force, wet and messy and stupid. I should have known. I should have paid better attention. Now Miles would know, and everyone would—

I stopped myself. That wasn't why I was upset.

I was upset because I couldn't tell. I couldn't tell that Bloody Miles wasn't real. I'd gotten—I *thought* I'd gotten so good at telling the difference. These pictures meant nothing. They told me nothing.

The door creaked open and a tiny body wedged its way inside my room. I opened my arms and Charlie climbed into my lap without hesitation. I buried my face in her hair. She was the only one I let myself cry in front of, because she was the only one who never asked what was wrong, or if I needed anything, or if she could help.

She was just there.

Am I crazy?

Concentrate and ask again

Am I crazy?

Reply hazy try again

Am I crazy?

Cannot predict now

Better not tell you now

Concentrate and ask again

Better not tell you now

Reply hazy try again

Cannot predict now

Ask again later

Ask again later

Ask again later

Part Two | The Lobsters

Chapter Seventeen

I spent the next three weeks in and out of the hospital.

By the end of the second week, I more often haunted my living room, but the Gravedigger rained medication on me like the London Blitz.

Every morning I woke up with the image of Bloody Miles burned into my memory, and every night I dreamed I stood on a gymnasium floor spray-painted red with the word *Communists*, while McCoy's scoreboard cackled on the wall behind me.

Nothing felt or tasted or looked good anymore. I didn't know if it was me or the new medication. Food made me want to throw up, blankets and clothes scratched and twisted, every light blinded me. The world had gone gray. Sometimes I felt like I was dying, or the Earth was breaking apart beneath my feet, or the sky might swallow me whole.

I couldn't go to work anymore. Not that I cared. Finnegan hated me anyway. This would be the perfect excuse for him to fire me.

I didn't even sneak out to Red Witch Bridge. I couldn't risk it. And a dark part of my mind imagined Bloody Miles standing in the trees, waiting for me.

Homework came in overwhelming waves, especially chemistry and calculus, which I had a hard enough time learning even with formal instruction. My mother tried to teach me, but she sucked at it, too. Some days I thought she'd break down in the hallway or the kitchen and fill the house with sobs. I don't know much about what my mother's life was like before she had kids, but I think she was happier. I think she didn't spend all her time caring for one child who was a high-maintenance musical prodigy and another who couldn't even manage her own medication schedule.

Charlie was a little different, because Charlie did what she always did when she was afraid or not sure how to handle a situation: she hid. She stayed out of the living room, my fortress, and only ventured into the kitchen when she knew I wasn't there. I hardly saw her at all those first two weeks, but after I had a particularly bad time with the Gravedigger, Charlie stood on the other side of the doorway, out of sight, and played me songs on her violin. Usually the *1812 Overture*.

The third week turned out to be the best of the three. That Sunday, Dad came home.

Rain thundered against the windows. I sat barricaded in my pillow fort, leaning against the couch, wondering about the contents of those eighteen-and-a-half lost minutes of the Nixon White House tapes, when rain-rippled headlights roamed across the far wall and gravel crunched as a car pulled into the driveway. Maybe my mother had left without me knowing and was just getting back. But she wasn't supposed to leave me alone. She wouldn't.

A car door shut. Someone pulled open the screen door.

"DADDY'S HOME!" Charlie screamed from the kitchen.

I peeked out of my fort. My mother stood right in the doorway, Charlie's fringe of red hair visible behind her.

And then a completely soaked, suntanned someone leaned around the doorframe. He grinned when he saw me, his warm dark eyes crinkling at the corners.

"Hey, Lexi."

I almost cracked my head open on the coffee table in my rush to get out of the fort. With my blanket still wrapped around me like a cloak, I threw my arms around his neck and hid my face in his collar.

"Hi, Dad," I mumbled.

He laughed and hugged me back. "Lex, I'm all wet."

"I don't care." It sounded more like *mfffmmph*.

"I came back as soon as I could," he said when I let him go. "Did you know? South Africa is *really* far away."

Chapter Eighteen

I dismantled the pillow fort enough to make the couch sit-able again. Dad and I watched the History Channel and played chess all day, and in the evening, my mother and Charlie joined us. Charlie played behind the life-size George Washington statue in the corner, reenacting the crossing of the Delaware.

When it was just me and Dad, he'd ask about school and what I'd been doing while he'd been gone. He carefully maneuvered around the word "friends," something I thanked him for. But I did reassure him.

"They're my friends. I mean, really, they are. Or were . . . I hope they're still my friends, if they know . . ."

"If they're really your friends, they won't care about your condition, Lexi." Dad hugged me closer to his side. He smelled like rain. "Tell me about them."

So I told him about the club. About the triplets. About Art and the fact that even though he could kill a small man with a poke to the chest, he still acted like a complete teddy bear. About Jetta and her French heritage. About Tucker and his conspiracies. I smiled more than I had for the past two weeks.

"Who's the kid who brought you home?" Dad asked suddenly, throwing me off kilter. "The one you punched?"

"How'd you know about that?"

"Mom told me," he said, smiling. "Punching? Is that how you wrangle boys these days?" He nudged me in the side. I swatted his elbow away and pulled my blanket tighter, trying to hide the blush in my cheeks. "Wrangling" boys hadn't been on my agenda lately.

"It's just Miles."

"*Just* Miles?"

I ignored him. "He runs the club."

"What, that's it? Nothing else?"

"Uh, what do you want to know? He's the valedictorian. He's really tall."

Dad made an approving sound at the word *valedictorian*.

"He knew who Acamapichtli was," I added after a second. "Along with most of the other Aztec emperors. And the Tlatocan."

Dad's approving noise rose an octave.

"And I'm pretty sure he can speak German."

Dad smiled. "That all?"

My face heated up again at the look he gave me. As if I *liked* Miles. As if I *wanted* to think about him.

Just thinking about his stupid face and his stupidly blue eyes turned me into the most confused person on the planet.

"No," I said, burrowing into my blanket. "He can also take a hit."

By the end of the third week, the world balanced on its axis. Dad stayed home, Mom stayed happy, and I got to go back to school on Monday. Sure, I wanted to puke from the anxiety rolling around in my stomach, but now I could get back to my (admittedly late) college search, catch up on all that schoolwork, and see my friends again.

Assuming Miles hadn't told them everything, of course. If he had, there was a real chance they wouldn't want to talk to me at all. But, reassuringly, I thought they had tried to contact me. The phone had been ringing more often than usual, and more than once someone knocked on the door and was turned away by my mother. I wished I had my own cell phone, but my mother probably would have taken that away from me, too.

Sunday night, as I tromped down the back hallway—I'd

just finished putting up all my pictures again—to the living room, I heard my parents' voices floating out of the kitchen. Talking about me. I pressed myself up against the wall outside the doorway.

"—that it's not a good idea, that's all. We can't pretend that it isn't as bad as it looks."

"I don't think we should resort to that yet. Lexi's a responsible girl. Something must have bothered her. I don't think she'd forget—"

My heard swelled painfully with appreciation for my dad.

"David, *really*," said my mother. "You can't know that. What if she didn't want to take it? It was my fault for not paying enough attention, but . . . but that's not the point. The medication isn't the problem. This has happened before, and it might happen again, and it keeps getting *worse*."

"So you want to hide her away? You really think that's best for her? Trying to convince her to stay in some asylum?"

The word rang in the air.

"Oh, David, please." My mother's voice lowered to a whisper. "You know they're not like that anymore. They're not even called asylums. It's a *mental hospital*."

I hurried to the living room and curled up on the couch, drawing my blanket tightly around me. So much for feeling good. My mother had removed my intestines and used them to tie a noose around my neck. She just hadn't kicked the stool out from under me yet.

She couldn't send me to one of those places. She was my mother. She was supposed to do what was best for me, not what would get me out of her hair the fastest. How could she even think of that?

It took a while for me to notice the big blue eyes watching me from the doorway.

"C'm'ere, Charlie." I spread my arms. Charlie hesitated, then ran across the room and climbed into my lap. I wrapped my arms and the blanket around her.

She saved me from trying to figure out how much I should tell her. "I don't like it when your head breaks."

I knew she was old enough and smart enough to know that my head didn't actually break, but she'd been calling it that for so long it didn't matter anymore. I think it made her feel better to think of it like something broken that could be fixed.

"I don't like it, either," I said. "You do know why it happens, right? Why my head breaks?"

Charlie removed the black castle from her mouth and nodded. "The brain chemicals make hallucinations. . . ."

"And do you know what a hallucination is?"

She nodded again. "I looked it up."

Word of the Week, maybe? I hugged her tighter. "You

know how you didn't want me to leave for that party a while back?"

"Mm-hmm."

"And how you didn't want me to go to the hospital three weeks ago?"

"Yeah."

I took a breath, pulling myself together. Better to prepare her for the worst than let it blindside her. My parents would never tell her this. Not until it was too late.

Maybe, if I told her now—if I prepared myself, too—I could still avoid it.

"Well, I might have to go away again. And it won't just be for a few hours or days or weeks." I absentmindedly pulled a bit of her hair back and began braiding it. "Okay? I might not come back. I wanted you to know."

"Do Mom and Dad know?" Charlie whispered.

"Yeah, they know."

It was better if she didn't know that it was our mother's idea. She'd figure it out one day, but for now she could go on believing that some higher power sent me where it thought I needed to be. She could keep trusting Mom and Dad, and keep being my whining, chess-playing, crusading Charlemagne.

Chapter Nineteen

Mono was my cover story.

Everyone believed me. Everyone except Miles, Tucker, and Art. Art, because he'd carried me during my episode. Tucker, because his parents were doctors and he could tell when someone didn't actually know the symptoms of mono.

Miles, for the obvious reasons.

I did my perimeter check three times while I hid Erwin behind his bushes on the front walk, and my eyes were drawn again to the roof, where the men in suits monitored the parking lot. It took me a few minutes to realize that public high schools didn't *have* men in suits watching their parking lots. I took a picture of them. I wasn't sure if the pictures would help anymore, but doing it made me feel better. Like I was doing something to help myself. Like that was still possible.

I still had so much make-up work—and no clue how to do most of it. When I slouched into the cafeteria after fourth period, I spent the hour doing homework instead of eating. I didn't have to check my food because I didn't eat my food.

I saw that damn snake hanging from the damn opening in the ceiling again on my way to seventh period. I arrived late, but Miles had already finished the lab by himself and, by some miracle, agreed to let me copy his results. I flipped open my notebook, glanced warily at Ms. Dalton, and began copying.

Miles watched me. When I got suspicious and looked up, he just quirked his eyebrow and kept staring. Like a bored house cat. I snorted and kept writing.

He followed me after class, hovering silently on my right side. The cat waiting for attention. Anyone else would have sparked a cascade of paranoia, but he didn't.

"Sorry you had to do that lab alone," I said, knowing full well that it had been no trouble for him. "Those results look like—"

"So where were you, really?" he cut me off. "I know it wasn't mono."

I stopped, looked around, waited for some kids to pass us. "It was mono."

Miles rolled his eyes. "Yeah, and my IQ is twenty-five. Really, what were you doing?"

"Having *mono*." I gave him the you-really-shouldn't-push-this-any-further look, but apparently Miles Richter didn't understand *everything*, because he scoffed and moved in front of me, blocking my path.

"Yes, the symptoms of mono include reacting to things that aren't there, screaming for no reason at all, and flailing on the ground like you're about to be ax murdered."

My face flushed with heat. "It was mono," I whispered.

"You're schizophrenic."

I stood there, blinking stupidly.

Say something, idiot!

If I didn't, he'd have no doubt.

Say something! Say something!

I turned and walked away.

I wanted to shoot Miles in the kneecaps more than ever. Accusations about my mental state were the cherry on top of the I-framed-you-for-setting-someone-on-fire sundae. The dickiest of dickery. I could go to *jail* for the fire thing—not only was Celia's dad a lawyer, but her family was loaded. We were so poor my mother took three quarters of my paycheck every week to supplement the family income.

Theo assured me that, if Miles really was the one running the job to set Celia's hair on fire, he wouldn't have let me take the fall for it. Not something that serious.

I didn't know if I believed her. Some of the things Miles did for money were pretty out there. He'd actually abducted someone's ex-boyfriend's beloved golden retriever.

After that I avoided him. I tried to avoid Celia, too. She walked around the school complaining about "attempts on her life." She glared at me constantly and flipped her hair whenever I was near, highlighting how short she'd been forced to cut it. Even Stacey and Britney seemed a little wary of Celia now, as if she'd set the fire herself.

I didn't talk to Miles for most of the week. Not even in our lab on Wednesday, when I broke our watch glass, spilling chemicals all over the table. Miles bent down to pick up the pieces. Then, since our lab was ruined, he fabricated data that ended up being more accurate than anyone else's.

When I walked into the gym at the end of the day on Thursday, Art and Jetta sat playing cards on one end of the bleachers. Miles was stretched out on the row above them, his battered notebook open over his face. The cheerleading squad practiced on the other side of the gym, their voices echoing off the walls.

As I approached the club, Art leaned back and nudged Miles in the ribs.

"Hey." I sat down beside Jetta. A solid two feet separated us, but it still counted.

"What's up?" said Art. "Did anyone say anything to you about the fire?"

Miles lifted the edge of his notebook and peeked out. When our eyes met, he groaned.

"Not really. Weird looks, but not much else. I didn't do it."

"We know. Celia did," said Art.

I stared at him. "What?"

"Celia did it to herself. We went back and interrogated her."

"You . . . you interrogated her? What'd you do, threaten to take her makeup off and reveal her secret identity?"

"*Mein Chef* said 'ee would shave 'er eyebrows off." Jetta smiled brightly. "Among uzzer zings. She told us everyzing—she set ze fire 'erself, Stacey and Britney had ze water, and she blamed eet on you."

Mein Chef? Was—was she talking about Miles? I looked up at him, but he only grunted.

"It's a good thing Stacey and Britney put her out when they did," said Art. "If they'd let her burn, you'd've been in deep shit."

"Oui," said Jetta. "Deep sheet."

Miles groaned again. I whipped around. "What's wrong with you?"

"Maybe I don't want to tell you," he snapped. He

sat up long enough to procure a pen from thin air and jot something down in his notebook. The side of his left hand was smeared with black ink from his pinkie to his wrist. Maybe his notebook contained a list of his mafia jobs. Or all the people who owed him money. Maybe—*ooh*, maybe it was a hit list.

Bet I was on there a couple hundred times.

Calculus homework by itself was a bitch, but when you added the screams and giggles of the East Shoal cheerleading squad, it became unbearable. I plowed my way through a half hour of derivatives before the cheerleaders quieted and the coach addressed them.

"So, ladies," said Coach Privett, a forty-something squat gym teacher with scraggly dark hair. "Basketball season is here, and it's time to pick another cheer captain. Hannah put in her two cents, and I agree with her."

"Who is it?" someone called. The whole group giggled.

Coach Privett said, "Drumroll, please," and the girls pounded their feet on the floor.

Art and Jetta stopped their card game long enough to shoot the cheerleaders dirty looks. Miles flopped onto his side in annoyance.

Celia sat among the cheerleaders, like a hyena in front of a bloody haunch of meat. She had that deadly obsessive look in her eyes that girls got when they knew what they wanted and were going to do anything to get it.

The same look she had whenever she laid eyes on Miles. Which made no sense to me. What girl in her right mind would be obsessed with Miles? *I* wasn't even obsessed with him. Me, who thought he might be Blue Eyes, and who had come to the unfortunate conclusion that even if he wasn't Blue Eyes, I still didn't mind noting the way he raked his hair to the side when it fell over his forehead, or how he stretched his legs out exactly twenty minutes into each class.

At least my attention to him was because I couldn't get away from him. Celia had to have a different reason.

Coach Privett clapped her hands together. "Aaaand . . . the new cheer captain is . . ."

They sucked in a collective breath.

" . . . Britney Carver!"

A ripple ran through the girls, and then lots of cheering and clapping and Britney squealed and stood and made a little bow.

Celia did not cheer, and she did not clap. Her entire face flushed with color as she gazed at her alleged best friend with cold-blooded murder in her wide, rabid eyes. I could imagine it as a cartoon—Celia's teeth turning into fangs and steam blowing out her ears as she grabbed Britney around the neck and throttled her until Britney's eyes popped out of her head.

When Coach Privett concluded the meeting and the cheerleaders dispersed, Celia still stood there, hands balled at her sides, jaw clenched. Her eyes made a quick sweep of the gym and saw me watching her. I looked down at my book. She turned and stomped across the gym and stood underneath the scoreboard.

Was it possible for someone to act the way she did because that was just the way she was? Or was there always a reason? I'd like to think, if someone saw me acting strangely, they wouldn't assume it was because I was a bad person. Or they'd at least ask if something was wrong before they made the decision.

"Boss, are we done here?" Art asked.

Miles, who had fallen asleep, jolted awake and mumbled something about going home. We gathered up our bags and headed to the exit. I was the last one out, and right before the doors closed, the yelling started.

But it wasn't Celia's voice.

I jerked around in surprise and stuck my head back into the gym. Standing under the scoreboard with Celia, her back to me, was a woman in a sharp business suit, her blond hair waving down to the middle of her back. I glanced over my shoulder; Miles and the others were still walking, too far away to have heard.

Celia's head was down, both hands up by her ears, like

she was ready to block out everything around her.

"I thought it would be okay . . . ," she said. "I thought . . ."

"That you had the situation under control?" The woman's voice was sickly sweet with an undercurrent of poisonous. I had heard that voice before, at the volleyball game on the first day of school.

"I did," Celia whined. "I don't know why . . . I knew they were going to pick me . . ."

"But they didn't. You want to explain that?"

"I don't know!" Celia fisted one hand in her hair. "I did everything exactly like you told me! I did it all right!"

"Apparently not," said the woman. "You wasted your time with that stunt you pulled at the bonfire. You've undermined yourself, and you're ruining my plans. Where do you expect to go now?"

"I don't even like cheerleading. And Britney's my friend—"

"Your friend? You call that bitch your friend? You need to do something about her, Celia. You need to show her that she doesn't deserve that position."

Celia whimpered something unintelligible.

"And then you go around thinking a boy will make this all better," the woman snapped. Blood-red fingernails tapped against her arm. "You've known him for five years and he's hardly looked at you. He threatened to shave your eyebrows off! He's an obstacle, Celia! One you need to remove."

"No, he's not!"

"I'm your mother—I know these things!"

Her mother?

Celia was crying now. She turned away from her mother to wipe her eyes, smudging her ugly mascara tears. Something slipped out of her hand and clattered to the floor, making her jump. Her cell phone.

When she bent down to get it, she saw me. Her eyes opened wide.

I ran from the gym as fast as I could.

Do you ever think about lobsters?

Very doubtful

I think about lobsters all the time. You knew that already; I've told you the stories.

Yes

Do you think the lobsters in the tank try to help the other lobsters? Is that why they pile up like that? Or is it just for company, because they know they're all doomed?

Better not tell you now

Either way, it must be nice to have someone.

Chapter Twenty

I told Tucker about Celia and her mother the next day, when we both had to work the late shift at Finnegan's.

"And her mom just *showed up* at school?" Tucker said. "I didn't think they got along."

I'd been considering the idea that the encounter had been some kind of hallucination, but there was confirmation— even Tucker knew about Celia's mom.

"Well they sure didn't sound happy to see each other. I think her mom must have been watching," I said. "She was there right after we walked out. But when Celia saw me, I swore she was going to fly across the gym and strangle me to death."

Tucker shook his head. "Add it to Celia's list of Weird Conversations."

"What does that mean?"

"Did you know McCoy talks to Celia all the time?" he asked. "He calls her to his office all the time. I used to be the front desk attendant sophomore year, and a week into September, Celia started showing up every other day. Into McCoy's office, stayed for half an hour, waltzed back out again. And she's been doing that ever since. Think that was included in her mom's 'plans'?"

"McCoy? No, I don't think McCoy is included in anyone's plans."

"Speaking of McCoy." Tucker leaned against the counter and clipped his mechanical pencil to the frames of his glasses. "Talking about the scoreboard legend a while back got me curious. I'm going to the library on Saturday to research—wanna come? I'll pick you up."

I thrust out my hand. "Deal."

Though I felt better after telling Tucker what I'd seen, I spent the next days wondering if Celia was going to jump out and stab me. She didn't, but she did shoot me warning looks that said I'd get shanked if I went near her.

I was still jittery on Friday. I sat on a bench outside school and waited for the parking lot to quiet down—there were still way too many cars around and I didn't want to take Erwin into that sort of hostile environment. The lights cast wide yellow pools on the asphalt. Most kids had stayed inside for some sort of basketball after-party in the gym, and anyone out here was in their car and gone within minutes.

Except for one person.

I spotted her when she crept out from behind a row of cars. Celia. She had a can of paint in one hand, and she shook it as she peered over her shoulder.

Abandoning my backpack on the bench, I darted down the next row of cars. I kneeled between two cars and watched her lean over the hood of a white convertible and paint the windshield.

I pointed my camera. A minute later, *Captain Bitch* in neon pink covered the convertible's windshield.

Oh, great. Celia listened to her mom. Cheerleader retribution.

The camera slipped from my fingers and clattered on the asphalt. Celia whipped around. Saw me kneeling there.

I scooped up the camera and sprinted in the other direction. Celia screamed something and the paint can hit the hood of a car as I passed by. It burst open, spraying fluorescent pink everywhere. I veered left, ducking down so Celia wouldn't see my head. I glanced through a car window. She raced down the row after me.

I crawled along, doubled back, and passed her before rolling underneath a van.

"RIDGEMONT!" I could see her sneakers. She walked

back the other way. I held my breath as she passed the van.

Please, please let me be hallucinating this. Because if I wasn't, that meant Celia Hendricks really was losing it. Maybe her mom was pushing her there, or maybe she'd always been like this, but I was pretty sure if she found me right now she was going to rip my hair out.

My salvation came a few seconds later.

"Milesie!" Celia squealed.

"What are you doing, Hendricks?" Miles's feet—shiny shoes and all—came into view. He always walked like that, heel-toe-*push,* like he'd knock over anyone who got in his way.

"Oh, nothing. Just hanging out. You?"

Now they were both planted right in front of the van.

"Nothing," he replied. His voice was low and sharp. "Just wondering why you're running around the parking lot, screaming your head off."

Celia hesitated. "No reason. I have to get going. But I'll see you tomorrow!"

She hurried off, and a moment later an engine started up.

Miles was still there. I held my breath—if he'd move, I could go get Erwin and leave. I wanted him to find me under this van about as much as I wanted Celia to. He couldn't see me like this.

But then he walked to the van's front bumper, kneeled down, and peered underneath. "Having fun?" he asked.

I let out a gust of breath and set my forehead against the asphalt. What an asshole.

"Running from crazy people is always fun," I replied.

Miles helped me out from under the van. As I brushed myself off, he asked, "So what was she chasing you for?"

"That depends," I said, bringing up the picture of Celia spray-painting Britney's car on my camera. I showed it to him. *Please be there. Please be there.* "What do you see?"

He pushed his glasses up and stared at it for a moment. "I see Celia getting angry about her cheerleading position and taking it out on Britney Carver's car with some offensively bright paint."

I almost hugged him. "Oh, good."

"Are you going to tell Britney?" he asked.

"Why? Do you think she'd believe me?"

"With this evidence? Sure. But good luck getting to her with Celia around."

"I'll probably give these to Mr. Gunthrie or someone on Monday."

"Give them to Claude."

"Why?"

"He'll give them to his dad, and he'll make sure everyone knows about it."

"That seems excessively mean."

"Celia was prepared to beat you to a bloody pulp a few minutes ago," he pointed out.

I made a mental note to go to the newspaper room Monday morning and give Claude the pictures.

Miles and I walked back up to the school. The crickets and cicadas had faded for the year, leaving the night quiet and undisturbed. Miles's truck was parked against the curb, near Erwin's bushes. The light outside the school's front entrance illuminated the whole front walk. I grabbed Erwin's handlebars.

The front half of my bike slipped free of the bush.

Only the front half.

Someone had cut my bike in half. It had been rusting away in the middle, but I was positive I'd get at least another semester out of the poor thing. Anger welled up in my chest.

Someone cut my bike in half.

Pressure built up behind my eyes. I had no transportation.

My mother would call me careless for letting this happen. She'd give me a lecture about respecting my possessions, even though I'd heard it a thousand times before. I wiped my eyes on the back of my sleeve and forced the knot back down my throat.

Dad had bought me Erwin. Brought Erwin all the way from Egypt. He was basically an artifact, and one of the few things I had from Dad that I knew for sure was real. He was priceless.

And now he was broken.

I grabbed the back half and rounded on Miles, who still stood a few feet behind me, looking mildly surprised. "Did you do this?" I asked.

"No."

"Right." I grabbed my bag from the bench and started down the sidewalk.

"You're going to walk home?"

"Yep."

"Great plan." He planted himself in front of me. "I can't let you. Not in the dark."

"Well that's too bad, isn't it?" I wondered when he'd decided to become a white knight. "I didn't ask for your permission."

"And I won't ask for yours," he retorted. "I *will* throw you in my truck."

"And I *will* scream rape," I replied evenly.

He rolled his eyes. "I didn't cut your bike in half. I swear."

"Why should I believe you? You're kind of notorious for being a lying, thieving bastard." He shrugged.

"You don't explain yourself to anyone, do you?"

He motioned to his truck. "Will you please get in?"

I looked around quickly; finding another ride home would be pretty impossible. And as I looked out at the dark, quiet street, it occurred to me that walking home wasn't the best idea ever. Sure, I hung out around Red Witch Bridge in the middle of the night, but that was in the cover of the trees with an urban legend and a baseball bat as weapons. Here, I was a teenaged girl with average upper body strength, hair like a signal beacon, and a mental condition that could make me think I was being attacked even when I wasn't.

At least I knew Miles well enough to understand that the look of frustration on his face wasn't a ploy. So I tossed the two halves of Erwin into the back of his truck and climbed into the passenger seat.

The cab still smelled like pastries and mint soap. I breathed in deeply without realizing it, and hastily let it out as a sigh. Miles glanced through the driver's side window, let out a quick curse, and grabbed a stack of papers on the seat.

"Sorry, I have to drop these off. I forgot. I'll be right back."

He hurried into the school. The papers must have been his stat charts for the week, but I found it hard to believe he'd forgotten them. Miles didn't forget things.

His truck was surprisingly clean. The dash had been stripped bare; the radio front was smashed in, and the knob for the heater was missing. Miles had stashed his backpack behind the driver's seat—apparently in a hurry, because it was on its side, and its contents spilled out in the cramped space.

The corner of his black notebook peeked out beneath his chemistry book.

This was my chance. I could just . . . take a look. Get a glimpse at the tip of Miles Richter's psychological iceberg. I checked to make sure he was still safely inside East Shoal, then pulled the notebook out.

It was bound in leather. There were several pieces of paper clipped to the inside back cover, but I ignored them and flipped it open to the middle. Both pages were covered with his untidy scrawl.

I went back to the beginning and skimmed through. Math equations filled whole pages. There were symbols I'd never seen and little notes scribbled off to the sides. There were quotes from books and more notes. There were lists of scientific classifications for plants and animals, and even more lists for words I'd never encountered. There were entire passages written in German, dated like journal entries. I noticed familiar names, like my own and the other members of the club.

And then, separated from the rest of the scribbles by a few blank pages, like he'd wanted to remember these things specifically, were short one- or two-sentence declarations, marked with the dates they'd been written.

Intelligence is not measured by how much you know, but by how much you have the capacity to learn.

You are never as great or as pitiful as you think you are.

Those who are picked last are the only ones who truly know what it feels like.

Schools without bike racks should be convicted of criminal negligence.

I stared at that last line, dated on the first day of school, urging it to change, to revert to its true form, because I knew I must have made it up. If that wasn't a quote from somewhere, if that was one of his own observations . . . then he'd lied about not standing up to Cliff for me. Celia'd scoffed at Erwin, and Cliff had stood in my way, and Miles had said he hadn't done any of it for me. . . .

This notebook didn't sound like Miles. It sounded like someone a lot more naïve than Miles. Someone who really liked to know things. Scientific classifications. Complex math. Words.

I looked up. Miles was coming out of the school. Groaning, I stuffed the notebook back under his chemistry book. I faced forward, trying to look inconspicuous. He slid into the driver's seat.

"Is something wrong?" he asked.

"You seem to have forgotten that someone cut my bike in half."

"And you seem to have forgotten that I have a truck," said Miles. "I can give you a ride. To school, at least."

"No thanks," I said.

"Really. I'm not joking. Unless you're that against having anything to do with me. I don't care. You can get in line."

He turned onto the main road. The line from the notebook felt like a dead weight in my stomach.

"No, not against it." I realized with a strange sort of happy dread that we were falling back into the easy conversation we'd had at the bonfire. "But I'd like to know why you're offering."

"What do you mean?" Honest confusion crossed his face. "Isn't that the good thing to do?"

I burst out laughing. "Since when have you been *good*? Are you feeling guilty or something?"

"A little sentimental, maybe. My first idea was to drive up and down in front of you a few times to prove I had a car and you didn't." His tone was light and he was smiling.

Holy crap, he was smiling. A real, teeth-showing, nose-scrunching, eyes-crinkling smile.

The smile slipped off his face. "What? What's wrong?"

"You were smiling," I said. "It was kind of weird."

"Oh," he said, frowning. "Thanks."

"No, no, don't do that! The smile was better." The

words felt wrong coming out of my mouth. I shouldn't say things like that to him, but they hung neatly in the air and cleared out the tension. Miles didn't smile again. He turned down my street and pulled into my driveway.

"Charlie's playing her violin again," I said. The music floated out of the house like a bird on a breeze. The *1812 Overture*. I had to throw my weight against the passenger door to get it open.

"The smile was better," I said again as I closed the door behind me, the words sounding less awkward now. "I think people would like you if you did it more."

"What's the point, though?" said Miles. "So, Monday."

"Monday."

"Should I be here?"

"Do you want to be here?"

He looked like a cat eyeing its prey. "Seven o'clock. After that I'm leaving without you. Do you work tonight?"

"Yes."

"Guess I'll see you there. And Alex?"

"Yeah?"

"I won't tell anyone. In case you were wondering."

I knew what he meant. And I knew he was telling the truth. There was something in his voice that said he understood. I believed him.

I fished Erwin out of the truck bed. Then I propped

the halves up against the garage door and headed inside as Miles drove down the street. My head spun with everything that had happened. Celia's revenge. Erwin. The increasingly plausible idea that Blue Eyes was not a hallucination at all, and never had been.

My mother let me get ten steps inside the front door before bombarding me with questions.

"Who was that?"

"What happened to your bike?"

"Did you forget you have work tonight?"

And my personal favorite, "Do we need to have *the talk*?"

I cringed. I did not need to think of Miles in that way. I was plenty confused about him as it was.

"No, we do not need to have the talk, Mom. I understand how boy and girl parts work. Yes, I have to go to Finnegan's. No, I don't know what happened to Erwin."

"Who was that in the truck?" She waved her empty coffee mug around. I couldn't tell if she was angry or excited—her zealotry managed to cover pretty much all the emotional bases.

"That was Miles."

Chapter
Twenty-one

I giggled a little when I found out the librarian I'd accused of being a Communist five years ago still worked at the library. I giggled a little more when Tucker and I walked in and she glared at me.

"She remembers me," I whispered to Tucker, grinning.

Tucker snorted and pulled me to a section of the library in the back, where several aging computers sat in a line against the wall. We took the two open computers at the end.

"I can't believe they don't have these records online," Tucker said, clicking incessantly at his yellowed mouse. The old computer wheezed as it started up. "I don't even think these are connected to the Internet. I don't think they have Ethernet ports. Oh God, what if they don't have *network cards*?"

"You make it sound like the nineties were hell," I said.

"They probably were. Our childish naiveté saved us."

The computers blinked to life and allowed us to access the newspaper archives from the desktop. The catalog seemed recently updated, despite looking like a victim of 1990s pattern choice.

"Okay, so I'm thinking there must have been something to spark this scoreboard legend," Tucker said. "Look for anything that says anything about East Shoal or the scoreboard itself."

I didn't mind scouring old newspaper articles—they were still forms of history, just slightly more recent than I was used to. Twenty minutes later, I found the first clue, one that I'd already seen before.

"'Scarlet Fletcher, captain of the East Shoal cheerleading squad, helps introduce "Scarlet's Scoreboard," a commemoration of the charity and goodwill her father, Randall Fletcher, has shown toward the school.'"

I turned my screen toward Tucker. He frowned. "I thought the scoreboard was older than that. This was twenty years ago."

In the picture, Scarlet beamed and flashed a set of white teeth. Her face wasn't obscured here; she looked vaguely familiar. There was another picture at the bottom of the article. Scarlet stood beneath the scoreboard with a boy with dark hair, wearing a football captain's uniform. His smile was strained.

"He's hot," I said absentmindedly.

"Sure, if you like the classical look," Tucker mumbled.

"What was that?"

"Nothing, nothing."

"Are you jealous, Mr. Soggy Potato Salad?"

"Jealous? When I've got this?" Tucker whipped off his glasses, bit the tip of the earpiece, and squinted at me. I laughed.

The librarian sprang out from behind a bookcase and shushed me. I clapped a hand over my mouth.

We returned our attention to our search. "Hey, here's something," Tucker said. "Not about the scoreboard, but it mentions Scarlet again." He turned his screen to me.

"'Though only numbering 151, East Shoal's graduating class of 1992 includes several remarkable names, including Scarlet Fletcher, daughter of politician Randall Fletcher, and the class valedictorian, Juniper Richter, who tested top in the nation in both math and language comprehension. . . .'" I let my voice fade away. "Is that . . . ?"

"It's Miles's mom, yeah."

"They went to school together? That means she was there when the scoreboard went up—maybe she could tell you something about it."

Tucker rubbed his neck. "That's . . . probably not going to happen."

"Why not?"

"She's, ah, in a mental hospital up in Goshen."

"A . . . a mental hospital?" I paused. "Why?"

Tucker shrugged. "I don't know anything else. She calls Finnegan's sometimes when he's there. One time I redialed after he'd hung up, and an orderly answered." He waved his hand around. "And now you see why I don't mind eavesdropping on people's personal lives."

I sank back in my chair. "You're sure?"

"Yeah. Are you okay?"

I nodded. That was why I'd trusted Miles when he'd said he wouldn't tell anyone. He knew what it meant to hide a secret like that.

I dove back into the articles, trying to shove thoughts of Miles and his mother and Blue Eyes to the back of my mind. I had a strange, intense desire to see him.

My eyes began to glaze over and my legs went numb right about the same time I found it. I was well into '97 when the headline reached right off the screen and smacked me in the face.

MEMORIAL SCOREBOARD FALLS, CRUSHES DONOR'S DAUGHTER

"You're kidding me," I whispered. "I think I just found your story, Tucker."

"What?"

"Scarlet died in ninety-seven," I said. "The scoreboard fell on her when she went back for the class reunion. And . . . Jesus, McCoy was the one who tried to lift it off of her. He was electrocuted. Scarlet died in the hospital a few hours later from sustained injuries, and they hung the scoreboard back up."

I showed him the article. His eyes widened as he read.

"McCoy went to school with Scarlet," Tucker said. "McCoy tried to save her and couldn't. Now he worships the scoreboard because . . . why? It *killed* somebody." He sat back, raked his hands through his neatly combed hair, and stared at me. "How messed up is this guy?"

"It didn't just kill *somebody*," I said. "It killed *Scarlet*. He's made it like . . . like a monument. A memorial for her."

A memorial for a dead woman.

There was definitely something strange going on. I just didn't know what it was.

Chapter
Twenty-two

I sat in the copse on the hill behind Red Witch Bridge that night, trying, for a little while, to forget what I'd learned in the library. Not the part about Scarlet, even though that was interesting. It was the information about Miles—about his mother—that had kept me from falling asleep.

The night was quiet aside from the breeze ruffling the leaves and the whisper of the stream. Most cars didn't come down this road at night because of the bridge. People said it was because they didn't trust the bridge's integrity, but the real reason was the witch.

A long time ago, back in the days when people still got pressed to death, a witch lived on this side of the river. Not the misunderstood kind of witch who only wants to heal with her chants and herbal remedies, but the creepy kind who cuts off crow heads and eats children and small pets.

So the witch was fine—or so the story goes—most of the time because everyone else lived on the other side of the river and didn't bother her. But then they built the bridge, and people started coming onto her land, and she got pissed. She would wait by the bridge at night and kill those unlucky enough to cross after dark.

Eventually she got pressed to death or something. But even now, when a car drove across the bridge at night, you could hear the witch scream. She was called the Red Witch because she was coated with the blood of her victims.

I was probably the only teenager in the state who wasn't scared of the witch. Not because I was extra fearless or anything, but because I knew where the legend came from.

Two sets of headlights appeared around the bend in the road. I scooted farther behind my tree, cracking twigs and fallen leaves, even though I knew they wouldn't see me. The cars pulled off on the shoulder. Doors opened and closed. Voices floated to me, words scrambled. A girl's high-pitched giggle, a boy's low murmur. Teenagers come to play with the witch. The headlights threw their long-legged shadows across the pavement.

There were five of them: four in the first car, one in the second. All with their shoulders huddled up around their ears in the chilly autumn air. The first four seemed to be reasoning with the fifth. The girl giggled again.

The fifth person broke away from the group and started across the bridge. His steps echoed against the old wood. Brave guy. Usually it took more persuasion. The others wouldn't be able to see him when he reached my side because of the trees, but if he walked up the hill, the moonlight would let me see him.

He crossed the bridge and stood in the darkness, looking around. Then he started up the hill.

"Miles?"

I stood and stepped out of the trees. I should have known. I didn't want to freak him out or anything, but he still stopped in his tracks and stared at me.

"Alex? What are you doing here?"

"What are *you* doing here?"

"No, I asked first, and since you are literally chilling here behind these trees, and no one does that at Red Witch Bridge at night, your answer is infinitely more important than mine."

"Well, you do it when you're the witch."

He stared at me. "You're the witch."

"I'm the witch." I shrugged.

"You sit out here at night and scare people?"

"No," I said. "I sit out here at night and watch people scare themselves. It's fun. What are you doing here?"

Miles motioned over his shoulder. "Cliff, Ria, and some others pooled their money to pay me to walk the bridge at night.

I didn't bother to tell them I don't believe in urban legends."

"Maybe they figured if the legend was true, the witch would get you out of their way."

"Richter! Find anything?" I recognized Cliff's voice.

Miles looked back and sighed.

"Want to mess with them?" I asked.

I pulled him down the hill with me and we stood at the other end of the bridge, in the darkness of the trees where the others couldn't see us. "Okay, all you have to do is yell at the top of your lungs."

"Right now?"

"Right now. Like you're being attacked."

Miles took a deep breath and yelled. Cliff and the others jumped, but didn't move. Miles's voice died out.

"Come on, Richter, we know you're trying to—"

I screamed. A good ear-shattering, chainsaw-killer, bloody-murder scream. Cliff stumbled backward, fell over, and had to scramble to his feet again. Ria screeched. The other two fled to their car, followed by Cliff and Ria, and peeled away. Miles and I stood there for another few moments, silent and waiting. The cold bit at my cheeks.

"Do you do this all the time?" Miles asked finally.

"No. Just today." I smiled.

He stared at me.

"What?" I said.

"Why are you here?"

"I told you—I'm the witch."

"*How* are you the witch?"

I sighed and swung my arms back and forth, wondering if I should tell him. He had that look on his face again, like he understood what was going on in my head.

Around us, the wind rustling the trees sounded like thousands of voices.

"Psithurism," Miles said, looking up at the forest around us.

"What?"

"Psithurism. It's a low whispering sound, like wind in leaves."

I sighed again. The wind blew his mint-soap-and-pastries scent toward me.

"I had a bad week a while back," I said finally, "when I was at Hillpark. I snuck out of the house at night because, y'know, I thought that Communists were kidnapping me. Came down here screaming my head off. Apparently I scared some potheads. My parents found me sleeping under the bridge the next morning. They were mortified."

"Because you slept under a bridge? 'Mortified' isn't the word I'd use."

"I was naked."

"Oh."

"They were angry, too. At least, my mother was. Dad was worried."

"Were you okay? The potheads didn't do anything to you?"

"No, I scared the crap out of those guys."

"That wasn't that long ago, then. How'd the story get around so fast?"

I shrugged. "Beats me. People communicate surprisingly well when they're scared—they just don't communicate the right things."

The breeze ruffled the leaves over our heads. Psithurism. I'd have to remember that. I desperately wanted to ask Miles about his mom, but I knew this wasn't the time. I sat down in the middle of the gravel road and patted a spot next to me.

"Cars rarely come down this way," I said.

Miles sat down. He folded his long legs and balanced his arms on his knees, bunching his bomber jacket up around his ears. The breeze had mussed his hair; I balled my hands in my lap to keep from reaching over and putting it back in place.

"I didn't see you at Finnegan's tonight," I said.

"I didn't get a shift at the store today. Went home after school."

Didn't get a shift. Like he wanted one.

"I don't understand you," I said, the realization hitting me at the same time I said it.

Miles leaned back on his hands. "Okay."

"'Okay'?"

He shrugged. "I don't understand you, either, so I guess we're even. But I don't understand most people."

"That's weird."

"How so?"

"People aren't hard to understand, except you. And you're so smart, I figured you had everyone on your puppet strings."

He snorted. "Puppet strings. Never heard it described like that before."

"I want to know what you do when you're not at school or work or running jobs. Where do you even live?"

"Why does it matter?"

I sighed again. He made me sigh a lot. "You're an enigma. You walk around doing stuff to people for money, and everyone's afraid to look you in the eye, and I'm pretty sure you're part of a mafia. You don't strike me as the kind of person who has a place to live. You're just there. You exist. You are where you are and you have no home."

The moonlight reflected off his glasses and lit up his eyes.

"I live a couple streets away from here," he said. "The Lakeview Trail subdivision."

Lakeview Trail was one of those half-and-half subdivisions—half pretty new houses like Downing Heights, half run-down hovels with crumbling sidewalks, like mine. I had a good feeling which side of the subdivision Miles belonged to.

"I'm not home most of the time. When I am, I try to sleep."

"But you don't." He was always tired. Always sleeping through first period. Always falling asleep over his meal at Finnegan's.

He nodded. "Most of the time I think about things. Write stuff down. Is that what you wanted to know?"

"I guess." I became aware that we were staring at each other. And had been for a while. I noticed and looked away, but Miles didn't. "It's rude to stare at people."

"Is it?" He sounded serious. "Tell me if I'm doing something weird. Sometimes I can't tell."

"What is up with you lately? Why are you being so nice?"

"I didn't realize I was." His face remained completely neutral. Except for that infuriating eyebrow.

I couldn't stand it anymore. I had to ask. "So you don't think it's creepy? My schizophrenia?"

"That would be stupid."

I laughed. I fell back into the gravel and laughed, my voice carrying up through the trees and into the sky. His response made me feel free. That was what I came down to Red Witch Bridge to feel anyway, but I'd never expected any help from Miles.

In a weird way, it felt like he belonged here. He belonged in the land of phoenixes and witches, the place where things were too fantastic to be real.

He leaned over and looked down at me. He seemed more confused than anything.

I pushed myself back up. He kept staring at me. I realized I wanted to kiss him.

I didn't know why. Maybe it was the way he looked at me like I was the only thing he wanted to look at.

How did one go about it? Ask him if I could? Or maybe quick and unexpected would be better. He made a pretty easy target, sitting there, docile for once, and kind of sleepy.

I really needed Finnegan's Magic 8 Ball. But I could guess what kind of answer it would give me. *Ask again later.* So freaking noncommittal.

No, none of that. Decision: Outright questioning.

Just say it, said the voice. *Ask him. Blurt it out. What can he say?*

He can laugh in my face.

Let him. It'll be a douche move on his part. You're only being honest.

I don't know.

Do you really think after all this, he'd brush you off like that?

Maybe.

Maybe he likes you, too. Maybe that's why he stares so much.

Maybe.

Screw it. I was chickening out. Quick and unexpected—GO!

I leaned forward and kissed him. I don't think he caught on until it was too late.

He froze up as soon as I touched him. Of course—he didn't like to be touched. I should have asked. I should have asked, *I should have asked* . . . . But then, like a building wave, I felt the heat pouring off of him. His fingertips brushed my neck. My heart tried to strangle me and I jumped away from him.

A band of moonlight lit up his eyes like fluorescent bulbs.

"Sorry," I said, standing and hurrying back up to the copse to find my baseball bat, trying to figure out what I'd been thinking.

He was still sitting there when I stumbled back into the street.

"So, um." My jaw tingled, lungs contracted, throat tightened. "I'll see you on Monday, I guess."

He didn't say anything.

I barely kept myself from sprinting through Red Witch Bridge. The wind thundered in the trees, and when I finally looked back, Miles stood at the door to his truck, outlined by moonlight, staring right back at me.

Chapter
Twenty-three

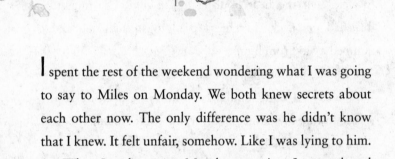

I spent the rest of the weekend wondering what I was going to say to Miles on Monday. We both knew secrets about each other now. The only difference was he didn't know that I knew. It felt unfair, somehow. Like I was lying to him.

When I woke up on Monday morning, I remembered the pictures on my camera and wondered how long it would take Celia to find me and kill me after I'd handed them over to Claude. Tucker and I had exhausted the library's databases on Scarlet and McCoy, with no further clues about McCoy's particular brand of psychosis. So either I asked Celia what exactly was going on with McCoy—she probably wouldn't give me a straight answer—or I found another source of information.

I told myself to drop it. I told myself it wasn't worth

it. But then I looked at the picture of Celia spray-painting that car, and all I could see was myself spray-painting the Hillpark gymnasium.

Two minutes before seven, Miles's truck idled in the driveway, tailpipe gushing exhaust into the frosty air. My mother stood at the front door, holding her coffee mug in both hands, her face pressed against the screen. I would've gotten mad at her, but she'd bought me a case of Yoo-hoo over the weekend. So I poked her out of the way as I shouldered my backpack and grabbed a Yoo-hoo from the hallway table.

"That's Miles?" My mother shifted to see better when Miles let his arm dangle out the truck window, as if that arm would give her his life story.

"Yes. He brought me home after the bonfire, remember? And on Friday."

"You should invite him over for dinner."

I laughed into the Yoo-hoo straw, making the drink bubble up. My face got hot. "Hah, right."

"You need to learn to be more sociable, Alexandra, or you're never going to—"

"Okay bye Mom love you!" I charged past her and out the door. She huffed loudly as the screen door clattered shut.

I jogged down the front yard, perimeter checking as I went, and climbed into Miles's pickup.

"So, how was your weekend?" I asked, trying to sound casual. His gaze snapped up to my face—I think he'd been staring at the Yoo-hoo bottle—and he shrugged.

"Same as usual." He left something hanging in the air, like he wanted to finish with *except for Saturday night.* Same here, buddy. He backed into the street.

"You work at Meijer, right?" I asked.

"Yeah," he said. The corner of his lips curled up. "I work at the deli counter. Have to give people their succulent, chemical-ridden salami and whatnot."

I pictured Miles in a dark room, standing at a butcher's block with a large knife in one hand a bloody cow's leg steadied under the other, a huge Cheshire grin spreading over his face—

"I bet the customers love you," I said.

"They do—when my manager is around."

"So do you run jobs there, too?"

"No. I don't *steal* from them, thank you very much," said Miles. "I'm above common thievery. Outside of school."

"Why do you do it all?" I asked. "It can't just be for the money."

"I have reasons."

"But, I mean, you know sometimes they just want to humiliate you. Like, don't you think if you'd gone back through Red Witch Bridge on Saturday, Cliff and the others would've tried to scare you?"

"Probably. Trust me, I know. I've had plenty of embarrassing jobs." He parked the truck and reached around his seat for his bag. "It's all *schadenfreude*. People just want to laugh at you."

"Can you really speak German?" I already knew the answer.

Miles glanced out the side window, and then said, almost too low for me to hear, "*Ja, ich spreche Deutsch*." A smile stretched across his face. "But don't ask me to do it—it makes me feel like a monkey doing parlor tricks."

We got out of the truck and started toward the school. "It must be awful for Jetta," I said.

"I think she's used to it. Whenever someone asks her to say something, she curses at them."

"She speaks French and Italian, right?"

"And German and Spanish and Greek and a little Gaelic."

"Wow. Can you speak all those?"

"Not really. I'm just . . . German." We crossed the parking lot. "Hey, since we were talking about it—I have another job to run on Thursday night. I want you to help."

"Why? What can I do?"

"Extra pair of hands. Art was the only one available. I'll

give you a cut of the reward, of course."

"It's nothing illegal, right?"

"Of course not. You'll be fine."

I had no idea how far Miles's definition of *legal* stretched, but maybe this was his form of a peace offering. He wasn't stupid—if it was really, truly dangerous, I don't think he would have asked. "Okay. I guess."

Miles went with me to the newspaper room, where I handed over my memory card to Claude Gunthrie, showing him the pictures of Britney's spray-painted car. First, Claude laughed. Then he downloaded them and sent an e-mail to his father, Assistant Principal Borruso, and McCoy.

I didn't miss all the weird looks we got on the way to English. I thought it might be because Miles was smiling, but that didn't seem like it, either. I didn't like this new attention. It made my neck itch.

I'd hardly finished my perimeter check when Ria Wolf slid into the desk next to mine, looking eager. Chills ran up my arms and legs at her predatory smile. I wanted to get as far away from her as humanly possible, but I dug my fingernails into the desktop and forced myself to stay put.

"Hey, what was Celia like when she was spray-painting Britney's car?" she asked.

"Huh?"

"You were there, weren't you?"

I looked around and realized Celia wasn't there, and most of the class was watching us and waiting for my answer. "I mean—yeah, I was there, but she was just painting the car. . . ."

Holy hell, had it really gotten out that fast? It had barely been five minutes.

"Are you out to get her or something?" Cliff appeared next to Ria, talking to me like we were best buddies. He was even worse than Ria; every time I saw him, I knew he was half a second from lunging out at me with a razor blade. "'Cause that's awesome; she deserves it."

"Hey, *Clifford*," Miles growled from his seat, "go find some other territory to mark."

"Hey, *Nazi*, go find some more Jews to gas," Cliff shot back, but even as he said it he stood up and moved back toward his desk.

"Do you understand what you're saying when those words come out of your mouth?" Miles asked. "Or do you just repeat what everyone else says because everyone else is saying it?"

Cliff settled into his seat. "What the hell are you talking about, Richter?"

"Everyone in this room knows what I'm talking about. Stop calling me a Nazi."

"Why should I?"

Miles's hand came down on the desk. "Because the systematic slaughter of millions of people *isn't funny*!" His sudden anger quieted the entire room. It even startled Mr. Gunthrie out of his newspaper.

I had thought he didn't care when people called him a Nazi. A mixed wave of relief and happiness rolled through me that he *did* care, but why did it make him so angry?

"ENOUGH TALKING." Mr. Gunthrie rose to his feet, looking between Miles and Cliff like he thought they might explode. "GET INTO YOUR LITERARY DISCUSSION PAIRS, AND I DON'T WANT TO HEAR A WORD OUT OF ANY OF YOU. UNDERSTOOD?"

"Yes, sir!"

"BEFORE WE BEGIN CLASS TODAY, I'D LIKE TO HAVE A NICE LITTLE CHAT ABOUT THE VALUE OF RESPECTING ANOTHER PERSON'S PROPERTY. DOES THAT SOUND NICE TO YOU ALL?"

And so began our twenty-eight-and-a-half-minute lesson on why spray paint and car windshields don't mix. Britney and Stacey watched him intently the whole time, nodding in agreement. Mr. Gunthrie gave us a last disappointed look and told us to get on with our discussion of *Heart of Darkness*.

Tucker, as usual, had already written up our discussion paper. He was being weird again, his expression closed like someone had shut a door inside him. I knew why as soon as he glanced over at Miles.

"So," he said, "are you two, like, friends now?"

I tried to keep my expression neutral.

"I . . . I guess. He gave me a ride here this morning." I paused, then said, "He spoke German."

"What?"

"You told me to tell you if he ever started talking with a German accent. I got him to speak German, so that's even better, right?"

If anything, Tucker looked more upset than before. "Why are you in his club?"

"Um. Community service."

"For what?"

"It's not a big deal. Just a misunderstanding at Hillpark."

A smart person would be able to put the Hillpark Gym Graffiti Incident—which most of East Shoal knew about—together with my community service. But no one knew enough about me. Hillpark and East Shoal hated each other so much it severed the lines of communication. Out here in the boonies of suburban Indiana, it was red versus green, Dragons versus Sabres. You didn't speak to someone from the other school unless you were spitting in their face. The only reason East Shoal knew about the graffiti at all was because Hillpark's main gym had been closed for several games while they cleaned the floor. My reputation at Hillpark hadn't bled into my time at East Shoal. Not yet.

But Tucker was separate from all that. He *did* know enough about me.

"When you two walked in, he was smiling." Tucker looked down at his desk, tracing the grooves in its top with his pencil. "I haven't seen him smile since eighth grade."

"He's only driving me to school," I reassured him. "I'm not going to start hanging out or figuring out scoreboard-related mysteries with him or anything."

"No, because that's my job." Tucker's face lifted, a smile tugging at his lips. "He's on transportation duty and I get mysteries. I see you building your harem of manservants."

"I'm looking at Ackerley next—I think he'd give a killer foot massage."

Tucker laughed, but glanced over his shoulder as if Cliff was going to appear behind him and slam his head into the desk.

I knew how he felt.

For the rest of that week, I felt strangely buoyant. At work, at school, even when I had to go near the scoreboard. Everything was good. Celia was suspended for the paint job. I got all my homework done on time (and even understood my calculus, which was a miracle in itself), took enough pictures and did enough perimeter checks to put my paranoia at ease, and I had people to talk to.

Real people. Not homicidal people.

Miles drove me to and from school. Like most people, he didn't act the same when you got him alone. He was still an asshat, but alone he was more Blue Eyes than jerk. On Wednesday, when the club stayed after school to work a swim meet, he even helped me bury Erwin.

"You named your bike Erwin?"

"Sure, why not?"

"After Erwin Rommel? You named your bike after a Nazi?" Miles narrowed his eyes at me. Erwin's back half swung at his side.

"My dad got him from the African desert. Plus, Rommel was humane. He got an order straight from Hitler to execute Jews, and he tore it up. And then he traded his family's protection for his own suicide."

"Yeah, but he still knew what he was doing and who he was fighting for," said Miles, but without conviction. "I thought you were scared of Nazis?"

My step faltered. "How did you know that?"

"You're a history buff; I assumed that whatever you were scared of would come from history, and Nazis were pretty scary." The corner of his lips twisted up. "There's that, and whenever someone calls me a Nazi, you get this look on your face like I tried to kill you."

"Oh. Good guess." I gripped Erwin's handlebars tighter. We rounded the back of the school and headed for the Dumpster behind the kitchen doors. I could smell tobacco and wood shavings and suspected Miles's jacket. He wore it every day now. He pushed the top off the Dumpster and we tossed Erwin's halves inside, closing the lid on my poor bike forever.

"Why does being called a Nazi make you so mad?" I asked. "I mean, I don't know why anyone would be happy about it, but I thought you were going to rip Cliff's teeth out the other day."

He shrugged. "People are ignorant. I don't know."

He knew. Miles always knew.

As we turned back toward the gym, he said, "Heard you've been on some sort of scavenger hunt with Beaumont."

"Yep. Jealous?"

It sort of slipped out. I was too paralyzed to say anything else. He didn't know about the library, did he? He couldn't know that I'd found out about his mom.

But then he snorted loudly and said, "Hardly."

I relaxed. "What is everyone's problem with him? I don't think he's that bad, honestly. Yeah, he's got a Cult in a Closet, but he's really nice. He hates you, but doesn't everyone?"

"He actually has a reason to hate me, though. Everyone else does it because it's expected."

"What reason?"

Miles paused. "We were friends in middle school," he said. "I thought he was a decent guy because we were both smart, we got along well, and I was new and he didn't make fun of my accent. But when we got here, I realized—he lets other people walk all over him. He's got no ambition. No drive, no end goal."

And what kind of ambition do you have? I thought. *The kind where you see how effectively you can kill someone's puppy?*

"He's smart," Miles continued, "he's really smart. But he doesn't put it to use. He could have as much leverage as I do, but he sits around with his stupid conspiracies and does his little chemistry equations and obsesses over girls who won't look twice at him."

"Like who?"

"Like Ria."

"Tucker likes Ria?" How did I not know that?

"Since I've known him. If he had any sense, he would've tossed out that romanticized idea of her he's had for so long and gotten to work doing something useful."

"So you ditched him," I said.

"Well . . . yeah."

"You ditched your friend—your only friend—because he didn't want to help you control the school."

Miles's lips tightened into a thin line. "No, not that . . ."

"Because he's got no ambition? No 'end goal'?"

"Yeah."

I scoffed at him. He looked over at me with the Magnificently Quirked Eyebrow, but I could tell his heart wasn't in it.

"You're a jerk," I said, walking off.

Miles went ahead to the pool while I searched the storage rooms behind the gym for extra towels for the swimmers. I had to walk past the gym doors to get there, and I stopped when I heard voices inside.

"You're not giving her the support she needs," said a sickly-sweet voice.

"I'm trying. I swear, I'm trying."

McCoy. Talking to Celia's mother.

So there *was* a connection between them. I couldn't let this pass me by. I ducked into the gym and under the bleachers, checking the scaffolding for microphones as I climbed through to the other side. McCoy stood before the scoreboard, his gray hair disheveled, his suit wrinkled. I crouched down as far as I could and turned my camera on, pointing it toward McCoy and the woman who stood with her back to me.

Today, her blond hair was done back in a tight braid.

"I know she's your daughter," McCoy said, "but she's not the sharpest knife in the drawer. She's not like you were."

"Celia is as smart as any of these idiots. She needs more focus, is all," drawled the woman. "She needs to get her head out of the clouds and see what's really important. What I'm handing her on a silver platter."

McCoy raised his hands pleadingly. "I want this to be easy. I want to be there for her."

Celia's mother scoffed. "Please, Richard. If you really want to help her, you'll show her this is about her future. Continuing the legacy I left her. She has potential to be *the best*." She paused, chewing on her words. Her bright nails tapped against her arm. "She failed in cheerleading. Surely you can do something about that?"

"I can't give Celia that spot just because she threw a tantrum. It'll have to be something else."

"Fine, then do something about the boy! Remove the distractions!"

"Richter *is* a problem. I don't understand what she sees in him. Or what she thinks is going to happen. He wants nothing to do with her."

"It doesn't matter what he wants. As long as Celia wants him, we have problems."

McCoy sighed. "I can only help as long as she doesn't try to fix the problem on her own. I have everything she needs."

"I'm glad you're putting that principal position to good use." Celia's mother's voice went sweet again. "Thank you, Richard. For everything." She reached out to stroke his face. Then she strode past him, out of the gym. He waited a minute, then followed.

I retreated underneath the bleachers, shut my camera off, and tried to make sense of what I'd just heard.

McCoy knew Celia's mother.

McCoy really *was* helping her with some strange destructive plan to make Celia the queen of the school.

They were going to remove the distractions.

That meant Miles.

Chapter Twenty-four

"**Q**uickly, another."

"I've got one."

"Do you play a sport?"

"Goddammit, you already know it, don't you?"

"You're Pelé."

Evan had been running his hand through his hair, and he ripped it away so fast he tore some out. "*How?* How did you get it without even asking me any questions?"

Miles laced his fingers together on his chest and stared at the ceiling of the gym, not answering. The rest of us sat in a circle around him while the boys' basketball team practiced on the court below. Jetta pulled a single grape out of her lunch box and dropped it in Miles's mouth. He took his sweet time chewing his reward.

"Last week, you said you had started getting really into football," he finally said.

"Soccer," Ian said.

"*Football,*" Jetta hissed, kicking Ian in the shin.

Miles ignored them. "Don't pick one of the most celebrated players in the sport next time."

"I have one, Boss," Art said.

"Are you alive?"

Miles started with that question when he wasn't quite sure where you were coming from. At least that's what I thought at first. After watching him play this game with the members of the club over a few months, I'd noticed a pattern. He smashed Theo, Evan, and Ian under his mental heel because it encouraged them to try to beat him, but he always gave Jetta and Art some leeway.

"Yes."

"Are you male?"

"Yes."

"Do you have a TV show?"

"No."

"Did you have a TV show at any point in your life?"

Art's smile never got very big, but it gave away every single thought in his head. "Yes."

"Did you wear bow ties?"

Art kept smiling. "No."

Miles had to tilt his head back against the bleacher to see Art. "Really? Interesting."

"Give up?" Art asked.

"No. You're Norm Abram. It was either Bill Nye or someone involved in woodworking."

Evan, Ian, and Theo let out a collective groan. Jetta fed Miles another grape. Art shrugged and said, "My dad got me hooked on *This Old House* when I was a kid."

Miles waved his hand toward me. "You go."

I hadn't had a turn at this since that first time, with the Aztec emperors. He'd never invited me, before now. "Okay, I have someone."

"Are you alive?"

"No."

"You're a historian; of course you're going to pick a dead person. Are you male?"

"Yes."

"Are you from North America or South America?"

"No."

He turned his head to stare me straight in the eye, like he could read my thoughts if he only focused hard enough.

"Europe is a trap . . . are you from Asia?"

"Yes."

"Did you have a significant effect on the development

of some strain of philosophy that profoundly impacted the world?"

"Why don't you ask *us* questions like that?" Theo blurted out.

I stifled a laugh. "Yes."

Miles sat and thought for a moment. He was only at five questions, and he was already getting pretty close.

"Are you from China?"

"No."

"Are you from India?"

"Nope."

He narrowed his eyes at me. "Are you from the Middle East?"

"Yes."

"Did you practice Islam?"

"Yes."

"Were you born before 1500 AD?"

"Yes."

"Did you contribute to the field of medicine?"

"Yes."

Miles turned to the ceiling again and closed his eyes. "Are you also known as the father of modern medicine?"

Ian frowned. "Hippocrates was a Muslim?"

"I'm not Hippocrates," I said. "I'm Ibn Sina."

"You know, part of the game is *not* telling Boss who

you are before he guesses it," Evan said.

I shrugged. "He already knew." I turned back to Miles. "And we got to twelve. But hey, at least you didn't drag it out just to show off, like you did last time."

He grunted.

Jetta looked up to the gym doors, then back to Miles. "*Mein Chef. Der Teufel ist hier.*"

We all turned to look. Mr. McCoy strode into the gym, straightening his jacket and tie, his gaze zeroed in on our group. He edged around the basketball practice and stopped at the foot of the bleachers. "Mr. Richter," he called up. He sounded like his jaw had been wired shut. "May I speak to you for a moment?"

"Yes," Miles said. He didn't move.

McCoy waited a total of four seconds before he added, "In *private*, Mr. Richter."

Miles pushed himself to his feet, stepped past me, and climbed down the bleachers. As he and McCoy walked to the far end of the gym, out of earshot, Evan and Ian gave identical exaggerated shudders.

"Careful, don't let them out of your sight," said Evan.

"Yeah," Ian added. "McCoy might pop out Boss's eyes with a melon baller and use them like olives in his martinis."

"What?" I said. "Why?"

"*Der Teufel hasst Chef,*" Jetta said.

"I don't know what that means."

"McCoy hates Boss," Theo explained. "I would say my brothers are being obnoxious, but there's a good chance McCoy actually has a melon baller in his desk drawer with Boss's name on it."

"Seriously though," I said. "Is it just the way everyone else hates him? Because it probably sucks to be the principal who has to deal with him." Please let it only be that way. Please let it not be anything out of the ordinary.

"No no," Evan said. "Listen. You could say Ian and I have . . . made the front office our second home. How many times would you say we've been sent in three years, Ian?"

Ian tapped his chin. "Give or take four times per semester? We're actually due."

"So we know a little bit about what goes on in that guy's office. He talks about Boss *all* the time. Boss is pretty careful with his . . . *stuff* . . . you know, so McCoy doesn't have anything on him, but he has all these theories he's always telling Assistant Principal Borruso. That Boss has weapons, or drugs, just a bunch of ridiculous stories. He legit wants Boss kicked out."

This was East Shoal; of course it was out of the ordinary.

"But . . . why?" I asked. "He can't just be annoyed. What would cause that?"

Evan shrugged. "All I know," said Ian, "is that McCoy

didn't just make this club and force Boss to lead it because he wanted to stop Boss from plastering people's homework on the ceiling. He did it because he wants to keep Boss in his sights."

So the possibly-mentally-unstable McCoy had his crosshairs locked on Miles. Why? Why would he care so much about Miles? Why would McCoy try to hurt him?

Or was I being paranoid? Was McCoy just dealing with an unruly student?

Could I take that chance?

"Don't worry, Alex," Jetta said, lounging back with her bundle of grapes. "If 'ee tries to 'urt *mein Chef*, we will send 'im back to the 'ell 'ee came from."

Coming from Jetta, that was refreshingly reassuring.

Miles returned to the bleachers a few minutes later, both eyes still in his head. I looked him over three times before doing a quick perimeter check. Nothing strange, but I couldn't deny the gut instinct that told me something bad was coming.

Blue Eyes was a little candle flame in the darkness, and even though I didn't know for sure if Miles really was Blue Eyes, I couldn't let him be snuffed out.

Chapter
Twenty-five

I sat by my window on the night of the job, waiting for the signal. My fingers jittered against the windowsill and my feet sweated in my shoes, despite the cold outside. Dad snored in the room down the hall, and if he was snoring, that meant both he and my mother were asleep. In the room next to mine, Charlie mumbled something about sugarcoated chess pieces. All they had to do was stay asleep for the next two hours, and everything would be fine.

I'd double- and triple-checked with Art to make sure the job was (mostly) safe and would definitely be over in two hours. I still didn't know exactly what the job was, or what I was supposed to do.

But then I realized I didn't care. I was going to enjoy tonight's adrenaline rush if it killed me. I wanted to be a teenager. I wanted to sneak out at night (not while under the impression I was being kidnapped by Communists) and do things I wasn't supposed to. I wanted to do them with *other people*. Real people. People who knew there was something different about me and didn't care.

Art's van rolled up at the end of the street, flashing its headlights. As quietly as I could, I removed the screen from my window, set it against the wall, climbed into the flowerbed outside, and slid the storm window shut behind me. Just like a nighttime trip to Red Witch Bridge. I set off down the slush-streaked street, squinted to make sure it was actually Art in the driver's seat, then climbed into the passenger side.

"Okay, now we have to go get Boss," Art said.

I buckled myself in. "Where are we going?"

"Downing Heights." Art smiled a little. "I know you love it there."

"Oh, but I do," I mumbled. "Tell me we're not going to Celia's."

"Nope. But first we have to get Boss, and he definitely doesn't live in Downing Heights."

Silent houses flicked by. In the distance, expensive Lakeview houses rose like dark mountains. But around us, each house was less friendly than the last. Suddenly my dirt-colored hovel of a home seemed so much nicer than before.

We turned a corner and the houses became downright scary. Like, Bloody Miles trying to murder me scary. I wouldn't have come down this way even at high noon.

Art stopped in front of a two-story house that looked like staples held it together at the corners. Shingles were missing all over the roof, half the windows had the glass broken out of them, and the porch sagged in the middle. Garbage littered a front lawn enclosed by a rusted chain-link fence. Miles's blue truck sat in the driveway, next to an aging Mustang that looked like it might be worth a lot of money if anyone tried to take care of it.

I knew something here must have been a delusion. Something. The darkness made everything worse, but this place . . . no one could live like this. This had to be fake.

"Uh-oh—Ohio's outside." Art nodded toward the side of the porch, where a makeshift doghouse gave shelter to the biggest Rottweiler I'd ever seen in my life. It looked like the kind of dog that ate babies for breakfast, old men for lunch, and virgin sacrifices for dinner.

No wonder he was Miles's dog.

"He lives here?" I leaned forward for a better look at the house. "How is this even habitable?"

"It's not, I don't think. His dad survives by constantly surrounding himself in a booze haze and setting the hell hound loose on the neighbors." Art shuddered. "The first time we ever picked Boss up, Ohio was awake. I thought he would bite my head off, and I never got out of the van."

I had never imagined big, bulky Art being scared of anything. I didn't know what I'd expected, but it wasn't this. So Miles wasn't rich. I'd still expected something a little nicer.

"What does his dad do?"

Art shrugged. "I think he's some kind of security guard downtown. There's only the two of them, so I don't think they're hard up for cash. But no one takes care of the place."

Movement on the second floor distracted me. The window on the far left slid open. A dark figure crept through the narrow opening like a cat and reached back in for a coat and a pair of shoes. He put the coat on but carried the shoes, then hurried to the side of the porch roof, lowered himself down the drainpipe like a ghost, and dropped silently on the balls of his feet, right on top of the doghouse.

Ohio gave a snort, but he didn't wake up.

The figure climbed off the doghouse, padded across the yard, hopped the fence, and ran around to the back of the van. I forced myself to start breathing again.

Miles climbed in through the back, shaking slush out of his hair and socks. He shoved his feet into his shoes. Art pulled away from the house.

"Damn dog." Miles flopped over, resting his head back.

It was still weird seeing him this way. Jeans and an old baseball shirt under his bomber jacket. Boots that looked like chew toys. He raked his hair back, cracked an eye open, and caught me staring.

"I live in Shitsville, I know." He looked at Art. "Did you get the stuff?"

"Behind me."

Miles grabbed the black duffel bag stashed behind the driver's seat and dumped the contents on the floor, where they rolled around.

A container of IcyHot, a bag of little black specks, five or six heavy-duty bungee cords, a screwdriver, a socket wrench, and a small sledgehammer.

"What'd you bring this for?" Miles asked, picking up the sledgehammer.

Art shrugged. "Thought it'd be fun. In case we need to smash anything."

I snorted. Art's hands were like two sledgehammers on their own.

"Don't smash anything too expensive. I told Alex we weren't committing any felonies."

"Uh, Boss? What do you call breaking and entering?"

"A felony," said Miles. "But it's not breaking and entering if you've got a key." He pulled a single key out of his pocket and held it up.

"Where the hell'd you get a key?"

"I've got someone on the inside. Turn here. He's the third house on the left."

We were back in Downing Heights, winding our way up the road toward the super-fancy houses. We stopped in front of one that looked like it could have been Bill Gates's second home. The front walk led up to a three-door garage and a huge porch with a stained-glass double door.

Miles shoved everything but the screwdriver, wrench, and sledgehammer into the duffel bag. "Art, you've got the car. Alex, you're coming with me." He checked his watch. "Hopefully no one wakes up. Let's go."

We got out of the van and jogged toward the house. Miles stopped beside the front door, flipped open the security keypad, and typed in a code. He turned to the door and unlocked it with the key. The doors swung open.

We stepped inside an entryway. Miles closed the door behind us and checked the other keypad inside the door, then motioned to another nearby door that must've led to the garage. Art headed through it with the screwdriver, wrench, and sledgehammer clutched in one hand.

This house belonged in Hollywood, not central Indiana. A huge staircase occupied the middle of the foyer (a *foyer*, they had a freaking foyer), splitting off in two directions upstairs. To the right of the foyer was a living room where the light from a TV flickered across the far wall. I hit Miles on the arm, pointing at the light. He shook his head and watched the doorway, and a second later a black-haired girl in paisley pajamas stepped into the foyer. She rubbed her eyes with one hand, staring straight at us.

"Hey, Angela," said Miles, calm as could be. The girl yawned and waved.

"Hi, Miles. He's fast asleep. I crushed those pills up in his dinner like you said."

"Awesome, thanks." Miles pulled out his wallet and handed Angela a twenty-dollar bill.

"Good work. He's still in the same room, right?"

"Fourth on the right," said Angela. "Mom and Dad are on the left, so you shouldn't have to worry about them."

"Thanks. Let's go."

The two of us set off up the stairs. At the top, we turned to the right and crept down a long hallway. It was all so disturbingly normal—besides the sheer amount of money that must have gone into it—that for a moment I thought the whole place might be a hallucination.

Miles stopped at the fourth door on the left, touched the handle hesitantly a few times as if he thought it'd be scalding hot, and then pushed the door open.

Whoever owned the room was incredibly disorganized. Clothes lay all over the floor. Papers and diagrams and maps of different places littered a desk against one wall. Models of cars and superheroes and mechanical animals covered the top of the dresser. Science posters were taped to every wall, including one of the periodic table that glowed in the dark.

The sleeper rolled over.

"Here." Miles unzipped the backpack and pulled out the container of IcyHot. "Go to the dresser. Should be one of the top drawers—smear this in the crotch of every pair of underwear you find."

"I—what?" I took the container. "That's disgusting."

"I'm paying you fifty dollars for this," Miles hissed, turning toward the bed.

I went to the dresser and yanked open the top drawer on the left. Empty. Crisp white underwear and boxers filled the one on the right.

Well . . . at least they were clean.

I picked up the first pair of underwear and uncapped the IcyHot. As I worked, I watched Miles out of the corner of my eye as he yanked the bedcovers back and harnessed the sleeper to the bed with the bungee cords, from his shoulders to his ankles. Then Miles upended the bag of black specks— fleas?—over the sleeper's head.

"Okay, I'm done," I whispered. I slid the drawer shut again.

"Now pick up every pair of underwear you can find on the floor and shove them under the dresser." Miles began setting the alarm clock on the bedside table.

With my index finger and thumb, I played a sort of crane game and picked up pairs of underwear, touching them as little as possible. I made a pile next to the dresser and shoved it under with my foot.

"The sleeping pills should wear off before the alarm goes," said Miles. I handed him back the IcyHot. "All we have to do is get out of here."

I crept over to the bed to get a better look at our poor, unsuspecting victim.

I froze.

"Oh my God, Miles."

"What?"

"It's *Tucker*!"

He looked so innocent in his Einstein T-shirt and pajama pants covered in atoms—and I'd put IcyHot in his *underwear*—

"Calm down!" Miles grabbed my wrist and pulled me out of the room. We hurried down the stairs and back into the foyer, where Angela waved to us from the living room. Then we were out on the porch. Miles locked the door and reset the security system, and we ran to the van. Art waited in the front.

"You *dick*!" I said once the doors were closed and Art stepped on the gas. I punched Miles's arm with all the anger welling up in me. "You didn't tell me it was *Tucker*!"

"Would you have done it if I had?" Miles asked.

"Of course not!"

"Yeah, but you're fine doing it if it's anyone else." Miles shoved his glasses up to rub his eyes. "Bit hypocritical, if you ask me."

"I didn't *ask you*." I crossed my arms and glared out the window. Awful guilt roiled in my stomach. "You should have told me."

"Why? Because you feel bad for him? Because he follows you around like a dog? He's never going to know you helped. He's going to be flustered and uncomfortable, and you'll be fifty dollars richer."

Another flood of anger shot through my limbs. "It doesn't matter—it's the principle of the thing!"

"No it's not, not when you suddenly decide it's bad because it's Beaumont!"

We glared at each other for a minute, until Art coughed. My arms tightened.

"You're an asshole," I said, looking away.

"Takes one to know one," Miles muttered back.

Chapter Twenty-six

The next morning, Miles actually showed up at my house. But I let seven o'clock come and go and asked Dad to drive me to school. He'd noticed something was wrong when I'd done a nosedive into my cereal without even checking it for trackers first. When he asked, I said that I hadn't been able to sleep.

Still, as soon as we hit the school parking lot, I was wide awake.

He dropped me off at the main entrance. I did a perimeter check, took note of the men—*real or not real?*—standing on the roof, and shouldered my backpack. I got the overwhelming feeling that people were staring at my hair. When I looked around, no one was even paying attention to me.

Miles was at the lockers, standing in front of his open door, stuffing books in. When I opened my locker, a crisp fifty-dollar bill fluttered to my feet. I scooped it up and shoved it at Miles.

"I don't want it."

He quirked an eyebrow. "Well, that's too bad, because it's yours."

"I'm not taking it." I threw the bill on top of his books.

"It's fifty dollars. Surely you could use that for something."

"Oh, I bet I could. Thing is, I won't."

"Why, because of a misplaced sense of morality?" Miles spat. "Trust me, Beaumont doesn't deserve your guilt."

"Who are you to decide that?" I tried very hard not to punch him in the face or kick him in the crotch. "You don't like him because he's a better person than you are. He doesn't resort to stealing and sabotage just to get other people to listen to him."

Miles looked like he was keeping himself from saying something nasty, but he shook his head and tucked the fifty into his back pocket.

As I walked to class, all I could think about was why I had ever wanted to kiss him. But then I heard the unearthly shrieks coming from Mr. Gunthrie's room. A large group of students had formed outside the door. I shoved my way through and jumped to the side in case of projectiles.

Celia was back, her fingers tangled in Stacey Burns's ponytail, screaming at the top of her lungs. Her hair, once blond, was now grass green. Britney Carver stood on Stacey's other side, trying to pry Celia's fingers away. Celia swung forward and planted her fist in Stacey's face with a crunch.

Claude Gunthrie tossed a few freshmen out of the doorway and sprinted into the room, grabbing Celia around the waist and lifting her off her feet.

"GET OFF ME! YOU FUCKERS DID THIS! I'M GOING TO KILL YOU!"

"We didn't do it!" Stacey yelled back, blood dripping from her lip. "Let me go!"

"Someone grab her arms!" Claude grunted under Celia's weight. "She's gonna—AUGH—"

Celia elbowed him in the face.

"WHAT?" Theo shot up and lunged for the arm Celia had hit Claude with, looking prepared to rip it off.

"WHAT'S GOING ON? BREAK IT UP, ALL OF YOU!"

As if he had the hands of God, Mr. Gunthrie thundered into the room, took Celia's collar in one hand and Stacey's in the other, and lifted them off their feet. They both looked so thoroughly shocked when he put them back down, they fell quiet and let each other go.

"CLAUDE, TAKE BURNS TO THE NURSE. HENDRICKS, YOU'RE COMING WITH ME." Mr. Gunthrie paused a moment, sizing Celia up, and then said, "WHY DID YOU DYE YOUR HAIR GREEN?"

Celia began screaming again and Mr. Gunthrie had to lock his arms around her to drag her from the room. Stacey, clutching her jaw, marched out without Claude. Claude, sporting a bloody nose, followed. Theo managed to slip out of the room with him.

I sank into a seat. Had Stacey and Britney really dyed Celia's hair green, or was it another one of Celia's stunts to draw attention to herself?

The whispers got louder. Miles walked in, looking a little put off by the half-empty room and everyone in the wrong seats. He sat down without acknowledging me.

Cliff and Ria were back at Ria's desk, snickering and glancing at the door every few seconds. Then Ria's face went so red and Cliff began laughing so hard that I turned and looked, too.

Tucker hobbled into the room, bowlegged. Deep bags ringed his eyes and both hands scrubbed at his uncombed black hair. His tie hung loose around his collar and his shirt was untucked. He gingerly lowered himself into his seat, wincing as he settled, and began scratching himself all over.

I slid out of my seat and hurried across the room. "Are you okay?"

Are you okay? is probably one of the top five stupidest questions ever. Ninety-nine percent of the time, it's easier to use a tiny bit of common sense. However, in the current situation I could think of nothing better to say, because *"I am so sorry for putting IcyHot in your underwear"* is not the first thing you want to tell a person who does not, in fact, know that you were the one who put IcyHot in his underwear.

Tucker folded his hands in his lap as if he'd finally realized he looked like a rabid monkey. "No," he said. "I woke up this morning and felt like I was on an acid trip. I'm itching all over and I don't know why." He leaned closer, shifting around uncomfortably in his seat. "And it feels like someone set my underwear on fire."

I pressed my fist to my forehead, my stomach twisting itself into knots.

"I know what happened," he began. I stared at him in horror, but he kept going. "Not the specifics, but I know what happened and why. And I know it was Richter. I know it was him, because he's the only person who could get in and out of my house in the middle of the night without tripping the alarm. At least, he's the only person who would do it for the sole purpose of screwing with *me*."

Tucker shot a glare over my shoulder at Miles. "Look at him; he's not even subtle about it. He's staring right at us now."

I didn't look. "It can't be that bad, right? What happened?"

He shook his head. "I don't know. My alarm went off an hour late, and everything's been going wrong since. I got halfway to school and my car broke down." Tucker paused for a moment to absentmindedly scratch his chest. "There was more than one person helping him, I think—Richter never did understand cars—probably someone in that club . . ."

Tucker stopped again.

"You didn't . . . you didn't help him, did you?"

Maybe it took me a second too long to answer. Maybe I looked in the wrong direction, or pulled a little too hard on my hair. But understanding washed over Tucker's face before I could start blurting out denials. He turned his whole body away from me.

Why had I hesitated? Why hadn't I done what I'd planned to do and told him everything?

Chapter Twenty-seven

By lunch, the story of what happened in Mr. Gunthrie's class had spread to the entire school. Claude's nose was swollen and bruised, and he winced every time he tried to talk. Stacey hadn't returned from the nurse, but Britney walked around complaining about Celia's bitchiness to anyone who would listen. I was 90 percent sure Celia herself had gotten suspended. Again.

I didn't see Tucker for the rest of the day, and it made me hate myself. I mean, forget that there wouldn't be another library trip to look up anything about McCoy, or any more conspiring at Finnegan's. I should've asked Miles whose house it was. And I knew Miles had been at least a little right when he'd called me a hypocrite for saying it was wrong just because it was Tucker. It should've been wrong no matter who it was. But I'd done it anyway.

By seventh period chemistry, the last thing I wanted to do was stand at a lab table for fifty minutes with Miles. I'd avoided talking to him all day, but the lab forced me to relay data about chemical reactions with certain types of metals so he could write it down. I don't know why he didn't just do it himself—the samples were easy enough to examine—but after every reaction he stood there looking at me, waiting for the result.

Apparently, this made him think I'd forgiven him. After class he followed me all the way to the lockers and then to the gym, quiet, until we saw Celia being led from the main office by her father and the school security guard.

"Celia was never like this before," Miles said. "She liked to bother me, but she never did anything to other people. I think something strange is going on, but I don't know what."

I turned and looked at the glass display case outside the gym, as if I couldn't care less about him or Celia. "You seem to be under the impression that I'm talking to you."

"You were in chemistry," said Miles.

"So we could do our lab."

I heard his molars grinding together. "Fine. I'm *sorry*." He said the word through gritted teeth. "Are you happy now?"

"Sorry for what?" I looked at Scarlet's picture again. The thing was entirely scribbled over in red now. I wished I had Finnegan's Magic 8 Ball.

Miles rolled his eyes. "For . . . I don't know, for not telling you it was Beaumont?"

"And?"

"And for making you put IcyHot in his underwear."

"It was cruel."

"So that makes you think it was *my* idea? I don't come up with this stuff; I just do it for people."

At the look I gave him next, his hands shot up in surrender. "Sorry, *sorry*, really—all right, if you're not going to talk to me, will you at least listen?"

"Depends on what you have to say."

Miles looked around to see if we were alone, then took a deep breath.

"I have some stuff I need to tell you, because I feel like . . . like I owe it to you. I don't know why I feel like that, and I don't like feeling like that, but there you go."

I was surprised, but didn't say anything. Miles took another deep breath.

"First of all—and if I don't tell anyone about you, you can't tell anyone about this—my mom is in a psychiatric hospital."

Was I supposed to be surprised? Confused? I didn't

think he'd actually tell me. But now I didn't have to feel bad about the imbalance of secrets between us. "What? No. You're lying."

"I'm not. She's in a hospital up north in Goshen. I visit her once a month. Twice if I can manage it."

"You're serious?"

"*Yes*. Again, you never believe me. I don't understand why someone would lie about that. I'm trying to make things better, but if you aren't going to listen then I'll stop talking—"

"No, no, sorry, keep going," I said quickly.

Miles gave me a shrewd look. "You're going to shut up and listen?"

"Yes. Promise."

"Well, since I know you want to know what she's in for—it's nothing. She's always been a little . . . off-kilter . . . but never bad enough to be committed. Never bad enough to stay in there. But denying that you're crazy tends to make people think you're more crazy—"

I made an understanding noise.

"—and that was how my dad convinced them at first. Said she denied it all the time. First he told them her bruises and the black eyes and the busted lips were all her fault. That she caused them in fits of depression and rage, that she was bipolar and he didn't trust her anymore. And of course as soon as she heard that, she was furious, which made it worse." He made a disgusted sort of noise in the back of his throat. "And then . . . the lake."

"The lake?"

"He threw her in a lake, 'rescued' her, and told them she tried to commit suicide. She was hysterical. No one bothered to look for evidence against him. That's when I started running jobs for people, and now I take all the late shifts I can at work, and forget the underage work laws, because I don't care. I'm getting her out of that place when I turn eighteen in May, and I need the money for her, so . . . so she has something, you know? Because my father's not gonna give her anything, and I can't let her go back to that house."

Miles stopped suddenly, eyes focused on a spot to the left of my head. Unease filled my stomach, the kind you get from suddenly knowing a whole lot more about a person than you thought you ever would.

"So. So are you—"

"Not done yet," he snapped. "Sometimes I have trouble understanding things. Emotional things. I don't understand why people get upset about certain stuff, I don't understand why Tucker doesn't try to be more than he is, and I still haven't figured out why you kissed me."

Okay. I could've died then. Just crawled on the floor and died.

"Have you heard the term *alexithymia* before?" he asked.

I shook my head.

"It means 'without words for emotions.' Except it's more than that. It's almost a mental disorder, but there's a sort of scale. The higher your alexithymia score, the more trouble you have interpreting emotions and things like that. My score isn't as high as some, but it's not the lowest."

"Oh."

"Yeah. So, sorry if I come across callous sometimes. Or, I don't know, defensive. Most of the time I'm just confused."

"So does that mean you don't care about the people you hurt when you run those jobs?" I asked.

"I'm not sociopathic; it just takes a while for me to process. I'm pretty good at turning off my guilt when I don't want it. But I can't stop. It's an easy way to get money, it keeps anyone from getting too close to me, and I feel . . . safe."

"What do you mean?"

"I mean that when I'm the one doing everyone else's dirty work, and everyone is afraid of me, I feel safe. I control what happens and to who."

"Whom," I mumbled, and to my surprise, he smiled.

"Right. Whom."

I got the feeling the smile wasn't only because I had

corrected his grammar. I wondered if he'd ever told anyone any of that before, and then wondered about his mother, in Goshen, and exactly how he planned to get her out while his dad was still around. I wondered what he would do if his little dictatorship over the school ever crumbled.

I peered back into the trophy case. Scarlet's picture screamed at me.

"I might know something about what's going on with Celia," I finally said. I told him everything I knew about Celia, Celia's mother, McCoy, Scarlet, and the scoreboard. How Tucker had been helping me look up information about it, but we'd reached a dead end.

"I know McCoy doesn't like you, and Celia does," I added. "And that . . . worries me. I think they're both really unstable. McCoy needs some kind of psychiatric help, and I don't think he's going to get it. I don't think he even knows, or cares. And I know—I *know*—it's like, I'm the crazy girl, making up crazy stories, why would you listen to me, but if you could just do me a favor and . . . watch out."

He stared at me. Blinked.

Then he nodded and said, "Okay. I'll be careful."

Chapter
Twenty-eight

Celia's second suspension wasn't announced, exactly, but everyone in the school knew the details. Thanks to her lawyer of a father (and some unforeseen intervention from Satan himself, because who else would come to her rescue?), Celia wasn't expelled. That was the bad news. The good news was that she'd be gone for the rest of the semester. The other bad news was that the semester was only ten more days. And the entire club saw the other *other* bad news coming from a mile away: when the semester was up, Celia would be back, and she'd be doing community service.

The only person who didn't seem to like the good news *or* the bad news was Principal McCoy, who only became more short-tempered and irritable after Celia was gone. His morning announcements were short and curt, and he didn't say anything about the scoreboard. In the afternoons, he could often be found outside the gym watching the club work. I knew Miles was a big boy who could take care of himself, but if there was ever a time to put my finely honed sense of paranoia to good use, it was now.

During those ten days, the school went back to relative normality. Maybe it was the Christmas spirit in the air, or the thought of a two-week vacation, but everyone seemed a lot more lighthearted, in spite of finals. Presents were exchanged. I saw small people dressed in red and green flitting between classrooms. I made everyone in the club Christmas cards and attached a Greek drachma from the 1800s to each one, unsure if they'd think it was stupid.

I gave Miles his first, to see how he'd react. I fixed my goggles on my face at the lab table as he weighed the card in his hand. Then he opened it up as if it had a bomb inside.

He pulled the coin out and studied it. "A drachma? Is . . . is it real? Where'd you get it?"

"My dad's an archaeologist. He picks up stuff all over the place." And the coins were one of the things he'd brought home that I knew were real.

"But this could be worth a lot of money," said Miles. "Why are you giving it to me?"

"Don't feel too special." I pulled out the test tubes and

test tube rack we'd need for our lab. "I put them in the cards for everyone in the club."

"But still. How do you know this isn't worth hundreds of dollars?"

"I don't, but I assume my dad wouldn't give it to me if it was worth a lot of money." I shrugged. "I have a bunch of stuff like that."

"Did you ever think that maybe he gives it to you *in spite* of the fact that it's worth a lot?"

"Do you want it or not?" I snapped.

Miles dipped his chin and stared balefully at me over his glasses, shoving the coin deep into his pocket. He turned back to the card.

"Did you make this?" he said. "Why's it only in green?"

"Charlie's on a green binge right now. It was the only color I could find."

He scanned what I'd written inside the card. *Dear Asshole: Thank you for keeping your word and believing me. It was more than I expected. Also, I'm sorry you were inconvenienced by my gluing your locker shut at the beginning of this year. However, I am not sorry that I did it, because it was a lot of fun. Love, Alex.*

When he finished reading, he did something so surprising that I almost dropped the Bunsen burner and set the kid across from me on fire.

He laughed.

Our neighbors turned to stare at us, because Miles Richter laughing was one of those things that the Mayans had predicted would signal the end of the world. He wasn't particularly loud about it, but it was Miles laughing, a sound no mortal had ever heard before.

I liked it.

"I'm definitely keeping this." Miles went to get his black notebook. He slid the card into it and came back to the lab table, where he continued to be completely oblivious to the staring and happily helped me start the lab.

The club seemed to really enjoy their gifts, even before I explained what the drachmas were. Jetta, who knew Greek, spoke it for the rest of the day. The triplets also wanted to know how much their coins were worth, and if they could pawn them.

"Probably, if you can find the right person," I said, "but I'll hunt you down if you do."

The club had a thing about giving one another gifts. Jetta, who planned on moving back to France someday to become a fashion designer, made everyone scarves. Art handed out amazingly realistic wooden figurines he'd made in shop class. (Mine looked like a long-haired Raggedy Ann doll.) The triplets actually sang a Christmas carol they'd composed themselves. Miles walked into the gym about five minutes after they'd finished, holding a large white box filled with giant cupcakes. Everyone gorged themselves while we watched the basketball practice. I didn't eat mine; I stacked it on top of the scarf and the figurines in a pile next to my backpack, with the excuse that I'd eat it later. I probably wouldn't. Not because I didn't trust Miles. He just wasn't as attuned to food poisons as I was.

Afterwards, the triplets started singing again, but this time they treated Miles to a nice round of "You're a Mean One, Mr. Grinch."

I got one other gift, and at first I wasn't sure if it was really a gift or a misplaced piece of sidewalk. A fist-sized chunk of rock sat on my desk without any explanation. I couldn't really blame the person who left it—I'd left one of my drachmas and a card full of apologies on Tucker's desk—but he could've at least explained what kind of message a rock was supposed to send.

But I kept it, partly because I was curious and partly because I'd never been one to throw away gifts.

Chapter
Twenty-nine

Christmas at the Ridgemont house was a lot like Christmas everywhere else. It was the only time of year my parents bought a lot of stuff. Most of what we got were things that had gone on sale after Christmas last year. Charlie didn't notice and I didn't care, because most of it was clothes anyway, and if they fit, they fit. Our presents appeared beneath the tree, both Charlie's and mine, with cards from Santa.

Every year on Christmas Eve, Charlie and I made Mom and Dad go out to dinner by themselves, and we made sure they went somewhere they'd actually eat the food and enjoy themselves. It meant my dad was happy and my mother was out of my hair.

At my request, Mom bought the ingredients for a Black Forest cake. Charlie got carried away eating the cherries while the cake was in the oven, but luckily we still had enough to cover the top edge. It looked delicious, and was guaranteed 100 percent poison- and tracer-free, which I was ecstatic about.

Sometimes it felt like I only got happy this way around Christmas. The rest of the year, I wondered if the point of Christmas was just spending money and getting fat and opening gifts. Indulging.

But when Christmas finally comes, and that warm, tingly, mints-and-sweaters-and-fireplace-fires feeling gathers in the bottom of your stomach, and you're lying on the floor with all the lights off but the ones on the Christmas tree, and listening to the silence of the snow falling outside, you see the point. For that one instance in time, everything is good in the world. It doesn't matter if everything isn't actually good. It's the one time of the year when pretending is enough.

The problem lies in getting yourself out of Christmas, because when you come out of it, you have to redefine the lines between reality and imagination.

I hated that.

After New Year's, a few days before we were due back at school, I asked my mother if I could go to Meijer with her. She gave me a strange look, but didn't ask why until I packed up a piece of our second attempt at a Black Forest cake.

"Miles works at Meijer. I wanted to see if he was there today."

Charlie demanded to go with us, and when we got into the supermarket, I held the plate of cake in one hand and steered Charlie toward the produce section with the other while Mom got a cart and went to shop.

I'd been in Meijer plenty of times since I was seven, of course. The deli counter hadn't changed at all, and the lobster tank was right in the same place. The lobsters still crawled over one another in their desperate search for escape. I propelled Charlie toward the tank, and she watched the lobsters as intently as I used to. The only difference was she never tried to set them free.

Despite the rush of post-holiday shoppers in town, the place was curiously empty. I worried that Miles wasn't working, but then a door behind the counter swung open and he walked out.

"Hey! You are here!"

Miles froze like a cat caught in a flashlight beam.

"What're you doing here?" he asked.

I balked. "Shopping, of course. Bit of a rude question to ask a customer, don't you think?" I passed the piece of cake over the glass case. "I hope you can keep this back there somewhere, or eat it really quick. Just think of it as an extra Christmas present. It's a *Sch . . . Schwarzw. . . .*"

Miles laughed. "*Schwarzwälder Kirschtorte*," he said. "A Black Forest cake. Did you—?"

"Charlie and I made it," I said, motioning over my shoulder to where Charlie stood, munching on a black knight.

Miles frowned over my shoulder. For a fleeting moment I wondered if he thought she looked like the seven-year-old me, standing next to the lobster tank with a seven-year-old him, asking for help in freeing the lobsters. Would he remember that, if I asked him?

Part of me was too scared to find out.

"She's cute at first," I said, "but trust me, it wears off once she crowns herself the pope and declares the bathroom 'religious grounds.'"

"She's done that before?" Miles asked.

"Oh yes. Several times. Last time I tried to take a shower, in fact. You could hear her screaming about blasphemers all the way down the street."

Miles laughed again—I was almost used to the sound by now. I looked back at Charlie, whose attention had started to wander. "I, uh, came to see if you were here, thought you'd like that cake. . . ." Suddenly there was nothing left to say. I was bothering him, I knew it. And why had I decided to bring him food at work? He plucked the cherry off the cake and stared at me as he chewed. I wished I had put more cherries on that slice. The whole jar of cherries. I could watch him eat a whole jar of cherries.

Jesus Christ on a pogo stick, what was happening to me?

I tugged hard on my hair and turned away, but he said, "Hey, wait, before you go. . ."

I turned back. He rubbed his neck, looking off to the side, and didn't say anything right away.

"I have another proposition for you," he said, and at the look on my face, he quickly added, "Not like the last one. This isn't a job, I swear. There's, ah, something I wanted to ask you. You said that you couldn't find anything else about Scarlet and McCoy? My mom went to school with both of them and I figured, if you wanted to . . . uh . . ."

"Yes?"

Miles took a deep breath, held it in with his chest puffed out, and looked at me warily. Then he let the breath out and said, "Do you want to meet her?"

I blinked at him. "What?"

"You know that monthly trip I was telling you about? I'm going up there again before school starts. I could pick you up on the way. It's almost an eight-hour round trip, though, so if you don't want to, that's okay—"

The more words that came out of his mouth, the more his face fell like he thought it was a bad idea. I let him run out of steam before I couldn't take his pitiful expression anymore and had to stifle a laugh.

"Yeah, I'll definitely go." I never thought I'd get such a golden opportunity to talk to his mom. There was no doubt she'd have whole treasure troves of information about Scarlet and McCoy.

And . . . oh, shit.

I swayed on the spot. This was about more than Scarlet or McCoy. He wanted me to meet his mom. I'd just agreed to meet his mom.

He perked up, but still looked apprehensive, like if he said, *"Really?"* I was going to say, *"No."*

"I'll have to ask first," I said, "but I should be able to. When are you going?"

"Saturday. I leave pretty early in the morning, so . . ."

"Don't worry about it; I'm an early bird." I saw my mother rounding the corner, heading for the lobster tank and Charlie. "There she is now, I can ask her."

"No, that's—you don't have to—" But I'd already waved her over.

"Miles invited me to go with him to visit his mom," I said.

My mother examined Miles, obviously remembering

when he'd brought me home during my episode, and Miles glanced from my mom to me, giving me a panic-stricken look I'd never seen on his face before.

"You're going to visit her?" my mother said with definite interest, but with that edge that suggested she thought Miles meant "visit her in jail."

"Uh, yeah." He swallowed thickly. "I go once a month—and it's nothing serious, really—but, uh, she's in a hospital in Goshen."

"A hospital?"

Miles looked at me again. "A psychiatric hospital."

My mother was completely silent for at least a whole minute. When she spoke again, her voice was careful, but almost . . . happy.

"Well, I think that sounds like a good idea," she said. Miles looked relieved, but my stomach sank to the depths of the ocean. Why was my own mother so okay with me visiting a mental hospital? Why was that a good idea at all?

It kind of felt like she was kicking me in the gut, and every kick said

I don't want you.

I don't need you.

I don't love you.

Chapter Thirty

Saturday morning, Miles stood on the doorstep in his bomber jacket with his hands shoved deep in his pockets. His breath fogged the pane of glass in the front door.

He looked me up and down. Pajamas and cat slippers. "Why aren't you ready to go?"

"My mom says I need to invite you in for breakfast."

Miles glanced over me, toward the kitchen. "I didn't realize you were eating. I can wait in the truck. . . ."

"No, no, it's okay." I grabbed his sleeve and pulled him inside. "Seriously, this'll all go over easier if you come and eat."

Miles looked toward the kitchen again. I knew he could smell the food—my mother had been wafting scents toward the front door since she'd started cooking this morning.

"Your dad is home?" Miles asked.

"Yeah," I said.

A line formed between his eyebrows.

"He's mostly harmless. But you have to remember your history." I lowered my voice to add, "Not everyone's dad is a complete asshole."

That seemed to convince him. He shrugged his jacket off. When I took it from him, it nearly pulled me to the floor.

"Christ almighty!" I heaved the unexpected weight back up. "Why is it so heavy?"

"It's a heavyweight flight jacket," said Miles. "I have another one that's lighter, but it makes me look like a greaser—what are you doing?"

"Smelling it." I stuck my nose in the collar. "It always smells like tobacco."

"Yeah, it would. *Opa* smoked a lot."

"Opa?"

"Sorry, my grandpa."

I hung the jacket on the coat hook next to the door and pushed Miles into the kitchen.

"Oh, you're here!" said my mother with fake surprise. "I've already set you a place at the table, right there next to Alex."

Miles's eyes glazed as they roamed over the scrambled eggs, sausage, bacon, toast, and orange juice on the table. I pushed him into a chair.

"It's nice to finally meet you, Miles." Dad reached over to shake Miles's hand. Miles stared at him like he'd lost the will to speak. "Staying for breakfast before you head out?"

"I guess," said Miles.

"Great! How much do you know about the French Revolution?"

"Like what?"

"When did it take place?"

"1789 to 1799."

"June twentieth, 1789 was the . . . ?"

"Tennis Court Oath."

"1793 to 1794 was the time period for the . . . ?"

"Reign of Terror," Miles answered, rubbing his neck.

"And Robespierre's full name was . . . ?"

"Maximilien François Marie Isidore de Robespierre."

"Well done, sir!" Dad grinned. "I like him, Lexi. Can we eat now?"

I filled Miles's plate for him, since he seemed to be paralyzed from the eyes down. Dad peppered him with history questions until they made it to World War II, and then they moved into an analytical discussion of wartime tactics.

Charlie didn't come out the entire time Miles was there, even though my mother had set a place for her. I'd been looking forward to introducing her to Miles—I had a feeling he wouldn't mind fueling her Word of the Week a thousand times over.

When the meal was left in scraps and ruins, Miles checked his watch and straightened up. "We'd better go. It's already nine."

I got dressed, and then we moved to the entryway to pull on coats and shoes.

"Oh, Alex, wait. Don't forget to take these." My mother sorted through a pile on the hall table. "The cell phone . . . your gloves . . . and here's some money if you stop for food on the way back."

I shoved all of it into my pockets and kissed her on the cheek. "Thanks, Mom." I turned back toward the kitchen. "Bye, Dad!"

"Bye, Lexi," Dad called back.

Miles stepped out the front door right before Charlie came barreling out of the kitchen, aiming for me.

She slammed into my legs. "When are you going to let me come with you?"

"Someday," I said. "Someday I'm going to travel the world, and you can come with me, okay?"

"Okay," she mumbled. But her eyes snapped up, and she jabbed a finger at me. "But I'm holding you to it!"

"I won't let you down, Charlemagne."

Chapter Thirty-one

I wondered how Miles made this trip every month without losing it. There was no music, no stereo, just an endless stretch of US-31 between Indianapolis and Goshen.

My delusion detector went off less and less while I was around Miles. Had his offer to meet his mother come any earlier this year, there wasn't an ice cube's chance in hell I would've taken him up on it. I would've gone nuts trying to figure out if he was lying, if it was some elaborate plan, or if he was just going to leave me in the middle of nowhere and laugh all the way home. But his presence didn't set me on edge anymore. The opposite, actually—since Tucker and I were no longer on speaking terms, Miles was the easiest person to be around. Maybe better than Tucker, even, because Miles *knew*. He knew, and he didn't care.

And he didn't seem to mind being around me, either.

"So what's your mom like?" I asked when we got off 465.

"I don't know," said Miles.

"What do you mean, 'I don't know'? She's your mom."

"I don't know—I've never had to explain her to anyone before."

"Well . . . what does she look like?"

"Like me."

I rolled my eyes. "What's her name?"

"Juniper," he said. "But she prefers June."

"I like it."

"She was a teacher. She's smart."

"Smart like you?"

"No one is smart like me."

"I've got a question," I said. "If you're such a brainiac, how come you never skipped grades?"

"Mom didn't want me to," he said. "She didn't want me to go through the things she went through when she skipped grades. She was always excluded from groups, people made fun of her. . . ."

"Oh."

"She probably won't stop smiling the entire time we're there. And don't mention anything about my dad or where I live. I don't like to worry her with stuff like that."

I nodded, thinking about Miles slinking across his

rooftop and dropping down onto the demon dog's roof.

"That, um, that dog . . ."

"Ohio," Miles said.

"Yeah. He's your dad's dog?"

"Yes. My dad got him partly to keep people from getting into our house, partly to keep me from getting out. He thinks I sneak out to meet people."

"But you do."

"He has no proof," Miles said. "Anyway, Ohio's not that smart and sleeps like a narcoleptic, so I guess he and my dad were kind of made for each other." He stared at the highway, then said with disgust, "I hate dogs. Cats are so much better."

I made my snort sound like a cough. We drove on in silence for another few minutes. I tried to burrow a little deeper into my coat.

"You didn't eat much at breakfast," I said.

"I wasn't that hungry," he replied.

"Liar. You were looking at that food like a kid from a third-world country."

"Your mom's cooking was really good."

"I know; that's why I eat it." After I check it for poison, of course. "Terrible deflection, by the way. You could have said, 'Because I felt awkward eating too much at a family gathering with people I've never met before,' and been done with it."

He coughed loudly, his fingers tapping the steering wheel.

Eventually Miles pulled off the highway and into a heavily wooded suburb. Everything was coated in blindingly white snow. He only took the backstreets, and the more houses we passed, the more I realized that this reminded me of where I lived. These could have been the same streets.

Maybe all paranoids had a sort of sixth sense for detecting places that wanted to lock them up. I knew the hospital as soon as I saw it. A squat, one-story brick building surrounded by a fence. Bare shrubs framed the front walk and snow-covered trees dotted the grounds. It was probably pretty during the rest of the year.

This whole McCoy-Scarlet-Celia thing seemed silly now. Hardly substantial enough to get me inside a mental hospital. McCoy could do what he wanted and Celia could deal with her own problems.

"Are you okay?" Miles asked, yanking my door open. I managed to unbuckle my seatbelt and slip out of the cab.

"Yep, I'm good." I balled my hands into fists and held them tight against my sides. Next to the front walk was a sign.

Welcome to Crimson Falls Residential Psychiatry Center.

Crimson Falls? It made me think of spilling blood. And in crimson lettering, no less.

My fingers itched to take pictures, but the little voice in the back of my head told me that if I did, orderlies would jump out of the bushes, throw a pair of shackles on me, and never let me leave. I'd never graduate high school. I'd never go to college. I'd never get to do the things normal people do because *normal people don't get so melodramatic about visiting mental hospitals, you idiot!*

That voice was so ambivalent sometimes.

It looked more like a hospital on the inside, where the floors were checked tile and the walls were exactly the right shade of taupe to make you want to kill yourself. A girl not much older than Miles and me sat behind the front desk.

"Oh, hi, Miles." She handed him a clipboard. Miles put both our names on the visitors' log. "You missed morning rec time. They're in the cafeteria right now. You can go on in and grab some food."

Miles handed her back the clipboard. "Thanks, Amy."

"Say hi to your mom for me, 'kay?"

"Sure."

I followed Miles down a hallway to the left of the reception area. We passed another set of double doors that led into a rec room being cleaned by attendants. A little farther on was a smallish cafeteria, filled with seven or eight patients.

Miles went in first. I followed in his shadow, tugging on

my hair and trying to shake the feeling that men in white coats were going to jump out and grab me.

There was only one food line in the cafeteria, and about ten square tables in the middle of the room. Large windows let in the sun. Miles navigated through the tables without so much as a glance at the patients, intent on only one of them, on the far side of the room.

He was right—she looked like him. Or, rather, he looked like her. She sat at a table near the windows, rolling around a few green beans on her plate and flipping through the pages of a book. She looked up and smiled a radiant smile—it was almost tooth-for-tooth the same as his, only easier, more used—and it was not the smile of a crazy person. Not the smile of someone who injured herself because of swinging moods. It was just the smile of someone who was very, very happy to see her son.

She stood to hug him. She was tall and willowy, and the sun gave her long sandy hair a golden halo. Her eyes were the same as his, too, the same color as the clear sky outside. The only things they didn't share were Miles's freckles.

Miles said something to his mother and motioned me over.

"So you're Alex," June said.

"Yeah." My throat felt suddenly dry. For some reason— maybe because Miles had so willingly hugged her—I felt no need to check her for weapons. I didn't feel anything strange about her at all. She was just . . . June. "It's nice to meet you."

"It's so nice to meet you, too—Miles talks about you all the time." And before I could think about that, she pulled me into a tight hug.

"I don't remember mentioning her before," Miles said, but he rubbed his neck and looked away.

"Don't listen to him. He's been pretending to forget things since he was seven years old," said June. "Sit down, you two; it's been a long drive!"

I kept quiet and watched them go at it, talking about anything and everything. When Miles explained things that happened at school, embellishing small facts and details, I'd jump in and correct him. June talked about what it had been like when she'd been in school, the people she'd known.

"Do you know what your senior prank is going to be yet?" she asked, face lighting up with excitement. I hadn't immediately taken her as a person who enjoyed pranks very much. "I thought up ours when I was a senior at East Shoal. Of course, not many people followed through with the entire plan—we only got to the first part of it."

"Which was . . . ?" asked Miles.

June smiled vaguely. "Setting Mr. Tinsley's Burmese python loose in the school."

Miles and I shot looks at each other, then back at June.

"It was you?" I asked incredulously. "You set the snake loose?"

June raised her eyebrows. "Oh yes. I don't think they ever caught it, though. That worried me a little."

"Mom, that snake is a myth now," said Miles. "People think it's still there."

I started to tell them that I'd seen the snake—that I'd *been* seeing it all year in the science hallway—but they pressed on, sweeping the conversation away.

The more she talked, the more I realized that June knew history. Not the history my parents were having an affair with, but personal histories. She learned the events that made up a person's life, and she used them to understand why they did the things they did. Miles knew words. She knew people.

So when I started explaining McCoy and Celia and everything that had happened this year, she absorbed it the way my parents absorbed war documentaries: with complete seriousness. I talked and she listened. The only thing I left out was the part about McCoy having it in for Miles.

"Celia sounds like a handful," she said after we'd vacated the cafeteria and moved into the rec room. "I went to school with a girl like that." June settled into her armchair, crossing her legs. Relaxed and thinking, June had the same catlike look about her that Miles did. "She was exactly like Celia sounds. Cheerleader, very high strung, very . . . what's the word I want . . ."

"Driven?" Miles offered.

"Ah! Yes, driven. And stubborn. All from her mother before her. The woman was a brute, hardly gave her a moment of rest from the time she could wear heels. Both of them got what they wanted." June shook her head. "We called her the Empress. *Empy* for short. Boys fell to their knees for her. Richard McCoy—you wanted to know about him, too? He was head over heels for her. And not in the cute puppy dog way. He had a shrine to her in his locker."

I snorted—it looked like McCoy was serving new mistresses now. Mainly, Celia's mother.

"But Empy was never interested in him, oh no," June continued. "I remember the day she started dating the captain of the football team, because when Daniel went to his locker after school that day, all of his things were scattered in the hallway, torn up. We all knew Richard did it, but no one could prove it. And he groveled at Empy's heels until the day she died."

"Do you remember that? What happened?"

"Well, it was a few years after they—Empy and the football captain—got married. Right after our senior year, she was pregnant and used it as leverage to make him marry her. She came back for our five-year reunion, and was standing under the scoreboard, talking about her glory days and her father's philanthropy, and it fell. They say she died at the hospital a few hours later, but I think the scoreboard caught her in the head just right, and she was gone on the gym floor. Richard was there—I heard that he still followed her around after high school—and he tried to lift it off of her. They said he looked . . . unreachable. Like his whole reason for being was pinned under that scoreboard, and nothing tethered him to the world anymore."

I shivered. "Do you think McCoy could be obsessed with someone else now? Like . . . he found a new tether?"

"It's possible."

Was that why Celia was doing all this terrible stuff to other people? Because McCoy was doing something to *her*? That changed things—I had really hoped Celia's involvement in all this was just some byproduct of her need to be popular. Something she'd wished on herself. But more and more it looked like she was caught up in something she couldn't control. And if that really was the case, how could I ignore it? After this semester, it wasn't like she had any friends. *Pariah* was practically tattooed on her forehead.

"I might be the only one who thinks something bad is going on," I said.

"Maybe you should talk to her," June said. "She might not think she can ask for help. Or she may not know how."

Wonderful—talking to Celia, one of my favorite things. Even if I wanted to, how could I get near her? Talking to anyone just seemed to make her angry, and we weren't exactly best friends.

"Keep her away from me, while you're at it," Miles said.

June laughed. "Oh dear, you've always had trouble talking to girls."

Miles turned red.

June looked at me. "When we were living in Germany, there was a nice girl who would ride down to the farm and talk to him. She brought him cake for his birthday. He never spoke more than three syllables to her, and he never accepted the cake."

"She knew I didn't like chocolate," Miles mumbled, turning a deeper shade of red and sinking into his chair.

That was a lie. He'd eaten the Black Forest cake I'd brought him.

"You lived in Germany?" I said, looking between the two of them. "On a farm?"

June's eyebrows shot up and she looked at Miles. "You haven't told her?"

"No, he hasn't told me."

June frowned at Miles, who shrugged.

"Well, we moved there when Miles was seven. And we came back a few months after his thirteenth birthday." June turned back to me. "He was so upset, but after my father died we couldn't stay anymore."

The airy way she said it made me think there was more to it than that, that she was skirting something important, but she didn't continue. Miles glared at the wall with his arms crossed.

"You seemed to make friends okay," June said.

"Right, Tucker Beaumont, the one kid in middle school who didn't make fun of my accent," Miles spat. "Great friend."

"I like accents," I said quietly.

"So do most other people, when they're coming from hot chicks and tan guys with muscles and nice smiles. Not when they're coming from a scrawny know-it-all with clothes that don't fit and no possible way to relate to other kids his age."

I couldn't think of anything to say to that. Neither could June, apparently. She put a hand up to her mouth and looked around as if she was searching for a misplaced book.

"I'm going to the restroom," said Miles suddenly, pushing himself out of his chair. "I'll be back in a minute."

When the double doors swung closed behind him, June lowered her hand.

"Did he tell you why I'm here?" she asked.

I nodded.

"He said it was because of his father, didn't he?"

Nodded again.

"It was. At first. I didn't want to leave Miles with him, and I fought to get out of here. It would have been better for Miles if I had been there, but I can't deny that this has helped me. I feel . . . more stable now. Still angry, but stable. And when I do leave, I'll be able to do what I couldn't before."

She paused and glanced at the door again.

"Alex, if I ask you a few questions, will you do your best to answer them honestly?"

"Yeah, sure."

"Does he have any friends? I know he's not the easiest to like, and I know he thinks people are . . . well, *cumbersome* to deal with, but there's someone for everyone, and I didn't know if. . . ." She paused and looked at me hopefully.

"I think he has friends," I said. "Everyone in the club is his friend. But I don't think he knows it."

June nodded. "Second question. Do people think he's . . . unpleasant?"

I would have laughed if June hadn't been so serious. "Most people do. But that's only because they never get to know him, and he never lets them. I think he likes it better that way."

June nodded again. "I don't know if you can answer this last one, but . . . ." She took a deep breath, much the same way Miles had before asking me if I wanted to come here. "Is he happy?"

That one caught me. Was he happy? Was I qualified to answer that? It seemed that the only person who knew if Miles was happy was Miles.

"I honestly don't know," I said. "Being here today—this is the happiest he's seemed in a while. But back home, at school . . . I'd say his happiness is probably on the low side."

June's face fell. "The only reason I ask is because he tries so hard. When he's not at school, he's working, and all he ever does is save money. I don't think I've ever seen him spend a dime on anything he didn't absolutely need. Even when he was little, he wouldn't accept things that people tried to buy him."

June sighed and relaxed back into the couch. "All he ever seemed to want was knowledge—numbers to crunch, history to learn, information to file away and use later . . ."

"He always carries around a black notebook with him, and he's writing in it all the time."

June smiled. "Ah, the notebooks. I got him started on those. Cleveland, his father, never liked the idea that his son was smarter than he was. He would get angry when Miles would correct him. I've always been afraid that Cleveland might have beaten that out of him, his love of teaching people. I told him to write what he knew in the notebooks instead of saying it out loud, and if he's still doing that, then his father hasn't changed him much at all."

I wanted to ask more, but I didn't want to give away the fact that I'd actually read the notebook. A different route, then.

"So what's he been saying about me?"

June laughed. "All good things. He's been very worried that you don't like him."

"He's been worried *I* don't like *him?*" I couldn't imagine Miles caring what anyone thought of him, least of all me. We'd been breaking into arguments all year, teetering on a seesaw of perpetual imbalance, because he was always either one way or the other. Miles the Jerk or Miles the Seven-Year-Old.

Oh God, I thought. *What if he told her about the kiss?*
He must have.
What did she think?
What did he think?
Better not tell you now.

"He remembers you," said June, and my stomach gave an odd stunted flop.

"Remembers me?"

"The girl who wanted to set the lobsters free. That was the day we left for Germany. I was shopping for a few last-minute things, and he wanted to talk to you. He liked your hair."

My throat tightened and my heart swelled painfully in my chest. *Please don't let this be a delusion. Please let this be real.* Here it was, finally and for certain, my proof. My first, completely real, not at all imaginary, friend was here. I'd found him, or he'd found me, or something.

He was real, I could touch him, we breathed the same air.

Miles chose that moment to walk back in, looking calmer than he had when he'd left. I tried not to stare as he sunk into his seat, but my brain scrambled to pull together fragments of memory, to put the boy from the lobster tank beside the boy in front of me now.

June said something to him in German, and a reluctant smile took over his face. He might've been confused about what he felt for other people, but it was obvious he knew exactly what he felt for his mother.

She was his reason.

It's him.

Cannot predict now

*No, I'm not asking, I'm telling. It's him. But what
if . . .*

Yes

What if he doesn't remember?

Concentrate and ask again

*Oh, sorry. I mean . . . it's like, if a tree falls in a
forest but no one's around to hear it, does it make a
sound? If he doesn't remember, did it happen? I know
June said we were there together, but she wasn't with
us. No one was.*

Most likely

*So you're saying it did happen? But . . . but if I'm
the only one who remembers the details . . .*

If I'm . . .

Chapter
Thirty-two

On the drive home, I huddled into my coat, going over everything we'd found out. It would be wrong to assume that something *wasn't* going on, that I was blowing all this up in my head. Something really was wrong with McCoy, and if we were the only ones who knew about it, we had to do something. But who would believe me? Who would believe Miles?

I stole glances at Miles whenever I could, wondering why it still shocked me that he was the boy from the lobster tank. I simultaneously wanted to kiss him and hit him for leaving.

Pressure built behind my eyes, a lump formed in my throat. I couldn't let him see me cry. He'd scoff at me or roll his eyes—he didn't seem like the kind of person that suffered tears gladly, and I didn't suffer anyone making fun of mine.

"You okay?" he asked after a half hour of silence.

"Yeah." My voice was definitely too high. Tucker would mock me so much.

"Hungry?" He scanned the horizon. "How does Wendy's sound?"

"Sure."

He drove into the Wendy's parking lot, to the drive-through. I picked out the cheapest sandwich on the menu. When he pulled around to the window to pay, I fished my money from my pocket.

He took one look at it and pushed it away. "I don't want it."

"I don't care, I have money, so take it."

"No."

I flung the ten-dollar bill at him, and he snatched it up and flung it back. This sparked a money-throwing war, which ended when Miles paid for our food, passed the drink carrier and bags to me, and then folded up the ten dollars and wedged it under my thigh. I scowled at him.

He backed into the parking space so we could sit in the bed of the truck and have a grand view of the highway. It wasn't much warmer in the cab, and stretching our legs seemed like a good idea.

"You're so skinny, I don't know how you're not turning blue," I said as I settled against the cab, sandwich in hand. Miles had already devoured half his french fries—the kid could definitely eat when he had food in front of him.

"It's this jacket," he said between fries. "So warm."

"Where'd you get it?"

"My *Opa*—sorry, again, grandpa—had it from World War II. He was a pilot." Miles took a bite of his sandwich. "We lived with him in Germany. He gave me some of his things before he died. Uniforms and old newspapers, medals, all sorts of stuff."

"So, after the war, he stayed in Germany?"

"What do you mean?"

"He didn't come back to America. Did he like it there, or something?"

Miles stared blankly at me for a second, and then he laughed. "Oh, you thought—no, no, Opa wasn't in the *United States* Air Force. He was in the Luftwaffe."

All the heat drained from my body.

"Well, don't look so shocked. I told you he was German."

"But that's a U.S. bomber jacket."

"Yeah, he got it from a U.S. pilot," Miles replied, and at my horrified expression, added, "What? He didn't kill the guy! They were friends! Why are you freaking out; you're supposed to be the history buff—you of all people should know that not all Nazis *wanted* to be Nazis."

I knew. Oh, I knew. That didn't stop me from being scared of them.

"You would've liked Opa. He was very down-to-earth."

"So is that why everyone calls you 'the Nazi' at school?"

"No. No one knows about Opa. They call me that because when I first started school here, I still had my accent, I liked to speak German a lot, and when I started running jobs, they thought it'd be a funny nickname. After a while, it stuck."

"Oh." I lowered my blushing face to my french fries. "So, um. What was the real reason you guys came back to the States? Your mom was acting sort of weird about it."

Miles curled his lip at his sandwich. "Cleveland. He wrote her letters for a long time, trying to persuade her to come back. I know she wanted to go, but Opa made sure she remembered why we were there. And when he died, it was the perfect excuse to leave." He rolled his eyes. "What'd she talk to you about?"

"Huh?"

"When I went to the restroom," Miles said. "What did my mom say to you?"

"Nothing important. Mom stuff."

Miles gave me a look that said he knew that much already, and he didn't want to ask the question again.

"She asked if you were doing okay in school. What people thought of you . . . if you had friends . . . if you were happy . . ."

Miles stared down at his sandwich, waiting.

"And I, you know, told her."

"Told her what?"

"The truth. Did you think I would lie to your mom?"

"No, but what exactly is 'the truth'?"

"Well, it was pretty easy," I said, annoyed now. "People think you're a jerk—"

Miles snorted derisively.

"—because they don't know you, and you don't let them. And I said yes, you do have friends—"

He scoffed. "Who, exactly? I was under the impression the entire school hated me."

"The club? You know, the people you hang out with all the time? The ones you talk to?"

"I don't know what jungle wilderness you've joined us from, but they are not my friends. Ever notice how none of them use my name? Even Jetta says 'mein Chef.' I'm just the person they're obliged to take orders from."

"You've got to be kidding me." I wanted to both

laugh and slap him, hard. "I don't even know how you can say they're not your friends. Are you trying to deny it so you don't get attached to anyone? Are you . . . I don't know . . . *how can you say that?* Do you not want friends or something? Even *I* want friends!"

He crammed the rest of his chicken sandwich into his mouth and stared off at the highway as he chewed. The rest of the meal was quiet, me pondering why anyone, even him, wouldn't want friends, and him glaring, the lights of the highway reflecting in his glasses. We cleaned up in silence, tossed the trash in a nearby bin in silence, and climbed back into the cab in silence.

And when Miles tried to start his truck, the engine clicked.

"I don't think that's supposed to happen," I said.

"No, really?" Miles shot me a look. He turned the key again. *Click. Click click click.* He stared at the dashboard for a few moments, tried the key once more, then went to open up the hood.

This isn't happening. A cold chill settled itself along my stomach lining. I didn't want to be stuck here, with Miles Richter, in the middle of nowhere, at night. *You are dreaming an impressively lucid dream, and you will wake up soon, and it will be okay.*

"I have no idea what's wrong," Miles said, his voice

hollow. I got out of the cab as well and shouldered him out of the way.

"Lemme look. . . ." I took a careful look at the engine, trying to remember what my dad had taught me about cars. I couldn't find anything, either.

Miles leaned against the side of the truck, scratching his head, gazing down at the ground like he'd lost something. Tucker had said Miles was awful with cars, and I thanked all that was holy that this hadn't happened while we were on the interstate.

"I can call," I said, flipping open the emergency family cell phone my mom had given me. "Do you know any auto repair places?"

"Do I look like I know any auto repair places?"

"You know everything else, so I figured I'd ask." I started to call home.

"Car trouble?"

I turned around; an older man, probably in his sixties or seventies, approached the truck with a concerned smile. For a split second I thought I knew him—his eyes looked exactly like Miles's. Miles clenched his jaw, so I figured I should do the talking. I looked the man over for any microphones or other strange objects.

"Yeah. It won't start, but it doesn't look like anything's wrong."

The man nodded. "Mind if I take a look?"

I shrugged, and the man shuffled over and stuck his head under the hood.

"Really, though," I said to Miles, who turned around, looking angry and confused. "If I had that many people as friends, I wouldn't be trying to act like I don't like them. And don't say you don't, because I know you do—"

"Why do you care so much?" he asked.

I gazed stonily back at him. "Really? You haven't figured that out yet?"

Deep breath, jaw clench. "They are *not* my friends," he said. "They don't want to be, like everyone else in that school. They're there because they have to be. Will you drop it?"

"Fine, How about this—you know your mom's last question? Are you happy? I told her that earlier today was the happiest I've ever seen you. That's a little pathetic, honestly." I couldn't stop the words from pouring out of my mouth. "You could have friends, you could be happy, but you choose not to be."

"What are you trying to tell me?" he barked so loudly I was sure the old man kept his head ducked out of courtesy. "Who are you to lecture me on being happy? You're the one taking your pills and all those stupid pictures, hoping the world doesn't go to hell when you finally slip up and someone finds out you're crazy. And you're trying to help me with my life when yours has been falling apart all year? Not to mention you've been dragging everyone else down with you—look at Tucker, who follows you around like a dog, and I'm sure you felt *so bad* about that job, so bad you couldn't even tell him what you did. So you know what? If I'm an arrogant douche bag, then you're a fucking hypocrite, and we're standing in a parking lot at a Wendy's in the middle of nowhere arguing about nothing, basically, and—and—" His voice lost steam. He dropped his arms, defeated, his expression was no longer full of rage, but guilt. "And I made you cry."

I wiped my eyes and looked at the hood of the truck, wishing very much that the old man wasn't there. "Yeah, well, isn't the first time."

I turned away and started walking.

Crazy. Falling apart. Hypocrite.

He was right. That's exactly what I was. I called him and Tucker and Celia and McCoy crazy when it was just me who was crazy, I was the crazy one, I was always the only crazy one.

I followed the red taillights. I didn't know where I was going, or what direction I was going in, or even where, exactly, I was right now. I was, as he'd so rightly pointed out, in a Wendy's parking lot in the middle of nowhere, and I was going there—nowhere.

I could feel him watching me as I walked away. Maybe a few words passed between him and the old man. I plopped down in the snow at the edge of the parking lot, about fifty feet away from the truck, pulled my knees up to my chest, and stared out over the highway. How many times had I tried walking away from Miles? Once at the bonfire—he'd stopped me—again when Erwin had died—and he'd stopped me again. This time he knew I had nowhere to go.

Shoes crunched a path behind me, and the sleeve of Miles's jacket tapped me on the shoulder.

"Here," he said.

I pushed the jacket away. "Don't want it." I wiped my eyes again, tried to stop my shivers. All those layers of sheepskin, it was probably like a toaster oven inside.

"I'm sorry I called you crazy."

"Why? It's true." I pulled my knees tighter. "I'm probably going to end up inside the hospital with your mom."

"No you're not." He sounded exasperated. "Your parents—"

"Have already considered it."

That stopped him.

"So you can take your stupid jacket 'cause you'll

probably freeze without it. What's your body fat percentage? Negative point-zero-zero—*oomph*."

He'd knelt down and flung the coat over my shoulders. Not looking at me, he pulled the coat tighter and said, "You're so damn stubborn." Though he tried to hide it, he shivered. "Come on, let's go." He offered a hand and I took it, using the other to keep the jacket on.

Strangely, he didn't let go of my hand when we got back to the truck. As an experiment, I squeezed a little. He squeezed back.

The old man peeked around the hood and smiled when he saw me wearing Miles's jacket.

"Well, it looks like your battery might need a little juice," said the man. "I've got jumper cables, should only take a second."

He popped the hood of his car and pulled a pair of jumper cables out of his trunk, and after a bit of instruction on his part, he and Miles set to work. I almost fell asleep standing up, and Miles had to prod me out of my stupor when it was time to go.

"Thanks again," he said to the old man. Miles's voice was weak, brittle.

"Really, it was no trouble." The man smiled and waved, stowing his jumper cables again. "You kids enjoy the rest of your night!" He got into his car and drove away.

Miles stared after him, a small crease between his eyebrows.

"What's wrong?" I asked, one hand on the passenger side door handle. Miles shook his head.

"It's nothing, I just . . ." He made an exasperated noise, his shoulders drooping a little. "He made me think of Opa." He walked around to the driver's side and got in.

"Oh, wait." I shrugged the jacket off, climbed into the truck, and handed it across the seat to him. "Seriously, your lips are turning blue. I'll be fine, really," I added when he started to protest. He feigned reluctance well as he slipped the jacket back on.

"He told me to give it to you," Miles said after a solid minute of staring out the windshield.

I was about to make a joke about how good that was, because someone needed to teach him some manners, but then I saw the look on his face.

"Let's go," I said softly. "We shouldn't be too far from home, right?" Miles nodded and threw the truck in drive.

Chapter
Thirty-three

Twenty minutes later I had to start talking to keep Miles awake. My lengthy lecture on the Napoleonic Wars (one of Charlie's favorite subjects) was cut short by the familiar streets of town and what I could only describe as a message from God.

The Meijer sign.

"Stop for a minute," I said, turning around to look at the store.

"What?"

"We need to go to Meijer."

"Why?"

"Trust me, we need to go to Meijer. Pull in and park."

He swung into the parking lot and drove as close as he could get to the doors. I almost had to drag him out of the cab and into the store.

"I work here all the time," he whined, yawning. "Why did we have to stop?"

"You're a baby when you're tired, you know that?"

I pulled him toward the deli counter. His coworkers gave us odd looks as we passed by. Miles waved them off. The main aisle was empty.

Miles nearly crashed into the lobster tank when I stopped in front of it. He blinked once, stared down at it, then looked at me.

"It's a lobster tank," he said.

I took a deep breath. Now or never.

"It's *the* lobster tank," I said. "Your mom told me you remembered."

Miles looked back at the tank, the water reflected in his glasses. At first I thought I'd been wrong, that the odds had been too high, that maybe my mother had been right this whole time and I had made the whole thing up. But then he said, "Do you do this all the time?"

"No," I replied. "Just today."

The corner of his mouth twitched. "You smell like lemons."

I rose up on my toes.

He turned, his hands finding my waist, his lips finding mine like he'd been preparing himself for this moment.

Saying I wasn't ready for it was an understatement.

I wasn't ready for the emotion, and I wasn't ready for the

way his long, chilly fingers worked their way under my jacket and sweatshirt and shirt and pressed into my hips, raising goose bumps on my skin. Everything around us drifted away. Miles groaned. The vibration rippled through my lips.

The heat. How did I not notice the heat? There was a furnace between the layers of clothing that separated us.

I pushed away. He breathed heavily, watching me with alert, hungry eyes.

"Miles."

"Sorry." His huskier-than-usual voice didn't sound sorry.

"No—I—do you want to come back to my house?"

He hesitated for a moment; in his eyes, I saw him working out the meaning of my words. It took him so much longer to figure it out than a math problem or a word puzzle. Those he got immediately. This took all his brain power.

I had to believe he'd been born with this confusion, this inability to understand people, because the alternative was that he'd been conditioned to think no one would ever suggest something like this to him, and he simply couldn't process it when someone did. And that was too sad to believe.

"You . . . you mean . . . ?" His eyebrows creased.

"Yes."

His breath hitched. "Are you sure?"

I let my fingers wander to the waistband of his jeans. "Yes."

Chapter
Thirty-four

We didn't talk on the way to my house. Miles's knuckles were white against the steering wheel, and he kept glancing over at me every few seconds. I knew this because I kept glancing over at him, too. Something wiggling and strange tunneled through my stomach, half excitement, half terror. When he pulled up the driveway and reached over to unbuckle his seatbelt, I held him back.

"Wait. Let me go in first. Drive down the street some, then walk back. You know which window is my room?"

"No."

I showed him. "Come to the window. I'll let you in."

◎ ◎ ◎

I marched up to the front door, perimeter checking the yard as I went, trying to be as casual as possible when I stepped into the house and flipped the bolt behind me. I kicked my shoes off in the hallway and tiptoed past the family room.

"Alex?"

My mother.

"Hey, Mom."

"I'm glad you're home." She stood from the couch and held out her hand. "I didn't realize you'd be out so late—you need to take this."

She gave me a pill. I swallowed it dry. "We stopped for dinner."

"Did you have fun?"

"Um, yeah, I guess." I wanted to be in my bedroom. Wanted to be shut in, safe, away from prying eyes. With Miles.

"How was Miles?"

"Good? I don't know what you mean."

"He was visiting his mother in a mental hospital. You'd think he'd have some sort of issues. Heaven knows the boy already seems a little . . . emotionally stunted. I'm half convinced he's autistic."

"So what if he is?"

She blinked at me. "What?"

"So what if Miles is autistic? And he's not 'emotionally stunted'—he has emotions like the rest of us. He just has trouble figuring out what they are, sometimes."

"Alex, he seems very smart, but I don't think he's the best influence."

I scoffed. If only she knew. "Then why'd you get so excited about the idea of me going with him? Because you wanted me to see where I'd be living after high school?"

"No, of course not! I didn't mean it like that."

I shrugged my jacket off and hung it on the coatrack. "I'm going to bed. Please don't bother me."

I left her standing in the dark entryway and slipped back to my room, closing and locking the door behind me. I didn't bother with a perimeter check. I didn't care. Joseph Stalin himself could've been standing in the corner and I wouldn't have cared. I lifted the window and popped out the screen.

"Be quiet," I said.

Miles had no trouble with that. He slinked into the room, blending into the darkness. I found him by touch and brought him close, helping him slide out of his jacket. The smell of pastries and mint soap filled my room. With him here, I knew everything really was okay. I wrapped my arms around him and pressed my face into his shirt. We tottered back, through the narrow shaft of yellow light from the streetlamp outside, and fell onto the bed.

The artifacts on the shelves rattled and my pictures fluttered. I sat up and pressed a finger to my lips. He nodded. The streetlight hit his eyes and turned them into blue stained glass.

He had to be real. Out of everything, he had to be real. I slipped his glasses off and set them on the nightstand. It struck me how open his face was, all clear blue eyes and sandy hair and golden freckles. My heart stuttered, but he hadn't done anything. I wondered for a second if maybe I was the one who'd been conditioned to think this couldn't happen. He laid there staring up at me, and while I was sure he couldn't see much, it still felt like he was analyzing the tiniest details.

My fingers fanned out over his abdomen. His muscles clenched and he released a breathless laugh. Ticklish. I smiled, but he'd closed his eyes. I eased the shirt up over his chest and he sat up to let me pull it off.

The feel of his skin under my fingers sent little jolts of fire up my arms, and when he carefully peeled my shirt off, I thought I would combust. I hated things like swimming and changing in locker rooms because I hated being so bare in front of other people. I was too exposed. It made me think of torture. But this wasn't torture at all.

Miles paused, wrapped around me, his neck craned over

my shoulder. I felt a small tug on my bra and I realized he was examining the clasp. I stifled my laugh in his shoulder. He'd gotten it unhooked and was re-hooking it. He unhooked and re-hooked it a few more times.

"Stop stalling," I whispered.

He unhooked it one last time and let me pull it off.

The rest of our clothes joined the shirts on the floor. I shivered and pressed myself closer to him, letting the heat build between our stomachs again, hiding my face in the crook of his neck. I rolled us to the side and he curled around me. I pulled the blanket up over us to create a little cocoon.

I loved being this close to him. I loved being able to touch so much of him. I loved how tightly he held me, the soft in-out of his breathing, and how I didn't feel the need to look over my shoulder when he was here. I loved being able to pretend that I was a normal teenager, sneaking around, and everything and everyone was

Just

All

Right.

Miles's fingers pressed into the small of my back. "Basorexia," he mumbled.

"Gesundheit."

He laughed. "It's an overwhelming desire to kiss."

"I thought you weren't good at figuring out what you felt."

"I'm probably using the word in the wrong context. But I'm pretty sure that's what this is."

I pressed a kiss to his shoulder. One of his thumbs brushed across my spine and. . . .

It was too much.

Too much, too fast.

"Don't hate me," I said. "But I don't think I want to do this. Not . . . not right now. Not here. I'm sorry; I didn't think I would change my mind."

He let out a whispery, relieved laugh. "That's actually good. I think I'm going to have a heart attack just from this. Anything more might kill me."

I wedged a hand between us. His heart beat fast and hard against my palm. I whipped it back. "Jesus, you're right, I think you might actually have a heart attack!"

I was mostly joking, but he pulled back, bashful. His breathing came a little harder. "It would help. If we could . . . reposition . . ."

We shifted away from each other. His breathing returned to normal. We faced each other in the dark, the covers pulled up over us. His hand found mine.

"Sorry," he said. "I'm not used to people touching me."

"Neither am I."

There was silence for a few long minutes, until I had an idea.

"Pick someone," I said.

"What?"

I smiled. "Pick someone."

He hesitated, then smiled back. "Okay. Go."

"Are you dead?"

"No."

"Are you a man?"

"No."

"Do you live in a foreign country?"

"No."

Female, alive, from the US. Maybe he *hadn't* gone for obscure.

"Do you have anything to do with East Shoal?" I asked.

"Yes."

Shot in the dark. "Are you in the club?"

He paused. "Yes."

"You're Jetta."

He shook his head.

I frowned. "Theo?"

"No."

"Well if you're not either of them, you'd have to be me."

He blinked.

"It's me?" I said.

"I couldn't think of anyone else," he said.

He inched closer and opened his arms; I crawled in and rested my head on his shoulder. He whispered something in German. I closed my eyes and placed my hand over his heart again.

Part Three | Rubber Bands

Chapter
Thirty-five

Miles fell out of bed at one-thirty in the morning, panic flooding his face.

"I have to go." He stumbled his way into his clothes. I sat up, shook off drowsiness, and pulled the comforter up to cover my chest.

"What's wrong?" I whispered back.

"Shoes . . . where are my shoes?"

"Next to the window."

He grabbed them and shoved them on his feet. "My dad knows I never work past midnight."

"What does he do if you're not there when you're supposed to be?"

Miles stopped and looked at me. Then he found his jacket on the floor and slung it over his shoulders.

"Come here." I opened my arms. He perched on the edge of the bed, body rigid. I turned his face toward me and kissed him. "Can you be here Monday morning?"

"Sure."

I kissed him again and handed him his glasses. "Here."

Chapter Thirty-six

I couldn't stop smiling at Finnegan's the next day. The customers definitely left me bigger tips, but that could've been because I wasn't staring at them like they were bugged.

Tucker noticed.

"Why're you so happy?" he grumbled, shoving bills into the register. The register shook when he slammed the drawer closed.

"Am I not allowed to be happy?" I asked. Still, I wiped my smile away. Guilt knotted my stomach. I wanted to tell him what I'd learned from June, but this was the most he'd spoken to me in days. I grabbed Finnegan's 8 Ball. *Did I do something wrong?*

My sources say no.

Tucker glanced sideways at me. "You're acting like you

won the lottery. Just tell me it doesn't have anything to do with Richter."

"Fine. I won't." I'd apologized a million and one times. I'd taken shifts for him at work, done my own discussion papers during English class, and hadn't asked him for a damn thing. I didn't care if he was mad at me. He had no right to comment on what I did with Miles.

He turned to face me. "You're kidding. You're still hanging out with him, after he did that to me? After everything he's done?"

"It's none of your business what I do with him, Tucker." I lowered my voice so the couple sitting at the closest table wouldn't overhear.

Tucker hesitated. "*What you do?* What are you doing with him?"

My entire face must've been as red as my hair. "I said it's none of your business, didn't I?"

Tucker's voice dropped until he was whispering. "You are *shitting* me. You slept with him?"

I pretended to check the cash register. "We're together, okay? That's all you need to know."

He grabbed my arm and pulled me toward the kitchen. "You have no idea what he's going to do to you! He's not a normal person, Alex! He doesn't understand how what he does affects other people!"

For a moment all I could do was stare at him. I'd had a snappy comment ready, but he hadn't said what I expected. He hadn't said, *"He's a dick"* or *"He's evil incarnate."*

Tucker had been through this before. Not exactly the same circumstances, but . . . Miles had hurt him a long time before I'd met either of them.

"I—I'll be fine, Tucker." I pulled my arm from his grip. "I'll be okay."

Tucker shook his head, his gaze dropping to the floor. He shouldered his way past me, muttering something I almost didn't catch.

"I hope so."

I'll be okay, won't I?

Without a doubt

Chapter Thirty-seven

Dad didn't seem to feel too bad about losing driving duties on Monday; he actually gave me a sly grin as I walked out the door.

I didn't know what I expected. Maybe for Miles to look happier than he did? Maybe for him to give me a reason to disbelieve what Tucker had said? It had only been a day since I'd last seen him, and I hadn't tried to quell the riot of excitement in my stomach. But as I climbed into the passenger seat, he only gave me the weakest smile before he dissolved into a sort of humiliated depression. He had dark bags under his eyes, like he hadn't slept.

"What's wrong?" I asked. "What did he do?"

"Nothing." He stared straight ahead as he drove.

I didn't say anything else until we'd parked and were

walking toward the building, and I noticed that he was doing his best to conceal a limp.

"Why are you limping? What happened?"

"Nothing. Nothing happened—I'm fine."

"Miles, what did he do to you?"

"Don't worry about it!" he snapped.

I shrank back. We didn't talk all the way to first period English, and when we sat down in our seats, a few snickers came from Cliff's corner of the room.

"Hey, Richter," Cliff called, "those Allies finally kick your ass?"

Miles gave Cliff the finger and laid his head down on the desk.

I stared at his back and his sandy hair, and my heart sank until it rested somewhere below my navel. Maybe I'd gotten my hopes up too much. Maybe Tucker had been right. Maybe that trip had been a one-time thing. Maybe he didn't. . . .

Stop thinking about him, idiot!

I looked at the flickering fluorescent light over my head, then at my classmates, fresh from winter break.

Celia's hair had turned a strange, moldy mixture of yellow and brown, but it was still green at the tips. She wore East Shoal sweats, and her blue contacts were gone; her eyes were brown. Her face looked weird until I realized it was because she wasn't wearing makeup. Even though she had no makeup on and she was acne-ridden, she was pretty.

Why did she try so hard?

Everyone was talking about her, making jokes and snide comments loud enough for her to hear. She just sat there, staring at the top of her desk, her eyebrows pushed together. She didn't seem to want to kill me. Or anyone. She didn't seem to have much fighting spirit left at all.

A tiny part of me, the part that forgot it had witnessed her screaming about her burning hair, and screaming about not getting what she wanted, and screaming about her friends, felt bad for her.

Miles slept through all our classes that day. Even if he didn't usually make an effort, he never just *slept*. The teachers must have realized something was wrong, because they didn't try to wake him up. Five minutes before each bell, he'd rise like the dead and shuffle on to the next class. Someone called him "Nazi" in the hallway after fifth period, and he just kept on walking.

I didn't like seeing him this upset. So when we left chemistry and headed for the gym, I shifted my books over to one arm and took his hand, threading our fingers together. I stood on my toes and kissed the corner of his mouth. For a few seconds, a real smile lit up his face.

It was gone by the time we got to the gym, though he still held tight to my hand. The club sat in a group on the bleachers, and a few feet away from them sat Celia. We'd all known this was going to happen, but no one seemed particularly happy about it.

"Hey, Boss. Alex," said Evan.

"Got something you want to tell us?" Ian asked, pointing to our hands.

Miles looked down as if he'd forgotten he was holding my hand, and then looked back up at Evan and Ian and their impish grins, and said quite plainly, "No."

I shook my head, let go of Miles's hand, and went to sit next to Jetta.

"As you probably all guessed, Hendricks is doing community service with us now." Miles waved a lazy hand in Celia's direction. She shot him a look, but it was gone in an instant.

"Can't you do anything, Boss?" asked Theo. "Can't you get her sent someplace else?"

"I don't like it," Miles snapped, "but I'm not a miracle worker. McCoy's own damn rules got her put here, and trust me, he wasn't happy about it, either. It's one semester—just deal with her. Evan and Ian, I'm leaving her under your control. Make sure she's doing something. Everyone else, normal stations."

Evan and Ian looked at Celia with twin expressions of glee on their faces, and then dragged her along to the storage rooms to get the ball carts. Jetta left to watch over Art's wrestling practice in the auxiliary gym, and Theo retreated to the concession stand. I started to follow her, but Miles grabbed my sleeve and gently tugged me back.

"You're with me." He motioned toward the scorer's table.

We sat down and got stat charts and rosters ready until the basketball teams came in and warmed up. I watched Celia the whole time as Evan made her sweep the gym floor by herself and Ian made her put new bags in all the trash cans.

When she was done, she sat down in the bleachers. Seconds later, her mother breezed in through the doors, blond hair swinging against her back. Celia didn't even look up when her mother stopped in front of her and began hissing.

"What are you doing now? Wallowing?"

Celia stared at her feet and said nothing. Her mother continued, casting a shadow over her. "You could have had everything, Celia. If you had done as I said, you could have had your pick of any college. Any one you wanted. You could have had everything. But now you're off the cheerleading squad, forced to spend time with these *delinquents*—"

"I'm sorry about earlier," Miles said. "I'm not used to dealing with . . . uh . . . not used to having someone to—"

"—and instead of trying to get back on top, I find you mooning over that *boy*—"

"—so yeah, it was him. Were you worried? I didn't mean to—"

"—I can tell you right now, Richard will have a thing or two to say about that. He's not going to let *my daughter* keep herself from her full potential—"

"—don't have to worry about it, okay? Everything's fine—"

"—Richard's going to put everything back in order. He'll make sure you're worthy of carrying on my legacy. And if that boy stands in his way, Richard will have him *removed*."

Miles pulled on my hand, jerking my focus completely to him. "You're shaking. Why are you shaking?"

"I'm just . . . nervous. And I feel bad for Celia. Her mother seems terrible, and McCoy . . . I want to tell someone, but I don't know who would listen."

"Maybe McCoy will slip, and we'll have evidence that something is going on."

Celia stood on the bleachers across the gym, staring back at us. Her mother had gone. When she saw me looking at her, she bolted down the stairs too fast and tripped the last three steps.

"You're an obstacle," I said.

"What?"

"Celia likes you."

"So I've been told."

"And McCoy and her mom think it's a bad thing. They think you're . . . impeding her potential, or something. And they really don't like it."

He hesitated. Doubt pressed his eyebrows together. Even Miles had a limit to his suspension of disbelief, and I'd been paranoid long enough to know I was pushing it.

"I know how it sounds," I said, "but I heard it straight from them, and I'm really afraid McCoy is going to hurt you. I'm not going to do anything stupid or weird or . . . just please tell me you'll stay away from him?"

He lifted my hand and held it against his chest. "I told you I'd be careful, didn't I?"

"Yeah."

Celia wiped her eyes and shuffled toward the door.

"What's she doing?" Miles rose from his seat. I pulled him back down again.

"Let her go," I said. "She'll be back."

Sure enough, about ten minutes later, Celia wandered back into the gym, her eyes redder and puffier than when she'd left. She sat down on the very end of the bottom row of the bleachers and stared at her hands. She looked . . . broken. Like the crazy bitch in her had finally died and left a shell behind.

June was right. I needed to talk to her.

Chapter
Thirty-eight

She tried to go down one of the back hallways after the game.

I didn't figure it'd be hard to stop her. Two words and she'd turn and pounce on me. But when I threw open the doors and called out her name, she looked over her shoulder, eyes wide, like she was afraid *I* was the one going to kill *her*.

And then she ran.

I chased her. I guess being a cheerleader had its perks— she was in better shape than me. But I knew where she was going. When we hit an intersection, Celia turned right and I kept going straight. I came out on the west side of the school, jumped down the handicap entrance ramp, and made it to the northwest corner in time to catch Celia in the stomach with my arm. My momentum slammed her into the wall.

"Stop . . . running . . ." I said, panting. She glared at me, rubbing the shoulder that had hit the brick.

"I . . . have to . . . ask you something . . ."

"So ask me," she snarled.

I took a deep breath. "McCoy. What's going on . . . with McCoy?"

Celia's eyes widened, then narrowed. "What are you talking about?"

"Look, I know about your mom. And I know about McCoy. I know he calls you down to his office all the time, and he's obsessed. If . . . if he's doing something, you should tell someone about it."

For half a second, real recognition flashed across Celia's face. But then her expression twisted and she bared her teeth.

"You don't know anything about me." She pushed me back. "Get out of my face. And don't mention Rich Dick McCoy or my mom to me again."

She shoulder checked me hard enough to make me stumble backward and almost lose my footing. I thought about following her again, questioning her until she admitted that something was going on, that she needed help, but I already knew.

I'd taken something she loved. She would never trust me.

She's not crazy at all, is she?

My sources say no

She's just . . . alone.

Most likely

But she never wants anyone around.

Reply hazy try again

She doesn't want help. Why doesn't she want help?

Cannot predict now

Chapter
Thirty-nine

The running theme of January seemed to be to make Celia's time a living hell. Evan and Ian forced her to pick up trash they'd knocked over. Theo had her clean the popcorn and hot dog machines for an entire week. Jetta made her jump into the pool in her clothes to get dive bricks that Jetta herself had thrown in, when the swimming team was standing less than ten feet away.

Celia never did anything to stop this. In fact, the only times she did get angry enough to put her foot down were the times I mentioned McCoy to her.

By mid-February, I began wondering what the club could possibly have against Celia that justified the things they did to her. Yes, she was a bitch. Yes, she'd done horrible things to people—or so I'd been told.

Miles and I didn't join in, but we didn't stop it, either, and that made me feel like we had. Whenever Celia saw us, whenever I'd catch her watching us after a quick kiss in the gym or holding hands in the hallway, I could swear she was about to burst into tears.

"They can do what they want to her," Miles said one day at the end of February, after the triplets had made Celia carry all the fishy-smelling towels to the laundry without a cart. She accidentally dropped some into the pool and had to get into the water to get them. Miles and I stood with our backs against the tiles. Miles was staring at the water with his nose turned up.

As Celia climbed back out of the pool, she looked at us—at Miles.

"Put those in the laundry room," Miles called to her.

Celia nodded. Miles was the only person she'd take orders from without cursing under her breath or glaring.

"Hey, Green Queen!" Evan, Ian, and Jetta came out of the locker rooms in bathing suits.

"What are you doing?" Miles asked, glancing at his watch. "It's six."

"Which means there's plenty of time to swim before we have to close!" Ian climbed the diving board.

"*Mein Chef!* Alex! You should come swimming wiz

us!" said Jetta, floating over to the side of the pool and looking up at us.

"Yeah! Boss, come on!" Ian cried before diving.

"No," said Miles. "I hate getting wet."

"That's what she s—" Evan began, before being dunked by his brother.

"You know I don't like swimming," said Miles when Jetta wouldn't stop giving him a very hurt-puppy-dog look.

"Zen we should play your game. I 'ave someone."

Miles fought a smile for a few seconds, but lost in the end. They started a game of twenty questions in German. I didn't know what they were saying, but I was pretty sure Miles was dragging the game out on purpose. When it was just him and Jetta, he could find any excuse not to speak English.

I was glad he had Jetta to talk to, but I was missing out. There was a whole other person inside him I couldn't see because I didn't speak his language.

When the game was over—Miles made it to fifteen questions before guessing correctly—Jetta lifted her arms toward him and wiggled her fingers.

"I'm *not* getting in," he said one last time, and Jetta admitted defeat and swam away.

"Don't tell me you can't swim," I said.

Miles scoffed. "Of course I can swim. If I couldn't swim I'd be dead by now," he said. Then, softer, "My dad used to take me fishing with him when I was little. You know, most sons fish with their dads; that's a nice family bonding experience, right? Well, add the attention span of a flea with ADHD, a bit of booze, and a large body of water, and you end up with a dad who thinks it's fun to throw his kid off the boat and watch him swim for shore."

"Like he did to your mom?"

He nodded. "He got me first."

"That's awful," I whispered. "You could have drowned! Or gotten really sick—there's all sorts of bacteria in lakes—or . . ."

"Or gotten pulled under by something I couldn't see?" Miles offered quietly. "Yeah, that was the best part. He knew I was scared of the things in those lakes. Bastard."

The smell of algae and pond scum.

"That was the day before my mom and I went to Germany," he went on. "She realized that Cleveland had done something and came looking for me. We stayed in the car that night, and the next day she decided we were leaving. We only went back to the house for a minute, for our passports. Then straight to Meijer so she could grab stuff she thought we'd need, and finally to the airport."

I hugged him, something I'd been doing a lot lately, sometimes because I could, most of the time because he seemed like he needed it.

So far, no one had tried to do anything to Miles. I'd hardly seen McCoy at all since the new semester started, and Celia didn't seem to have it in her to hurt anyone. Whenever I caught her staring, I only had to look at her to get her to go away again. But she was always hovering, like a ghost waiting for someone to join her on the other side.

Miles had been taking fewer and fewer of his mafia hit man jobs, and it was clear that he didn't have enough occupying his mind. He frequently paced the length of the gym, wrote so often in his notebook that he had to get a new one, and would occasionally start his sentences in the middle of a thought. His limp went away, but he wore his sleeves rolled down and came to school one day with a black eye. His mood infected the club like a disease; nothing ran smoothly anymore. And soon his gloom infested the whole school.

Mr. Gunthrie went on an hour-long rant about the flickering light over my desk, throwing away an entire class period. Ms. Dalton couldn't find any of her notes and even forgot her Diet Coke. Students who normally paid Miles for his services began taking matters into their own hands, and detention was full for the first time all year.

I wondered if the gloom was affecting me, too, but I got the feeling it had more to do with the thin envelopes I kept getting from colleges and scholarship foundations. Most of them started with *"We regret to inform you . . ."* I tried not to take it personally—how many mentally ill, lower-class high school girls could there be in Indiana? Probably more than I thought—but handing each one over to my mother was like running the gauntlet of passive-aggressive pep talks. *Are you sure you signed up right? Maybe you just forgot something. Should I have Leann explain things to them?*

Needless to say, I didn't enjoy spending time at home. But school wasn't much better.

In March, I began to notice people pointing at me as I walked by in the hallway, ignoring me when I tried to talk to them, and blatantly not believing things I said. I wouldn't have cared so much if it hadn't been exactly what had happened at Hillpark after they'd found out.

At the end of March, the entire club was assembled in the main gym for the band competition. The bleachers were full with spectators, along with the bands from other schools. McCoy employed half the students in seventh-period gym to string up golden ribbons around the scoreboard and create a "tribute table" where people could sign a petition to finally get the scoreboard plated in gold and pick up a complimentary tiny scoreboard magnet. (Obviously, it was a smashing success.)

From what I saw, most people thought this was a joke: honoring the scoreboard like this was a quirky little thing we East Shoalers did to cover up the fact that it had killed someone. I never got wind of anyone accusing McCoy of losing his marbles.

When the competition started, we were kicked out of the scorer's table by the guy announcing the bands. We stood next to the main doors with our backs pressed to the wall. I stuck close to Miles, because there I didn't feel the need to check every instrument for contraband items and Communist propaganda. If something strange was actually going on, Miles would tell me.

One band finished their set, and another came in to take its place. The announcer left his post, complaining about never getting restroom breaks. In the relative quiet, I began to nod off against Miles's shoulder.

"Excuse me, everyone?" Celia's voice filled the gym. I jerked awake. The room went silent.

"Hi," she waved from the scorer's table. "I just wanted to take a moment to remind everyone that all proceeds from today's concession sales are going to benefit the American Schizophrenia Association."

You're the obstacle, idiot! the little voice roared.

"Alex," Miles said urgently, pulling me toward the door. "Alex, you have to get out of here—"

But I was rooted to the spot, my brain frozen.

"All of this is in honor of our own paranoid schizophrenic, Alexandra Ridgemont, who transferred to our school after graffitiing the Hillpark School gymnasium." Celia turned and looked at me, along with everyone else. She waved, smiling. "Hi, Alex."

Her last words were lost in the empty air of the gym; Miles had shot across the bottom of the bleachers and ripped her microphone's power cord from its extension. He charged up to the scorer's table and took the microphone itself away from her, but the damage was done.

I was in a tank full of sharks.

Eyes bore down on me from all sides. The band members stopped moving their instruments. A few people on the other side of the bleachers stood up for a better look. Theo had come in from the concession stand and now hovered by the far doors with Evan and Ian, their faces pale.

My hand fumbled for the door. The push bar slipped under my fingers once, twice—finally I was able to push it open, and I sprinted for the nearest restroom.

I locked myself in a stall, threw up, and curled into a ball on the tile and squeezed my eyes shut. I tugged on my hair, wishing it wasn't so damned red, wishing my mind worked the way it should, wishing things would go back to the way they were when I was seven, when everything was real and I didn't know any better.

When I finally calmed down enough to open my eyes. I was still sitting on the floor in a bathroom stall in a public high school, I was still crazy, and my hair still looked like I'd dunked my head in a tank of ketchup.

Miles must've been keeping people out of the bathroom, because no one came, and every so often he would pound on the door and call my name and say that he hadn't told anyone.

I wanted to tell him that I believed him, that Celia could have found out other ways. But I couldn't get myself to move, and I couldn't open my mouth.

"Lexi?"

I pushed myself to my feet, wiping away whatever tears were left, and cracked open the bathroom door. Dad stood there, smelling like freshly dug dirt and wild herbs. Behind him, the hallway was empty. Miles had gone. Dad didn't say anything, just pulled me into a hug and walked me out to the car.

Chapter Forty

My dad was better at calming me down than I ever gave him credit for. I think some of it was the way he smelled. The other part was his choice in movies.

"Dad, you could be Indiana Jones."

"You think so?" he replied. "I'd have to grow a bit more scruff than I have now." He rubbed his unshaven face. "Ooh, I could go as Indiana Jones for Halloween next year. Think your mom would agree to dress up as my spunky yet sexy female companion?"

"I dunno. You'd have to look really good. And probably bribe her with chocolate."

He laughed, and the doorbell rang. He went to answer it while I settled into the couch with the bowl of popcorn. Charlie had avoided the living room since we'd returned, and my mother—thank God—had been at the grocery when Miles had called my house.

I tried to ignore what was going on in the hallway. Dad would scare away anyone, unless it was Miles. But I had a feeling Miles was going to give me some space.

"I wanted to check on Alex and make sure she was okay. I heard about what happened at school."

Tucker.

"Yes, she's fine," Dad replied. He peeked into the living room. "Hey, Lex Luthor, you feel up to guests?"

I pushed myself off the couch and peered around the doorframe into the hallway. Tucker stood on the front step, worry on his face. His hand brushed nervously through the huge pot of fresh white geraniums my mother had set on the porch. Behind him, the trees along the street were in full bloom, bursting with the colors of spring.

"Oh, hey, Alex. Are you okay?"

"Dad, it's fine. I'll talk to him outside." I set the popcorn bowl down and moved past my dad to join Tucker on the porch. "It's okay, really," I said one last time, and with a reluctant smile, Dad closed the door.

"So . . . you're okay?" Tucker said quickly. "Are you coming back to school?"

"No, I'm really not okay," I said. "But yeah, I am coming back. We only have two months left, after all. And if I don't go back, things are only going to get worse."

High school dropout. That was exactly what colleges wanted to see on applications.

Tucker stood there for a moment, running his hand through his black hair, fixing his glasses, spinning his watch around his wrist.

"How'd you find out?" I asked.

"Text message." He held up his phone. "I think . . . most everyone in the school got one."

I nodded. I had figured that pretty much everyone knew by now—that's why they'd been ignoring me, and whispering behind my back the past few days. Celia'd been leaking the information for at least a week now. The band competition was just a way to scare me.

"So . . . now you know," I said.

"I'm sorry."

"For what? It's not your fault I'm crazy."

"No, I . . . I don't care about that. My dad has schizophrenic patients. He calls them 'normal people with more quirks.' I'm sorry that I got so mad at you. And ignored you for so long. And I'm sorry I didn't trust that you could handle Miles. I shouldn't have butted in."

"But you were right—I shouldn't have done that to you. Or to anyone. I should've stopped him."

Tucker laughed hesitantly. "Well. I kind of deserved it."

I waited.

Tucker sighed and sat down on the porch swing. "He got that job from Cliff. I'd been waiting for it all semester. Do you remember Celia's bonfire, on Scoreboard Day?"

"Yeah . . ." My stomach sank. I knew where this was going.

He blushed and looked away. "I slept with Ria."

Before I knew what I was doing, I had his face in my hands and was yelling, "TUCKER. THAT IS NOT TRUE. You are the one source of GOOD in this godforsaken place! You can't have gone along with Ria's plans—*I'm* the one who screwed up and put IcyHot in your underwear!"

Tucker shook his head, and I dropped my hands.

"No, you're not a bad person," he said. "And Richter isn't a bad person, and I'm not a bad person. We're just people, and people sometimes do stupid things."

I stared at him. After a few seconds, I said, "So. You and Ria."

"Me and Ria," he replied.

"You had sex with Ria Wolf."

"I had sex with Ria Wolf," he admitted, raising his hands in defeat.

"And how was that?"

"It *sucked*," he said, laughing suddenly. "It was awful. I've never felt more awkward in my life. I mean, it was pretty obvious from the beginning that she was using me, but you've seen her—she's hot. Like, beyond hot. Like hotness to the nth power."

"Tucker, I get it."

"You'd think hotness would make it better, you know? But it's kind of hard to enjoy yourself when the other person keeps hitting you and telling you how terrible you are at it and what you're doing wrong."

"That *would* suck." I laughed only because he did. "Why'd you do it? I mean, it couldn't have been because she was hot."

Tucker turned a little red again. "Honestly? Richter and I sort of had a war going over her during middle school."

"Over Ria?" I laughed again.

"Yeah, that's why he hates her," Tucker said. "I mean, we both knew it was pointless, but he never understood why she'd pick brawn over brains. She came up to me at Celia's bonfire and started flirting with me—"

So it was Tucker with Ria in that bedroom, and I had almost walked in on them.

Peachy.

"—and then it sort of happened. I knew she was just doing it to make Cliff mad—everyone knows that, she does it every year—and I knew I'd have to deal with him afterward. That's why Richter had you guys break into my house and do all that stuff to me, because Cliff paid him, so really it was my fault in the first place—"

"Tucker, shut up."

"Okay."

We lapsed into silence, staring across the street at my neighbor's bright green lawn. After a few minutes, Tucker said, "So, you still think something is up with McCoy?"

"Yeah," I said. "I never told you—I got to talk to Miles's mom."

I explained everything I'd learned from June. Then I told him about confronting Celia outside the gym, and about Miles being an obstacle.

"I think McCoy's going to do something. But I don't know when, or how. And I'm afraid that if I don't figure it out, something bad will happen."

"And you're *positive*," he said slowly, "that this is all actually happening?"

I rolled my eyes. "I'm never positive of anything, Tucker, I'm just telling you what I know. But you said earlier this year that Celia and her mom didn't get along, right?"

"I—well, I mean, I've seen them come into school a few times before, and I've heard things, but it's not like I'm in with their family."

"Well, look—even if I am making up parts of it, I know that *something* is going on. I know McCoy is messed up and I know he's taking Celia along for the ride. And I feel like . . . like if I don't do something about it, then no one will."

Tucker was quiet for a moment. Then, finally, he said, "I don't know if I should tell you this, but . . . I know where McCoy lives. You won't find anything incriminating in his office or at school. If there *is* anything, you'll find it where he lives."

"Mr. Soggy Potato Salad," I said, putting my hand over my heart. "Are . . . are you suggesting we *break into* someone's house?"

Tucker shrugged. "Not to take anything. Just to look around."

"Should I ask Miles to come with us? He has more experience breaking and entering than we do."

"He knows about all of this?"

"If McCoy is really after him, I figured he could keep himself safer than I could alone," I said. "Besides, he's known about me since October."

"Oh, well." Tucker thought for a moment. "Yeah, I guess we'd be stupid not to ask him. His house is only a few streets away from McCoy's."

"What?"

"Yeah—McCoy lives in Lakeview Trail."

Chapter
Forty-one

Dad took me to school the next day. In the hallways, everyone stared at me like I'd imagined them doing all year. My hair had become a blight, just like at Hillpark; people saw me coming and jumped from my path.

I tried to perform my perimeter checks like usual, but by the time I'd left my locker, there were so many eyes watching me it became difficult to keep my panic down. The only good place was English, where Mr. Gunthrie seemed to have reined in the class so well they ignored me completely.

Miles ignored me, too. He sat with his head bowed, scribbling furiously in his notebook.

The lines he made were thick and dark, and covered whole pages.

In true Miles the Jerk fashion, he didn't talk to me until I forced him to, when we were walking together toward the gym. It was the day of the one baseball game I'd been dreading all year—East Shoal vs. Hillpark—and part of the reason I'd decided to come back to school. The other part was a joint threat between my mother and the Gravedigger to burn me in the fires of hell if I stayed home. (I told Dad that; he said I might be exaggerating.)

I had to face this. But before I could even think about it, I had to make sure Miles was okay.

I checked to make sure no one was around, then asked Miles, "What's going on?"

He ran a shaky hand through his hair, his eyes flicking back and forth over the empty rotunda. "I—sorry—I couldn't think at all today. Everyone knows. They've been talking about it all day, and I can't figure out *how* they know. . . ."

They knew about his mom. I grabbed his hand and pulled it away from his hair, holding it between both of mine. "What's the worst they can do with it, right? We only have a couple months left."

"It's that they *know*," he said. "I don't like them knowing things about my mom, because they're going to start making judgments. And will anyone even take me seriously anymore? What are they going to ask me to do now? Even if it's ridiculous, I'll have to do it—I can't say no, because then I go from die-hard genius back to punching-bag nerd, and no one will be safe anymore. *I* won't be safe anymore."

I looked around again—just him saying he didn't feel safe made me think McCoy was hiding around a corner with a lighter and a can of hairspray.

Finally he said, "My mom called me. Last night, at Finnegan's."

"How come?"

"My dad. He went up to see her. She told me not to visit anymore."

"Miles . . ." I wasn't good at comforting people. So I did what I'd done before, and dragged him into my plans.

"I think Celia told everyone," I said. "Like she told them about me. And I think McCoy was the one who told *her*."

Miles's expression flattened out the way it always did when he was dealing with information rather than emotions. To anyone else, he probably looked bored or annoyed. To me, he looked relaxed. The content cat. "That makes sense. He would have access to records. It would've been harder for him to find out about my mother, but . . ."

I rubbed my head. "I honestly didn't think Celia would hurt you. I thought . . . I thought she still liked you too much."

"I guess she's had enough."

"Tucker and I think we can figure out what McCoy's master plan is, but we need your help."

"With what?"

"We're going to break into his house."

Miles brought out the Magnificent Quirked Eyebrow, which made me feel better. That expression meant that things were at least kind of okay.

"Are you sure that's what you want to do?"

"Tucker said if we're going to find anything incriminating, it won't be at school, and he's right. It'll be at McCoy's. While I'm sure I could just John McClane my way into his house by shooting down the front door, I figured you might be able to do the job a little more discreetly."

"So basically you're saying if I don't agree, you're going to go anyway, but you're pretty sure you'll get caught."

"Basically."

"But you know I don't want you to get caught."

"Yes."

"So you're blackmailing me."

"Yep."

He narrowed his eyes. "I can get behind that," he said. "When?"

"I don't know. Are you sure you won't mind it if Tucker's there? Can you two play nice?"

"Maybe."

"Would it help if I told you this was Tucker's idea?"

Now both eyebrows were up. "Well, fuck me."

"I'll take that as a yes."

He leaned over and kissed my temple. The times *he* kissed *me* were so few and far between, I couldn't help but smile.

"I'll meet you by the track," he said, walking away without further explanation.

Chapter Forty-two

When I arrived at the baseball field minutes later, the visitor stands were already packed full of red-clad Hillpark fans, many of whom I recognized even from a distance. They formed one undulating mass of red, the head of a dragon rising from their midst. Its scales glimmered in the sun and flames licked from its mouth. The Hillpark side was separated from the East Shoal side by the concession stand and press box planted behind home plate.

I kept my eyes peeled for any sign of Miles.

What I saw instead were Cliff and Ria, on their way to the bleachers from the concession stand. I froze like a deer in headlights when they neared—this was what I got for not doing a good perimeter check. If I'd done the perimeter check, I wouldn't have run into them, I wouldn't look like an idiot, I wouldn't . . .

"Watch out, babe, she's dangerous," Cliff said to Ria, holding out an arm like he was going to protect her from something. *Protect her from you, idiot.* I gritted my teeth and tried not to look at them.

"I'm not dangerous," I said, keeping my voice level.

"Yeah, and your boyfriend isn't a Nazi," Ria scoffed.

For a second I wondered what Miles ever saw in her. She must've been horrible to him, because nothing else would make him hate her so much.

Now I understood why the nicknames made Miles so upset, and I couldn't listen to it anymore. "Don't call him that."

"Really?" Ria blinked, eyes wide and innocent. "Because he's kind of asking for it today."

Anger balled up in my chest. "And you're kind of asking to be called a bitch."

I hardly realized I was saying the words until they were out of my mouth.

Ria almost dropped her soda. Her voice turned flat and sharp and deadly. "What did you just call me?"

I couldn't back down now. "You're a bitch. Sleeping with other guys just to make him jealous"—I jabbed a finger at Cliff—"is pretty far into the definition of *bitch*, I think."

Ria's knuckles turned white around the soda bottle. I

really really hoped she didn't charge at me—my legs weren't going to move very fast, even if I asked them.

"Take that back," she said, voice tight. "Fucking take it back, or I swear to God—"

I didn't listen to the rest of her threat—I lowered my head and walked past them, toward the concession stand, to wherever Miles was. Coming to this game didn't seem like such an awesome idea anymore. I took deep gulps of air, thinking about the trouble I could get into for saying things like that to people like Ria. I could already imagine them formulating a plan. Fuck. Oh, fuck.

I needed to find Miles.

I didn't have to look far. I spotted him walking toward the visitors' bleachers. My heart jumped into my throat and my stomach dropped, leaving a gaping void in my chest where vital things belonged.

He was a Nazi.

Or he was dressed like one. The brown suit. The black boots and gloves. The hat. The glaring armband. A saber hung at his side and the German flag from East Shoal's Flags-of-the-World entryway rested against one shoulder. He pulled his hat off and wiped his forehead. He'd gelled his hair back, finally putting it in some kind of order.

It wasn't until his eyes met mine that the realization this was really happening hit me. When he saw me, his gaze didn't turn glassy and hard and cold. It softened into something deeper than recognition. The eyes were his. The rest was not.

I hurried over to him, stopped ten feet away, and hugged my chest so he wouldn't see me shaking.

"You're going to get arrested!" I hissed, barely daring to raise my voice above a whisper. "What are you doing?"

"They can't arrest me for wearing an outfit," Miles said, his eyebrows creasing. "Besides, I'm the mascot, see?" He nudged the saber sheathed at his hip.

"Hey, it's Schizo Ridgemont!"

Some kids I knew from Hillpark walked by, looking shocked to see me alive. Miles whipped around, yelling at them in rapid German. The Hillpark kids shut up in surprise.

"I realize that you think you have to keep doing this, but . . ." I yanked on my hair. "But you're dressed up like a *Nazi*. What about everything you said to Cliff? About not wanting people to call you that?" I hesitated. "How much . . . how much did they pay you to do this?"

Miles didn't reply.

Someone passing by laughed loudly, and I caught the words, "The Nazi and the Communist."

"*Shut up!*" I yelled. "You're all so fucking inconsiderate! I'm trying to talk!" I turned back to Miles, lowering my voice again. "You don't need to degrade yourself like this."

That was a terrible cover-up, and he knew it, and I could tell that he knew it. The truth was that I was terrified of Nazis, and here one stood. "Please take the uniform off," I whispered. "Please."

He stared at me with a strange expression on his face and took a few steps forward, reaching out for me; I took a few steps back in response. He pulled his hat off and blinked at the sun in his eyes.

"Okay. Just give me a few minutes. My other clothes are in the pool locker room."

He headed toward the school. I escaped up to the press box where Evan and Ian worked the baseball scoreboard controls and explained to them where Miles was and how I planned on hiding with them for the entire game.

"Isn't this your old school?" Evan asked.

I nodded. "Unfortunately."

"What happened? What got you thrown out?"

"I, uh, spray-painted the word *Communists* on the gym floor. Things got out of hand; I was having a few problems at the time. Everything's fine now."

"It's okay," Ian laughed. "We really don't care about your—problem? I guess, is what we're calling it."

"Well, that's good." Relief washed through me. I looked over at the Hillpark stands, then back at Evan and Ian, and remembered how much it had sucked the first time: how people hadn't trusted me, how they made fun of the way I spun around every time I entered a room, my incessant picture taking, and how I hadn't been that lonely since I was seven years old and my only friend had left me for Germany.

Out of the corner of my eye, I saw someone climbing the stairs to the press box. A brown uniform flew up and landed on the scoreboard controls. "Your Nazi boyfriend won't need that anymore!"

I spun, catching a flash of Ria's blond hair. I looked down at Miles's uniform, then over at Evan and Ian, and all three of us understood at the same time.

"Theo!" Evan called to the concession stand below us. "Come up here and run this thing for a second!"

The three of us sprinted to the school, each holding a different piece of Miles's uniform. We barreled into the hallways behind the gym, through the locker rooms, and into the connected natatorium.

It had finally happened. McCoy had used Cliff and Ria as a distraction and Miles was laying on the tiled floor in a puddle of his own blood.

The natatorium was dark when we arrived. A lone figure sat on the bench next to the pool, soaking wet and clad in nothing but a pair of boxer shorts.

"Go get towels," I said to Evan and Ian. They vanished into the locker rooms.

I sat down next to Miles. His glasses were missing and his eyes were unfocused. "I hate water," he mumbled.

"I know."

He looked like a waterlogged cat. His hair was plastered to his head. Goose bumps covered his skin, layered over fading bruises that dotted his torso and ran down along his ribs. A horrible green-yellow-blue one ran diagonally across his back. They were all old, not inflicted here.

"What happened?" I asked.

"I went into the locker room to change," he said. "They ambushed me. Took my glasses. Threw me in the pool. They were gone by the time I got out, but it was slippery and I fell back in. Now you're here. The end."

He scratched at his legs, his arms, picked at his skin like there was something there. I remembered all the bandages. The smell of pond scum and algae. *Animalia Annelida Hirudinea.*

Leeches.

"You can't let them do things like this to you," I said.

"It won't be much longer."

He said it softly, his voice like every part of him I'd ever met—the jerk, the seven-year-old, the genius—and none of them, all at the same time. This was something new, something unknown. Something that scared me. Maybe he meant it wouldn't be much longer until the end of the school year, that when we were out of high school he'd have more freedom to do what he needed to do.

Are you sure, idiot?

You're so stupid.

He never talks about college, or anything after this.

Are you really so naïve?

All he wanted—all he knew to do—was to get his mother out of that hospital. But he had to get rid of Cleveland first. He had a plan. I knew that.

I hadn't realized how far he was willing to go.

Some deep instinct made me reach out and grab his arm, hold it tightly as if I could keep him right where he was, alive and sound.

I could not lose him again.

No—I could not let him get lost.

I was suddenly more afraid than I had ever been my entire life, more afraid than when Bloody Miles had shown up at Celia's bonfire, more afraid than when my mother said she would send me away. This was worse than the idea of McCoy trying to hurt Miles. I could stop McCoy. I could yell and scream and even if they didn't believe me, they would stop and look.

I had no sway over Miles himself. Not when it came to this.

Evan and Ian returned laden with towels and Miles's

school clothes, and Miles dried himself off. Neither of them said anything about the bruises as Miles pulled his pants and shirt on.

We followed him out of the natatorium. As we passed the main gym, I heard voices and glanced inside, but only McCoy was there. He paced below the scoreboard, talking aloud like he was gearing up for a big speech. No Celia, no Celia's mother. Fear spiked through me that he was so close, that the only thing separating him from Miles was a closed door.

Then the fear was gone again, and McCoy was just a lonely man in a lonely room, talking to himself.

"What's wrong?" Miles asked.

Even if I told him, I wasn't sure he'd understand.

"Nothing," I said.

Will he be okay?

Outlook not so good

Can I do something to make him okay?

Very doubtful

. . . can I do anything?

Don't count on it

Chapter
Forty-three

I saw what Miles had meant when he'd said people would start paying him to do ridiculous things. In chemistry, someone gave him thirty dollars to call Ms. Dalton a Coke-sucking whore in German, which of course she didn't understand. He got twenty dollars to put tape on the bridge of his glasses, wear too-short pants, and don argyle socks for three days. Cliff, the asshole, paid Miles fifty dollars to be able to deck him in the jaw, and one punch turned into several punches and a kick to the gut. The triplets speculated that Cliff had been aiming for the genitals, but Miles's incessant stare had thrown him radically off target.

Every day he threw away another piece of his pride and dignity for a few dollars, but I couldn't stop him.

I don't think anyone could have.

Chapter
Forty-four

"RIDGEMONT." Mr. Gunthrie slapped his newspaper down on his desk.

"Yessir?"

"I AM TIRED OF THAT DAMN LIGHT FLICKERING."

The light over my desk flickered as he said it, mocking him.

"Do you want me to do something about it, sir?" I asked. I could hardly keep my eyes open. My dreams had been less than restful lately.

"I DAMN SURE DO. THE MAINTENANCE MEN HAVE REPLACED THE LIGHT THREE TIMES. GET UP THERE AND TELL ME WHAT IT LOOKS LIKE."

I wasn't about to ask him why he didn't just ask the

maintenance guys to check. While the rest of the class turned back to their work, I climbed onto my desk and lifted away the ceiling tile next to the light. Putting my hands on either side of the opening and standing on tiptoes, I looked up into the darkness.

"Something's gnawed on the wiring." I squinted into the dim space, trying to focus on the frayed wire. It hadn't just been gnawed on—it had been completely ripped in two.

Something near my head hissed.

I turned and saw the python there, its tongue flicking out at me. I rolled my eyes. I didn't have time for this. Damn delusions needed to leave me the hell alone.

I ducked my head back down but kept my hands up for balance. Something touched my arm, but I ignored it. "Hey, Miles, you wanna give me a boost? I think there are mice or something up here. I might be able to see it better."

Miles turned, rose halfway out of his seat, and looked up at me.

The snake hissed again.

I looked at the snake. I looked at Miles.

The snake. Miles.

The snake.

Miles.

"Alex." He held up a hand. "Don't. Move."

Several kids screamed; desks shifted and scraped against

the floor as they jumped up and ran from the room. Mr. Gunthrie shot out of his seat, cursing loudly and yelling about snakes and Vietnam.

The python coiled down my arm, passed behind my head, and wrapped over my left shoulder and across my chest. It looped itself once around my waist, then down my left leg. Its body spilled out of the ceiling like scaly water, lighter than it looked.

"Holy shit." Miles stood fully now. "Holy shit, Alex, it's the snake."

"You can see it?" I hissed the words out through my teeth.

"Yeah, I can see it."

"What do I do?"

"Uh—let me think—" He pressed his palms to his forehead and spoke rapidly. "They can live over twenty years—feed on large rodents or other mammals—average about twelve feet but can reach nineteen—" He groaned loudly and spoke even faster. "Trinomial name is *python molorus bivittatus*, can be domesticated, nonvenomous, can kill a child when they're young and crush a full-grown man when they're older—"

"Miles! Shut up!" My voice rose an octave, my heart pounding against my ribs. The snake shifted against me. I fought the urge to scream.

"Someone call Animal Control!" Theo cried.

"No, that'll take too long!" Tucker was suddenly beside me. "It's hungry. C'mon, Alex, you have to get down from there."

"How do you know it won't"—I shivered as the snake's waving head brushed my calf—"kill me?"

"It's hungry," Tucker insisted, avoiding the question. "I can help get him off; you have to come down here."

"Him?" I squeaked.

"Please, please get down! It's going to be okay."

"God, Beaumont! What the hell is wrong with you?" Miles shoved Tucker out of the way and held out a hand. I slowly lowered my left hand from the ceiling to reach out and take his.

"No more facts," I whispered.

"No more facts," Miles agreed. "Go slow—step down."

I moved slowly.

The snake hissed.

"Tucker!" I waved my other hand, the one attached to the arm that had the snake's tail wrapped around it. Tucker looked surprised, but took my hand. "Where are we going?"

"The janitors' closet," he said.

"Lead, lead."

We headed toward the door, passing stunned classmates and a freaked-out Mr. Gunthrie.

I crushed their hands. We shambled out into the hallway and toward the stairs.

"I think you're breaking my fingers," said Miles.

"Shut up."

As we painstakingly descended the stairs, they kept up a steady stream of small talk. We stopped at the bottom and took our time turning, then set off for Tucker's Cult in a Closet. The snake weighed on me like the heaviest piece of clothing I would ever wear.

"So, um, Miles." I squeezed his hand harder. "Have I said how much I really don't want to be stuck in Crimson Falls? But I'm pretty sure my mom is going to put me there anyway, and this situation made me realize the direness of that whole thing. . . ."

"Crimson Falls," Miles repeated. "What's Crimson Falls?"

God, we were not about to play this game. "The psychiatric hospital. Where your mom is."

"Alex, the hospital is called Woodlands. Where'd you get Crimson Falls?"

I sucked in a breath under the snake's weight, trying to keep calm. "That's what the sign out front said. It said Crimson Falls."

"The sign in front says Woodlands."

Panic gripped me. Made Miles panic.

"Hey," he continued quickly, "what'd you do with my Christmas present?"

"What present?" I breathed out. "The cupcake? I ate it."

"No, not the cupcake—oh dammit, I forgot to explain." He flexed his hand in mine. "I left it on your desk before we got out for Christmas break."

"The rock? The one that's been sitting in my locker all semester?"

"Yeah."

"That was you?"

"It's a piece of the Berlin Wall. I thought you'd like it."

I looked over at him, felt the snake constrict again, and could only say, "Shut up."

"God, Alex, I am so sorry," Tucker breathed. "I never thought this would happen—I thought it would die soon. . . ."

"Do you even have a club in that closet, Beaumont?" Miles growled.

"No! Of course not! You seriously think I have friends?" Tucker shot him a glare over my head. "You have a club. I have a python. You can stop rubbing it in my face now, all right?"

"Both of you! Shut. Up."

Somehow we made it to the janitors' closet. Tucker

hurried to the back of the small room and pulled open a freezer. The snake swung its head up, tasting the air. Tucker pulled a whole frozen raccoon from the freezer. He dangled it near the snake, and then tossed it on the floor.

The snake slithered off me.

I stumbled back and fell on my butt in the middle of the hallway.

Miles backed out of the room and turned to me.

"You gave me a piece of the Berlin Wall," I whispered.

"What?"

"You gave me a piece of the *Berlin Wall*."

"Yeah, Opa gave it to me. I've had it for a really long time, and I thought you'd like—"

"MILES." I grabbed the front of his shirt and hoisted myself up to his level. "YOU GAVE ME A PIECE OF THE SYMBOL OF THE DOWNFALL OF COMMUNISM IN EUROPE."

"I—well, yeah—"

"Crimson Falls isn't Crimson Falls."

"No, it's—"

"I almost got killed by a fucking snake."

"Yeah—"

"I think I'm going to faint."

My hands fell away from his shirt, blood rushed to my head, and the world went black.

Chapter
Forty-five

I spent the rest of first period and all of second in the nurse's office, watching Animal Control pass through the hallway. I had to answer a lot of questions, then talk to my dad on the phone. (Apparently my mother thought I'd hallucinated the snake, but then she found out half my English class was now paranoid as hell, and the other half was so excited they couldn't stay in their seats.) Miles helped Tucker get rid of the snake food fridge, but they refused to tell me exactly how they snuck it out past the teachers and Animal Control. Miles looked grim. Tucker was sweating.

"What'd you have to do, kill someone?" I asked. "Did you have to hide a body, too?"

They glanced at each other. Tucker pulled on his collar. "Not exactly."

"Don't worry about it," Miles said at the same time.

I decided to leave that one alone.

I went back to class during third period and was bombarded with requests to retell the story. It was so bad that the teacher decided we weren't learning anything and we got a free study period instead.

The problem with retelling the story was that it made me relive it, and I didn't want to remember the feeling of coming close to having my ribs crushed. I didn't want to remember how that python had gone from fake to real in five seconds. Looking back on an event and realizing how easily you could have died—without even comprehending the deadliness of the thing that killed you—was a little like getting a bucket of ice water thrown in your face. Mostly harmless, but no less shocking.

I spent my lunch period combing my food for poison and thinking about how I could have been gone forever.

Poof. Kaput.

Forget college—bye-bye, all the other years of my life.

I would have died in this lobster tank.

Chapter
Forty-six

I was working at Finnegan's on Friday when a swarm of East Shoalers stormed the place. Everyone from the club to Cliff and Ria showed up, cramming every corner of the restaurant.

Finnegan himself always stopped by on Friday nights, and this royally screwed me over because I couldn't take pictures or do my perimeter checks or my food inspections. He sat in his office and made sure we were doing what we were supposed to. He was an average-looking guy—average height, average build, average black-brown hair and gray-blue eyes. He reminded me of a vulture, his neck too long and bent at odd angles.

Miles wandered in and took a seat with the rest of the club. Gus slid his burger and fries through the kitchen window before I could ask for it.

"Thanks," Miles said when I set the food in front of him. Art and Jetta sat across from him, the triplets at the next table over.

"Sorry I can't stay and talk," I said. "Finnegan's here. He'll crucify me if it looks like I'm not working." I tugged on Miles's white shirtsleeve with two fingers as I said it. A sorry replacement for a kiss, but the best I could do under Finnegan's watch.

"Pretend like we're ordering something else," Theo said. "And answer this question: You're going to prom, right?"

Miles rolled a french fry between his thumb and index finger.

"I—no, I can't." I pulled out my notepad and pretended to write something down. "I have to work that night."

"Oh, but Jetta could make the perfect dress for you," whined Theo. "Please? Please go. Ask off work. I did, and I never ask off."

"I really can't, Theo; I'm sorry." I didn't have the money for it, and neither did Miles.

"Don't look now," Art whispered. "Cliff's giving you the evil eye."

In my peripheral, I noticed Cliff and Ria staring at me from a few tables over.

"They can do what they want," I said. "They probably

just want to make some more jokes about me being a snake charmer."

I didn't expect anything else from them at this point. After the snake incident, I saw them in the cafeteria, reenacting what had happened for their friends. According to them, I'd fainted straightaway, and Miles had tried to beat the snake to death while it was still wrapped around me. A-plus performances, really, but if they were going to make fun of my near-death experience, they could have at least gotten the details right.

I ignored them and returned to the counter, pretending to look for another notepad but actually searching for the Magic 8 Ball. Was that snake real every time I saw it, or only sometimes? Were there other things I had thought were hallucinations, but were actually real? Even if the answer to that one was *yes*, it wasn't like the 8 Ball could tell me exactly what they were. . . .

The 8 Ball's usual spot beside the register was empty. I grabbed Tucker. "Hey. Where's the 8 Ball?"

"What?"

"The 8 Ball. Finnegan's Magic 8 Ball. I can't find it."

Tucker gave me a weird look, said, "Finnegan doesn't have a Magic 8 Ball," and hurried off.

I stared at the countertop and let that sink in. I'd used that 8 Ball so many times I couldn't remember all the questions I'd asked it. And I'd never once suspected it of being a hallucination. It didn't even seem like a hallucination. There was nothing strange about it. The blue water wasn't purple or orange or green. It never said strange things. It was just an old Magic 8 Ball, red scuff mark and all. It was just there.

I looked up. The restaurant was a living, breathing creature, ready to eat me alive. I braced my hands against the edge of the counter and took a few deep breaths.

"Alexandra!" Now Finnegan was leaning forward in his computer chair, craning his vulture neck around the office door to see me. "Get back to work!"

I scrambled for my water pitcher. Tucker was already going around with the Coke and tea. I nodded as I passed him, refilling drinks on the way. When I stopped at Cliff and Ria's table, everyone there was strangely cordial to me. I liked it that way. It was like they didn't really notice me. I ignored them and they ignored me. Good.

Until I turned to move on to the next table. My foot caught on something. I stumbled. The water pitcher, after sloshing its contents across my front, caught me in the jaw. Pain throbbed through my lip, and coppery blood spread across my tongue.

I cursed and pushed myself up. Laughter arced over my head. Cliff pulled his foot back under the table.

Then Miles rose from his seat and dragged Cliff out of his, slamming him back against the table. Ria and the others cried out as their glasses rattled.

"What the hell is wrong with you?" Miles growled. Every muscle in his hands and arms stood out, strained, his jaw tight. This was worse than yelling. This was even worse than in English class. His glasses had slipped down his nose, and he nailed Cliff to the table with an unrelenting stare. "When are you going to stop? What did she do to you?"

"Chill out, Richter—"

"YOU FUCKING CHILL OUT, CLIFFORD." Miles slammed him against the table again. "If you've got a problem with anyone, it's me. So deal with me."

I stood, grabbing my water pitcher. "Miles, stop. He's not worth it. It's not a big deal."

Miles's eyes flickered over to me. "He hurt you."

I touched the spot on my lip where I'd bitten myself. My fingers came away bloody. "I'll be fine. I bit my lip. It was an accident."

Miles looked less than thrilled, but he released Cliff.

"Damn, Richter. You know your girlfriend is screwy in the head, right?" Cliff tugged on his collar. "But I guess you're used to that, huh? I figure you like her because she reminds you of your dear old *Mutter*." He paused and folded his arms, getting a serious, concentrated look on his face. "It's really kind of creepy, when you think about it, because that means that you want to fuck your mom."

I felt the shock wave move through the room. It started with Miles, knocking him slightly backward, seeming to ripple through every last inch of him. It silenced the rest of the restaurant. I saw Tucker in the far corner, forgetting that he was refilling someone's tea and letting the cup overflow.

In the world of high school insults, it was actually pretty tame, but Miles's reaction made it terrible. Even Ria seemed scared. The muscles in Miles's throat worked as though he was trying to speak or swallow, but his lips pressed together so tightly they turned white. He closed his eyes.

"Miles," I said.

He exhaled sharply through his nose, opened his eyes, and reached out for me.

Cliff punched him in the ear.

Miles gasped and staggered to the side, clutching his head. I dropped the water pitcher and threw myself at Cliff before he could get another hit in. The next thing I knew, I had Ria grabbing at my hair and shirt, and Cliff trying to pry me off. Then Art was there, holding off two other football players from joining the fray, and Jetta and the triplets and Tucker jumped in around him, trying to help me, and the whole place went to hell.

Eventually, someone grabbed me underneath the arms

and lifted me right out of the fight. I was set on my feet behind the counter, and turned to see Gus—big, potbellied Gus, the cigarette still clamped between his lips. He nodded, looking worried.

Pitying.

I hated that look.

He trundled off to break up the fight, leaving a fuming Finnegan in his wake. Finnegan's face went from red to purple to white. Plates shattered. Drinks flew across the room. Blood dripped from my lip.

Finnegan only got two words out before he apparently lost the ability to speak.

"You're fired."

Chapter Forty-seven

My mother was not amused.

As soon as she saw my lip, she knew what had happened. Like Finnegan had some sort of telepathic link with her or something.

Or, more likely, that Finnegan had a sister called the Gravedigger.

She sat me in my room with my pictures and my artifacts, and she forced me to stay there for the rest of the night. Charlie kept me company, curled up in my lap, my arms around her. The gravity of the situation didn't hit me until Saturday afternoon, when Miles showed up on the doorstep, apologizing.

"I didn't mean to get you fired," he said.

I'd invited him in, but he still stood on the welcome

mat outside the door, his hands stuffed in his pockets. Shadows ringed his eyes. A bruise was forming along his left cheekbone that may or may not have come from the fight at Finnegan's.

"It's not your fault Cliff punched you in the ear," I said. "He's a two-hundred-pound human wrecking ball. Did you really think I was going to stand there and wait for him to hit you again?"

He stared at me.

"The answer is *no, you didn't,* because *no, I wasn't.* Besides, Finnegan was going to find something to fire me for sooner or later. I'm glad it was something worth getting fired over."

"I could have handled Cliff," Miles said. "I have some general experience getting the shit kicked out of me. But you needed that job."

I wanted to argue with him, but sometimes he had a terrible way of being right. I hadn't just gotten fired; I'd gotten fired for starting a fight. So much for ever using Finnegan as a work reference.

I glanced back into the house to make sure no one was listening, but Mom had gone to the store with Charlie, and Dad had fallen asleep reading a *National Geographic* on the couch. I stepped out onto the porch and closed the door behind me.

"Well, it's too late now," I said, then offered up a pitiful smile. "But hey, that means I'll have more time to figure out what McCoy's doing, right?"

I was joking, but Miles frowned. "You still want to break into his house?"

"I have to figure out what's going on. As long as we don't get caught, it'll be fine." I was positive it would, if Miles was still in on the plan. I waited, but his frown only deepened until he pushed his glasses up to rub at his eyes.

"I remember lifting you up, you know," he finally said.

"What?"

"With the lobsters. I remember lifting you up. You were heavy."

"Uh . . . thanks?"

He shook his head. "When are we doing this?"

"The day before the spring sports awards."

"That's soon."

"I know. Tucker found out from the front desk secretary that McCoy is staying late that day for preparations, so we know he won't be home. I told my mom I'd have to go back to school to help the club set up the gym—I'd sneak out, but my parents have been watching me constantly."

Miles exhaled sharply through his nose.

"Okay," he said. "Am I picking you up?"

"Tucker said he could, and we'd meet you there. Since you already live so close."

"Fine." He hesitated a second, then turned to go.

"Wait!" I caught his sleeve between my fingers. "Are you angry?"

He only turned halfway back. "I'm a lot of things," he snapped. "I don't know."

"You could . . . you could hang out here for a while. You don't have to go home."

"I shouldn't—" he began. Then my mother's Firenza turned down the street and pulled into the driveway, boxing in Miles's truck. Charlie bounced in the passenger seat. My mother got out and called for help bringing in the groceries.

"Well," he said, and I swear he sounded relieved, "I guess I could stay for a while."

Chapter
Forty-eight

The day before the spring sports awards, Tucker picked me up just as the shadows of the trees began slanting the other direction. I ran out to his SUV as fast as I could, ignoring the perimeter check, so my mother wouldn't have time to see who was driving. The Hannibal's Rest phoenix soared overhead. I didn't mention it to Tucker.

"I didn't need anything, right?" I asked, checking myself over. Converse. Jeans. Striped T-shirt.

"Nope. Richter said he knows a quick way in." Tucker pulled out of the driveway and started toward Lakeview.

"Why do you still call him 'Richter'? You've called him 'Miles' before."

Tucker shrugged. "Habit, I guess. I don't know if I'll ever be able to call him anything else."

We made it to Lakeview in ten minutes. Tucker passed Miles's street and went two more, to a cul-de-sac where rainbows and unicorns came to die. Miles's truck was already parked along the curb. Tucker pulled up behind it and pointed to a house a little farther down.

"That's his."

The place had probably looked good once, but now unchecked ivy grew up its sides. The house must've been red and white, but the white was peeling and yellowed, and the red had been bleached to a Pepto-Bismol pink.

We got out and met Miles.

"He hasn't been home since I've been here," said Miles.

"How long do you think we have?" I asked.

"An hour—Evan and Ian said they could hold McCoy at the school until at least four. Should be plenty."

"Are you sure you can get in?" Tucker asked.

Miles scoffed. "Have some faith, Beaumont. I got into your house, didn't I?"

Tucker rolled his eyes. "Fine then. Lead on."

The two of them started down the sidewalk. But as soon as I took a step, a flash of red behind the driver's seat in Tucker's SUV caught my eye. I looked back, wondering if it was some sort of hallucination, and then realized—I knew that shade of red.

"Hold on."

The two of them stopped as I marched back to the SUV and threw open the back door. Charlie crouched in between the seats, curled so tightly I hadn't seen her there on the drive over. She stared at me, eyes wide and frightened. The black king was in one curled fist, shiny with spit and dented with teeth marks.

"Charlie!"

"Sorry!" she whined. "I thought you were going to your school and I wanted to see it! You never take me anywhere with you!"

I tugged on my hair. "Seriously? Ugh—I can't take you home now."

"Let me come with you!" She tried to jump out of the car. I shoved her back into the SUV. I didn't want her walking around in the middle of the crappy side of Lakeview Trail.

"Where are we?" she asked.

"Stay here. Are you listening to me? Do *not* leave this car." I fixed her with my most searing gaze. "Do. Not. Leave. This. Spot. Got it?"

She nodded, but still tried to get a better look outside. I got the feeling that she hadn't actually heard a word I'd said.

"What is it?" Miles called.

I pointed a warning finger at Charlie and slammed the door closed. She sat back in the seat and crossed her arms, pouting.

"Charlie hitched a ride," I said. "I never even saw her get in. I told her to stay put while we're in there."

Miles and Tucker glanced at each other, but said nothing.

We walked up to McCoy's front door. I did my perimeter check, glancing back at the SUV to make sure Charlie didn't sneak out. Miles went straight for a ledge created by the edge of the porch roof. He felt around for a second, then pulled down a key.

"How'd you know that was there?" Tucker asked.

Miles shrugged. "He probably has them all over the place." He kicked the welcome mat aside, and there was another key underneath. "See?" He kicked the mat back in place, then unlocked the door and pulled it open.

Inside, the smell of mustiness coated everything like a thick layer of bad cologne. Tucker sneezed. Miles closed the door behind us.

"It looks so . . . normal." Tucker said.

We passed a staircase and went into a dining room lined with cabinets.

"Maybe for a retired octogenarian," I said. Antique furniture filled every available inch of space, some of it broken and some of it in usable condition. I thought I saw a WWII gas mask wedged between a broken scale and a worn cookie tin, but I grabbed Miles's hand and told myself that it wasn't really there.

We scoured the entire lower level of the house, from the dining room to a narrow, dirty kitchen to a living room with the ugliest orange shag carpet I'd ever seen in my life. For half a second I was tempted to leave McCoy a handwritten note expressing my profound and sincere astonishment that he had the balls to keep such a carpet in his home.

Nothing seemed out of the ordinary, except for the gas mask and a few magnets shaped like swastikas on the refrigerator.

"I haven't seen anything," I said.

"No." Tucker shrugged. "But there's still upstairs."

I turned toward the staircase again and saw a flash of red.

"Charlie!" I hissed, darting after her. I *knew* I shouldn't have trusted her to stay in that car. She was too much like me to stay put. She froze halfway up the stairs, looking back.

"I told you to stay in the car!" I said.

"But I want to help!" she cried, stomping her foot.

"Get down here right now."

"No!"

"Charlemagne!"

"You sound like Mom!" She charged the rest of the way up the stairs. I ran after her. Miles and Tucker were right behind me. I shouldered open the door Charlie had gone through.

And then I froze.

"Look at all the dresses," Charlie crooned.

The room was a museum exhibit. Dresses—prom, homecoming, cocktail, formal, even wedding—were displayed on mannequins. The mannequins all wore blond wigs. Plastered on the walls behind them were pictures upon pictures upon pictures, all of one person: Scarlet.

My stomach lurched. These could be *my* walls.

There was a large wooden desk on the far side of the room, strewn with papers and more pictures in frames. A pair of silver heels sat on the corner.

"What the actual fuck." Tucker walked in, then Miles a moment later.

I put an arm around Charlie and moved her behind me as Tucker, Miles, and I moved to search through the papers on the desk. There were all sorts of things—bills, official-looking documents from school, taxes that hadn't been filed yet, a half-completed crossword puzzle.

"This is all just junk," Tucker grumbled, picking up a stack of blank printer paper. It didn't even look like McCoy had a computer, much less a printer.

"Keep looking," I said. "There's got to be something. . . ." I grabbed the corner of a photograph and slid it out of the mess, careful not to dislodge anything else.

It was a picture of Celia and an older, dark-haired man

with an arm around her shoulders. Both of them were smiling. Celia's father, maybe? The man's eyes had been burned out, the edges of his face crinkled and red.

But why would McCoy burn Celia's father's eyes out? Why would he burn *anyone's* eyes out? How could anyone go this far down the rabbit hole without realizing they needed help?

And more importantly, what would he do if he found us here, looking through his things?

I stuffed the picture back where I'd found it, grabbed Miles and Tucker, and pushed them both toward the door. We needed to get out of here, now. "We're not going to find anything else. Let's go." Eyes peeked out of the dark space under the desk. "Charlie! Come on!"

No one asked any questions. Miles pulled the key from his pocket and locked the front door behind us.

"Uh-oh," Tucker said.

McCoy's junker of a car trundled down the street. Miles shoved the key above the doorframe, then grabbed us both and yanked us off the porch. He pushed Tucker and me behind the dead shrubs that hugged the side of McCoy's house, then ducked in after us. Sharp branches dug into my arms and head, and sweat trickled down my neck. McCoy pulled into his driveway, got out of his car, and went inside.

"Is he gone?" Miles whispered, his neck cranked toward

me so the shrubs didn't poke his eyes out.

"Yeah," I said.

As quietly as possible, we climbed out of the shrubs and dashed for Miles's truck and Tucker's SUV.

Charlie wasn't behind me. I jerked to a halt, pulling Miles with me.

"What? What is it?" he asked.

"Charlie! Where'd Charlie go?" I looked around, back to McCoy's house. "She came out with us, didn't she? You saw her come out?"

"Alex—" Miles pulled me forward.

"Miles, if she's still in that house—we have to go back!"

He kept pulling. I dug my heels in. Stupid, *stupid* Charlie, had to follow us. I couldn't believe her. I knew she was only eight, but I couldn't believe she could be this stupid.

Miles grabbed my shoulders and dragged me to the cars, swung me around so I was pinned between him and his truck. Tucker stood behind him, his face twisted with that awful pity.

"Alex."

Miles's voice was low but forceful. His bright blue eyes pierced me.

"Charlie's not real."

Why did you leave?

Chapter Forty-nine

The world tipped sideways. "W-what?" I stuttered.

"Charlie's not real. There's no one there. There never was." Miles pulled me around to the other side of his truck. The words buzzed in my ears, and everything stopped. The wind stopped rustling the trees; even the bug on Miles's windshield froze in its tracks.

"No." I tore my arm from Miles's grasp. Shock radiated out through my limbs. "No. You're lying. She was there— she was right there!" I'd seen her leave the house with us; I was sure. "Don't lie to me, Miles. Don't you fucking lie."

"He's not lying." Tucker came around on my other side, his hands up.

"She's real, Tucker. She's . . . she's got to be . . ." I looked toward McCoy's again, expecting Charlie to pop out from the other side of the house, playing a game. I'd yell at her for scaring me, and I wouldn't let her out of my sight again until we got home.

But she didn't appear.

"Go home, Beaumont," Miles said to Tucker. "I'll take care of her."

"Alex," Tucker said again, moving closer to me. I stepped away, wiping my eyes. I couldn't cry. Charlie wasn't here. She was at home. But the more I wiped my eyes, the more tears spilled out.

Home. I had to go home.

I climbed into the passenger seat of Miles's truck, buckled myself in. Home.

"It'll be okay." Tucker leaned through the window, holding my hand and speaking softly.

What was "okay"?

Miles's door slammed. The truck roared to life. Tucker slipped away with the rest of the scenery.

Miles kept talking to me, but I couldn't hear what he said.

She was just there. She had always been there.

The front door slammed against the hallway wall when I threw it open.

My parents were at the kitchen table. Eating dinner. Like nothing was wrong. Their heads shot up when I appeared in the doorway. I suddenly realized I couldn't breathe.

"Charlie," I choked out.

My mother stood first. She still had her napkin clutched in one hand, and she came at me with it like I was a baby who'd spit up. I backed away from her.

"Why didn't you tell me?"

"Alex, honey . . ."

"How can she not be real?"

A whimper came from behind me. Charlie stood in the hallway, her chess set held in both trembling hands. It was the chess set she'd had to get new black pawns for, because I'd flushed all the old ones down the toilet. One of the pawns was wedged between her teeth. When she whimpered again, it fell out of her mouth.

"What's going on, Alex?" Charlie asked, her voice shaking as much as her hands. "What are you talking about?"

"Charlie . . ." A knot formed in my throat. My vision blurred again. "But . . . but I remember you bringing her home from the hospital. Feeding her and taking care of her and watching her grow up and . . . and she always had Christmas presents under the tree, and you always set a place for her at the table . . . and she has to be . . ."

"She *was* real," my mother said. Her voice had gone tight, strained in a way I'd never heard it before. "But she died. Four years ago."

Dad stood up as well. I didn't like that everyone was standing.

"Charlie died before she turned five. As—" Dad's voice broke. "Asphyxiation," he said. "I should never have let her play with my chess set—"

I backed away, shielding Charlie from view. She whimpered again. The chessboard tumbled from her hands, and now all the other pieces joined the black pawn on the floor.

"I'm calling Leann." My mother went for the phone. "We shouldn't have waited so long. This has gone too far. There's got to be a stronger medication she can prescribe."

"She doesn't need stronger medication." A hand wrapped around my arm. Miles stood where Charlie had just been, glaring at my mother. Anger radiated off him, deep and cold. "She needs parents who give a shit about telling her what's real and what's not."

My parents stared at him, both of them rooted to the spot and completely silent.

"Miles," I whispered.

"How could you not tell her?" He got louder by the second. "Charlie's been dead for years, and you think it's okay to pretend she's not? Did you think Alex wouldn't find out? Was she too crazy for that?"

"No, it's nothing like—" my mother began.

"Like what? What could justify that?" Miles's fingers dug into my arm. "It better be pretty damn good, because that's fucked up. That's really fucked up. You're the ones she's supposed to be able to trust—you're supposed to be the ones she can go to when she can't tell. But instead she has to take a bunch of pictures because if she tells you anything, you threaten to send her to an asylum!"

Tears filled my mother's eyes. "You have no right to come in my house and tell me how to treat my daughter!"

"Oh, really? Because I know terrible parents, and you're one of them!"

"We tried," Dad finally said, his voice barely above a whisper. "We tried to tell her. Alex was in the hospital at the time—she'd just had an episode, she wasn't doing well—and no matter what we said, it just . . . rolled off." He looked at me. "Like you couldn't hear us. At first we thought you were just in shock. We thought you understood. But then you came home, and you were talking to her, and we realized that . . . that you didn't."

The room was too small, too close, too hot. An awful sob escaped my throat before I could catch it. I clapped my hand over my mouth. It seemed to break Miles's anger; his face rearranged itself into a soft expression of pity that I hated. I didn't want that look from anyone, least of all Miles. Never him. I darted across the kitchen to the back door. I could hardly see, but I knew exactly where I was going.

I wrenched the door open, tripped down the steps, and sprinted across the backyard.

When I got to Red Witch Bridge, I slid down the embankment of the creek and climbed under the bridge, where no one could see me. My lungs burned, and my eyes stung from the tears.

Blue Eyes. Bloody Miles. Scarlet. The 8 Ball. And now Charlie.

Charlie. Charlemagne. My own sister. If Charlie wasn't real, then what was?

Was everything made up? Was this whole world inside my head? If I ever woke up from it, would I be inside a padded room somewhere, drooling all over myself?

Would I even *be* myself?

Charlie had been a constant. Never once had I suspected she wasn't real. She'd always been real. Soft and warm and there when I needed her.

I couldn't breathe. I pressed a hand to my stomach and sucked in air, but bile rose to block it. My throat closed up.

"Alex! Alex, calm down!" Miles slid down the embankment, planted himself in front of me, and grabbed my shoulders. "Breathe. Just breathe. Relax."

He took my hand and pressed it to his chest, over his heart. It beat frantically under my palm.

Was that real? His heart? Was he real?

I stared back at the blue eyes I'd always thought were too good to be true. So were they? Was Miles real? Because if Charlie wasn't real and he wasn't real, I didn't want this anymore. I didn't want any of this.

"Hey."

"Are you real?" I asked.

"Yes, I am," he said resolutely. He pressed my hand harder to his chest. His heart beat like a drum.

"I am real. This"—he put his other hand over the first—"is real. You see me interacting with other people all day long, don't you? I talk to people; I affect things in the world. I cause things to happen. I am real."

"But—but what if this whole place"—I had to suck in air again—"what if everything is inside my head? East Shoal and Scarlet and this bridge and you—what if you're not real because nothing is real?"

"If nothing's real, then what does it matter?" he said. "You live here. Doesn't that make it real enough?"

Chapter Fifty

Miles and I sat under Red Witch Bridge until darkness settled in for good around us. My parents hadn't come looking for me—I guess they knew I wouldn't go far. Or they had amazing faith in Miles's ability to find me. Or maybe they didn't want to face either of us.

At the house, the kitchen light was still on. I stopped in the backyard, taking a long minute to search the area. It seemed stupid now, but I couldn't stop myself. I turned slowly on the spot. House, door, street, woods.

We went in through the front door. I closed it loud enough to make sure my parents knew we were back. I didn't want another confrontation. I didn't want Miles and my mother going at each other's throats again.

I did another perimeter check in my room, opened one

of my photo albums on the dresser.

It was all Charlie. Charlie smiling, Charlie playing chess, Charlie asleep with her violin tucked under her arm.

I showed Miles the album. "What do you see?"

He flipped through a few pages. "Furniture. Your backyard. Your kitchen. The street. What should I see?"

I took the album back from him, closed it, and set it on the dresser. No medicine would ever be strong enough for this.

Miles glanced at the clock on my nightstand. It was almost one in the morning.

"Will your dad be angry?" I asked.

"Probably. He gets angry about everything."

Over his shoulder I got a glimpse of white and red; Bloody Miles stood in the corner, grinning at me with his stained teeth.

I squeezed my eyes shut. "Do . . . um . . . do you have to go?"

"Are you okay?" He brushed my arm. I opened my eyes.

"I'm fine. I'm good." I turned toward the bed and the window.

Charlie stood outside, a horrible sad grimace on her face. All sixteen black chess pieces stuck out of her mouth like finely carved tumors. I gasped and jumped; Miles's arms came around me.

"What do you see?"

"Charlie's at the window. And . . . and you're in the corner."

"Me?"

I nodded. "From Celia's bonfire. Please don't ask."

"I can stay."

I nodded. I pushed open his arms and walked to the closet, opening the door in Bloody Miles's face. I peeled my shirt and jeans off and put on my pajamas.

Miles sat on the edge of the bed and took off his shoes.

"Your parents?" he asked.

"We're not doing anything." Besides, they might not be real.

"I think your mom hates me," he said.

"I kind of hate her," I said, realizing with a jolt that I meant it. "She needed to hear that. Thank you for telling her."

I closed the closet door. Bloody Miles's foul breath fanned over my ear and cheek. I pulled away from him and slid past Miles, into the bed. He lay down and slung an arm over my waist. I didn't know how to position myself: facing away from him, Charlie stared at me through the window. Facing him, Bloody Miles loomed overhead. I turned to the pillow, eyes shut.

This wasn't real. They weren't real.

Miles pressed up against me and buried his face in my hair. He could say he didn't understand emotions all he wanted, but sometimes it felt like he understood them better than anyone else I knew.

The hard ridge of his glasses pressed into my temple. I liked the pressure. It reminded me that he was there.

"Miles?"

"Yeah?"

"Don't go away."

"I won't."

Chapter
Fifty-one

Morning sunlight crept into the room, lighting up my artifacts and the freckles on Miles's face. The sheets were tangled around us. One of his hands was curled in my shirt, warm against my stomach, and the other was tucked beneath his chin. The rise of his body blocked most of the room, so I had to peek slowly over him to check the surroundings.

Bloody Miles was gone.

So was Charlie.

I stopped the thought as soon as I noticed it creeping up on me and allowed it to get no farther than that: Charlie was gone. No amount of hoping or wishing would bring her back. Not really.

The door opened a crack. My mother. I met her eye, expecting her to barge in, to yell at us, to put me under house arrest for lying to her yesterday, for running out so late, for letting Miles sleep in my room. But she didn't.

She nodded and turned away.

Miles sighed. His glasses were askew on his nose. I didn't want to wake him up, but I also didn't want to be alone. I kissed his cheekbone. He sighed again. I huffed and said, "Miles."

He grunted, cracking his eyes open.

"Morning," I said.

"How did you sleep?" he asked.

"Okay, I guess." I wouldn't have slept at all if he hadn't stayed awake until I drifted off. The night was a blur now; I couldn't remember any dreams, just flashes of red hair and chess pieces, wisps of violin music. "You?"

"Better than usual."

I reached up to fix his glasses. He smiled a little.

"Do we have to go to school today?" I asked. "Can we at least skip the awards?"

"The awards are the one thing we have to go to," he said. "I have to be there for the club, and if you don't go you'll be violating your community service."

"But McCoy will be there. I don't want you near him."

McCoy will burn his eyes out.

"If we don't go, McCoy will have a reason to call me to his office. Then he'll have me alone and it will be even worse."

God, he was humoring me and I couldn't stop myself. "Then you have to stay away from him. Don't let him anywhere near you. Don't even let him look at you—"

"I know." His fist pressed into my stomach. "I know."

If I looked at him any longer, I was going to start crying, so I pushed myself up and crawled over him to dig my school uniform out of the mess on the floor.

When I'd finished changing clothes, I had Miles wait by the front door while I crept into the kitchen.

Dad was alone, staring out the window over the kitchen sink. I tapped on the doorframe to get his attention.

"Your mom's on the phone with Leann," he said. I checked the clock. Seven in the morning—that had to be a new record for her.

"I'm going to school," I said.

He turned away from the sink. "Lexi, I don't think—"

"I don't want to be here all day."

"Your mom doesn't want you to go."

"Just today, please?" I wasn't letting Miles go by himself, and I knew, if I kept pushing, Dad would cave. "If it makes you feel better, Miles will be with me all day."

He shoved his hands into his pockets. "Actually, it does. But you know she's going to be pissed if I let you leave."

I waited.

He waved a hand in defeat. "Go. But promise me you'll

come home if you get scared or panicked or—or if anything happens—tell Miles this, too, so he can bring you back here!"

He had to raise his voice for the last part; I was already marching to the front door.

Believing something existed and then finding out it didn't was like reaching the top of the stairs and thinking there was one more step. Except when the thing was Charlie, the stairs were five miles high, and your foot never found the floor again.

Being back in school after that kind of drop was surreal, like I was falling past everyone else so quickly they couldn't even see me.

Everyone ignored us, for the most part. After classes were over, Miles and I retreated to the gym and sat behind the scorer's table. He barked out orders; all hands were on deck to set up for the awards.

"Celia!" Miles snapped. "Why are you late?"

Celia hurried into the gym, her lank brown hair hanging around her pallid face.

"Sorry!" she whimpered as she settled onto the bleachers, wiping her eyes. "Richar—Mr. McCoy wanted to talk to me."

My heart sank. Why did he want to talk to her? What

were they doing in his office? Why did McCoy have a picture of her and her father in his house?

Miles scrutinized her. "About what?"

Celia squirmed. "Nothing."

"Celia. What did he tell you?"

"It's none of your business, douche." A little of Celia's old self resurfaced. She huffed and went to sit at the end of the bleachers, then dropped her head into her hands and began sobbing.

This was worse than usual. Much worse.

I forced my breathing to remain even. If McCoy came anywhere near Miles, I'd be on him like a snake. Like that python.

Be the snake, the little voice said. *Be the snake. Squeeze the life out of him.*

Miles glanced toward the gym doors that led to the rotunda. "McCoy will be here soon," he said. I couldn't tell if he was worried or scared.

"Do you think he's still in his office?" I asked. Miles nodded.

Celia was having a breakdown. McCoy was probably sharpening his executioner's axe.

If I went now, I might be able to head him off. Stop him before he ever left his office. It could work.

"I'll be right back," I told Miles. "Restroom break. Stay

away from McCoy if he comes in here, okay?"

"Okay."

As soon as I was out of Miles's sight I began jogging. The rotunda was dotted in red—trophies, pictures, whole pieces of wall dripped with red paint. A long wavy red line led the way from the gym to the main office at the far end of the main hallway. I followed it.

Be the snake.

I strode past the front desk, ignoring the protests of the secretary, and pushed my way into McCoy's office.

He sat behind his desk, looking unusually put together. Suit. Tie. Hands folded in front of him. Bloodshot eyes. The office was just an office—certificates framed on the walls, books on a bookshelf, computer humming on the desk.

"It's okay, Mary," he said to the secretary. She huffed and went back to her seat.

"What are you going to do?" I asked, balling my fists at my sides.

McCoy picked a piece of lint off his sleeve. "What do you mean?"

"I know you've been calling Celia down to your office for the past four years. I know you've been working on some kind of *plan* with her mother. And I know you hate Miles. I know you're trying to get rid of him because . . . because Celia's mom said he's an obstacle."

"I'm afraid I don't know what you're talking about, Miss Ridgemont."

"You know *exactly* what I'm talking about." I glanced out the door to make sure the secretary wasn't listening. "I'm not crazy, all right? I know about Scarlet. I know about your *obsessions*. I'm not letting this get past me. And I'm not going to let you hurt Miles."

McCoy rearranged the nameplate on his desk. "You're mistaken. I don't plan on doing anything to Mr. Richter."

"If not you, then who? Celia?"

"I can't say I know what Celia Hendricks has to do with it."

"Look, psycho—"

"I realize you've had a difficult year, but are you sure you've taken your medication regularly?"

"I have, actually. You're not my mother, so please don't ask me that again. Now tell me what you're going to do to Miles."

"Again, Miss Ridgemont, I'm not going to harm a hair on Mr. Richter's Aryan head." He paused, and it took all my willpower not to look away from those searing eyes. "You should hurry back. It would be a shame if you failed your community service requirements right at the end of the year."

I hesitated. If McCoy revoked my community service

hours, I would definitely get sent away somewhere—Woodlands, or worse—and I would probably lose all class credit for this year. He had leverage; I had pieces of a story and a psychiatrist on speed dial.

He laced his fingers together with a benign smile. "I think we're finally seeing eye to eye."

No we're not, you asshole. But I couldn't say that. I couldn't say anything if I wanted to get out of here in one piece. I stood on the other side of his desk, shaking with fury.

"Have a nice day, Miss Ridgemont."

I trudged back to the gym in silence.

I couldn't stop McCoy on my own, but if I told anyone about this, who would believe me? It might sound vaguely believable coming from someone like Tucker, but from *me* . . . There was no way. If I even breathed a word of something this big, my mother would have me committed before I could say *just kidding*.

I entered the gym on the other end of the bleachers, near the scoreboard. The bleachers had already filled with athletes and their parents. The members of the club were stationed around the room near the doors. Miles stood beneath the scoreboard, his back to me. Celia stood beside him, like she was on a leash.

McCoy was already there. He was already standing at the mic in the middle of the gym. Already talking.

But if he was here, who had I spoken to in his office?

"Good afternoon, ladies and gentlemen. I'd like to welcome you to our annual spring sports awards. We'll begin with our league-winning baseball team, who've had a great season. . . ."

My shoe squeaked against the floor. Celia turned and saw me there; she was still crying, but harder than before.

Her mother was standing in the shadow of the bleachers on the opposite side of the gym, with her business suit and her long blond hair. But her face—I had seen her face before. In the newspaper. In the display cases outside this gym. In Celia's own expression—because when they stood side-by-side, the similarities were unmistakable.

But Scarlet—Scarlet was dead. Scarlet had been dead for *years*.

"Remember, Celia," she said, her voice filling the gym, "I'm doing this for you."

Celia didn't react.

"Richard and I have sorted everything out. It'll be over soon."

Celia didn't react because Celia *couldn't* react because Scarlet was dead.

"You can move on."

The scoreboard gave an ominous creak. Scarlet smiled. McCoy spoke a little louder at his microphone when the scoreboard creaked a second time. No one noticed. I couldn't be the only one seeing this. It was *happening*—it had to be—except Scarlet—Scarlet wasn't smiling at Celia; she was smiling at *me*. And she lifted one pointed, cherry-red nail toward the scoreboard.

I looked up. Red paint dripped down the wall. Each letter was ten feet tall; the two words crunched the scoreboard between them like bloody teeth.

CRIMSON

FALLS

The scoreboard screamed too loudly for McCoy to cover it up. Celia jumped away, scrambling onto the bleachers. Miles turned to hiss at her.

The scoreboard's supports snapped.

My feet stuttered; Scarlet's high laughter pealed across the gym.

I shoved myself off the doorframe and slammed into Miles's back.

Chapter Fifty-two

Here's the thing about dying in a sudden and tragic accident, like getting crushed by a scoreboard:

You don't expect it.

I expected it. So I think that's probably why I didn't die.

Chapter Fifty-three

I forced one eye open. Then the other.

My head had been caught in a vise. My mouth was lined with cotton. The light in the room was low, but enough for me to make out the ridge of my legs and feet underneath the covers of a bed and the dark alcove around the corner, where the door would be. A white-noise machine hummed in the corner, and a sterile smell crept up on me.

I was in the hospital. Bed. Bathroom. Machines hanging from the ceiling. Red-eyed camera by the door. No hallucinations here.

My body was still asleep. I flexed my fingers and toes to make sure I could, then looked around.

The curtains were pulled back from my bed. The bed next to mine was empty. On the other side of me, a figure swaddled in a blanket slept soundly in a chair that looked like it had been designed by a torture expert.

My mother.

I coughed to clear my throat. She jerked awake, stared at me blankly until she seemed to realize I was staring back at her. Then she was right in front of me, brushing my hair from my face.

"Oh, Alex." Her eyes had already glazed over with tears. She held me carefully, like I'd break.

"What happened?"

"That scoreboard fell on you," she said, sniffling. "Don't you remember?"

"Sort of." I did. I remembered running, then pain, then the light closing off around me like I was being smashed between pages of a book.

"They said . . . they weren't sure if you were going to wake up." A sob escaped her, and she clapped a hand over her mouth.

"Where is Miles? Is he okay?"

"Yeah. Yeah, honey, he's fine."

"Is he here?"

"Not right now, no."

I had to figure out where he was. I had to make sure he was safe. "How long was I asleep?"

"Three days."

"Mom." I said it mostly from surprise. The tears were spilling down her face.

"I was so scared," she said. "When your dad told me you went to school, I wanted to bring you home, but he said you'd be okay. . . ."

"This wasn't his fault."

"I know it wasn't."

"It wasn't my fault either."

"I know, I know." She wiped her eyes with the collar of her shirt. "I don't blame you; of course I don't blame you. I just want to keep you safe, and I . . . I don't think I know how to do that anymore."

Carefully, making sure nothing hurt too badly, I propped myself up on my elbows. She took the hint and put her arms around me, hugging me to her.

Why had she waited so long to tell me about Charlie? Was it because she couldn't bring herself to think about it? Or because I was happier when Charlie was around?

And was this why she wanted me to go to the mental hospital? Not to get me out of her hair, but to save me from myself, because she couldn't do it anymore?

"I bought you . . . some Yoo-hoos. . . ." she said when she finally pulled away, sniffing. "I put them in the fridge, because I know you like them cold. . . ."

And I thought she poisoned my food.

So apparently crying *did* hurt. My tears stung. I felt the pulse in my head as my face heated up.

"Love you, Mom," I said.

She leaned over and kissed my forehead.

Chapter Fifty-four

The next day, while Mom went for lunch, I got an unexpected visitor.

Celia. She stood at the edge of the room, looking a little more like her old self—blond hair, too-short skirt, layer of makeup topped by a coat of strawberry-colored lip gloss.

"You know," I began, finishing off a drink of water from my sippy cup, "everyone says history repeats itself, but I did *not* expect it to be so literal."

Her jaw tightened, her hands fisting in the hem of her shirt. Tough crowd. She stood there, staring, like I was going to whip a couple of throwing knives out from under the covers and use her for target practice.

Finally, she said, "How did you know?"

"I'm crazy, didn't you hear?" I said. "The real question is, why didn't you tell anyone?"

Celia shrugged. "I . . . I don't know. I didn't think anyone would care. They'd say I was just trying to get attention. Or that it was my fault. Or . . . I don't know."

She suddenly looked very, very old. "I'm tired of this. I'm tired of being alone. I'm tired of the way people look at me and the things they say. And I'm tired of trying to deal with it on my own."

"So don't," I said. "You're allowed to ask for help."

"Why doesn't anyone tell us that?"

"Because . . . maybe no one told them."

"Do you think I'm a bad person?" Celia asked quietly.

"No," I replied. "I don't think you're crazy, either."

She smiled.

It wasn't until a few hours later that the nurse came in and said, "We're all so surprised you haven't had any visitors yet!"

Chapter
Fifty-five

The club visited later, when Mom and the nurse were in the room so I knew they were real. They brought candy and flowers and history textbooks. You know, things they thought would cheer me up. They sat around the bed for most of the day, recounting with great detail and enthusiasm how heroic I looked knocking Miles out of the way right before the scoreboard hit him, and how everyone in the gym freaked out, and how I was still all over the news.

Apparently, Miles hadn't been McCoy's target at all. The scoreboard was meant for Celia. She had moved out of the way because she thought I was attacking her. McCoy, enraged, had tried to strangle Miles and had been dragged off by Mr. Gunthrie. A weight lifted off my chest. McCoy had slipped up. The threat was gone.

"But you're never going to believe *why* he tried to drop a scoreboard on her," said Evan.

"You know how McCoy is always calling Celia to his office?" said Ian.

"Apparently McCoy was obsessed with Celia's mom," Theo said, cutting to the chase. "And she got crushed under that thing years ago. Since he couldn't have her, he settled for Celia, but Celia wasn't . . . living up to his standards, or something. So finally he decided he'd immortalize her by dropping the same scoreboard on her that killed her mom. The cops found all sorts of incriminating stuff in his house. Journals and plans and, like, videos. Of Celia. When they got to the school after McCoy tried to strangle her, Celia told them everything, right in front of all of us. It was horrible."

"It was so weird," Evan added. "It was going on for two years, and nobody knew. Why wouldn't you tell someone about that?"

"Maybe she didn't think she could," I said.

Theo nodded. "I believe it. I talked to Stacey and Brittney after the awards—apparently Celia's dad got remarried a few years ago, and Celia's stepmother was planning on kicking her out of the house as soon as she graduated, and her dad was on board. Stacey and Brittney said Celia hardly ever told *them* anything, and they were her only friends."

"She has a stepmother?" I said.

"I've seen her a few times," Theo replied. "Short, brown hair, looks like she should be really nice, but I'm not totally surprised to know that she isn't."

Was this why Tucker and Miles hadn't questioned me all year when I said I'd seen Celia and McCoy speaking to Celia's mother? Because they thought I was talking about her stepmother? How many more hallucinations had gotten past me because of miscommunication?

"How did no one suspect McCoy before this?" I asked.

"'Ee 'as been voted number one principal in the township three times," Jetta said. "And 'is office was spotless."

"Apparently he did a pretty damn good job cleaning up after himself," said Ian. "If he didn't have all that stuff at his house, he probably could have said Celia was making things up. At least they still would have gotten him for trying to strangle Boss."

Theo huffed. "At least now when Celia testifies against him in court, they'll have a houseful of hard evidence to back her up."

"Does anyone know if she's okay?" I asked.

"She was molested by a psychopath for two years," Art said. "So, no."

Only after I threatened to rip out the stitches in the side of my head did they finally tell me what Miles had done.

"He went all white," said Art. "I've never seen someone lose all their coloring like that. Then he screamed at me to cut the power, and he ran over and started trying to lift the scoreboard off you. We had to pull him away so he didn't electrocute himself."

They all looked suddenly guilty.

"We wanted to help you," Theo said.

"Mr. Gunthrie came back right after that," Evan said, "with the paramedics and everything. They lifted it off you, but Miles was still there, and he made this noise—"

"And Mr. Gunthrie made us shut him in the boys' locker room before he did something stupid, like going after McCoy in front of all those cops," Ian finished.

I took a long draw from the straw jammed into my Yoo-hoo bottle, trying to calm myself. "Where is he? I haven't seen him. He knows I'm awake, right?"

They shared uncertain looks.

"We 'aven't seen 'im since," said Jetta. "'Ee 'asn't called any of us."

"We drove by his house, but his truck wasn't in the driveway." Evan looked at Ian and Theo, who nodded. "And we checked at Meijer, but he hasn't gone in to work."

"I thought he might be at Finnegan's," said Art. "He did get banned, but I didn't think that would stop him."

"So none of you have seen him since the scoreboard fell?"

They all shook their heads.

A lead weight sunk in my stomach. The threat from McCoy might be gone, but there was another threat to Miles.

One I couldn't fight.

Chapter Fifty-six

My hands itched for my Magic 8 Ball. For Charlie. For soft, dark, quiet safety. For answers to questions I couldn't answer myself. For escape from this world by retreating so far into my own head, I never had to question whether it was real or not.

But I couldn't stop worrying about Miles.

It was Wednesday night—six days after the scoreboard fell, three days after I'd woken up, half a day before I was scheduled to leave the hospital—when Tucker burst into my room, his coat dripping with rain.

"Oh, finally decided to come visit?" I put the finishing touches on my newest Crayola masterpiece, a picture of a T-Rex. It reminded me of something, but I couldn't think of exactly what. "I didn't figure it'd take you this long to show up."

"Alex."

The tone caught me, made me look up again.

"What? What is it?"

"Miles. I think he's doing something stupid."

I threw my legs over the side of the bed and hunted for the shoes Mom had brought me. "Have you talked to him? What did he say?"

"He hasn't been coming to school." Tucker's words came out short and fast. "I haven't seen him until just before I came here. He was at my house—he looked really freaked out, like someone was after him. He apologized. Except he kept tripping over his words."

I stood, grabbed Tucker's hand, and pulled him toward the door. "What else?" I peeked around the doorframe.

"He . . . he wanted me to make sure you were okay. He said he couldn't come himself."

I ignored the invisible buzz saws cutting holes in my stomach. "Give me your coat."

"What?"

"Give me your coat. You're sneaking me out of here."

"But you're hurt!"

"I don't care if I'm missing a leg, Tucker. We're going

to Miles's house, and you're driving. Give me your coat."

He did. I pulled it on, zipping it all the way up. I balled my hair back and pulled the hood up to cover it.

"Lead the way," I said.

Chapter
Fifty-seven

My perimeter checks were useful, but it was Tucker's knowledge of medical-speak that got us out of the hospital.

I knew I'd never be able to repay him for sneaking me out. And I'd never really be able to thank him for being worried about me when he found out Miles and I were together, instead of being angry.

We sprinted across the rain-soaked parking lot to Tucker's black SUV and peeled our way out to the street. He didn't ask me what I thought was going on. They used to be best friends. He probably already knew.

I couldn't see Hannibal's Rest because of the dark sheeting rain, but I knew when we passed my street because the phoenix sat atop the stop sign, its feathers flaming red in the rain. We swerved through the Lakeview Trail entrance. Tucker pulled up in front of Miles's house. I spotted Miles's truck in the driveway, but not the Mustang that had been there before.

"We have to get inside." I jumped out of the SUV.

"What?"

"We're going into the house! Come on."

Together we climbed the fence into the front yard. I desperately hoped Ohio wasn't out, or couldn't hear or smell us in this rain. The monster dog would tear us both to pieces. The front door of the house was shut tight and all the first floor lights were off, but a light was on upstairs.

I pulled Tucker to the doghouse, freezing when I saw the hulking silhouette of the huge Rottweiler, apparently asleep. But there was something unnatural about Ohio's stillness.

Chills ran up my arms. This was it; this was the night. I climbed up on the doghouse and reached for the drainpipe, like I'd seen Miles do when he'd left the house that night. It had been reinforced with pieces of wood that stuck out at odd angles and made perfect hand- and footholds. Miles must have put them there. The trick to climbing them was not combusting from the fiery soreness burning through my entire body.

Within minutes, both Tucker and I were on the rain-slicked porch roof and making our way to the room with the light.

The window was open enough for me to wedge my fingers underneath and pull it up. Tucker and I tumbled inside.

I started out noticing the little things: the notebooks spilling from the closet; the hunk of Berlin Wall sitting on the dresser, crumbling on one side like part had been broken off; the words scribbled on the walls. A picture frame sat on his nightstand. The black-and-white picture was of a man who looked almost exactly like Miles, one eyebrow quirked up, wearing a black flight jacket and standing next to a WWII-era fighter plane.

"He's not here," I said. "We have to search the rest of the house."

"What about Cleveland?" Tucker asked.

"I think he's gone. His car is gone."

Tucker didn't look so sure.

"Come on." I walked to the door and wrenched it open. A stale smell hit me straight in the face, and I realized how much Miles's room had smelled like him, like mint soap and pastries.

Tucker followed me out into a narrow hallway lined with doors, all open. The rain and wind howled outside. This place was so cold, so sad, I wondered how Miles managed to live here at all. Tucker walked toward the opposite end of the hallway, where a staircase descended to the first floor. A single lightbulb over the stairs cast a halo on his black hair.

He sucked in a breath. "Oh, shit."

"What?"

"Oh shit, Alex, oh shit." He started down the stairs, two at a time. I ran to the top of the stairs and looked down.

Miles sat against the wall at the bottom, slouched over.

One second I was at the top of the stairs and the next I was at the bottom. Tucker was already at his cellphone, speaking to a 911 operator. I knelt next to Miles, wanting to touch him but afraid of what I'd feel. Blood dripped slowly onto his glasses; the extra weight pulled them down until they hung off one ear.

Would he be cold? As dead and empty as the house around him?

This could not be happening. I was hallucinating all of this. I could make it all go away if I tried hard enough.

But I couldn't. And it was real.

I placed a shaky hand over his heart. I couldn't feel anything. I pressed my ear against his chest, closed my eyes, and prayed, really prayed, for the first time in my life, to whatever god was listening.

Don't go away. Don't go away.

Then I heard it. And I felt the almost unnoticeable rise-and-fall motion of his chest as he breathed.

Tucker dragged me back.

"Is he breathing?" I asked. "Is he really breathing?"

"Yeah," Tucker said, "yeah, he's breathing."

Chapter
Fifty-eight

We sat on the front steps as the paramedics took Miles out of the house on a stretcher. The cops found Cleveland's car not far away, wrapped around a tree, and Cleveland stumbling around in an angry drunken stupor. Connections weren't hard to make.

Tucker took me back to the hospital. To my surprise, no one yelled at me, but I did pull a few stitches, blow up my blood pressure, and get a couple more days in the hospital under strict confinement to my room.

I was okay with that. Because the next morning, I got a roommate.

Chapter Fifty-nine

"**M**r. Lobster. Do you think my hair is more Communist red, or your red?"

Morning sunlight swept across the tiled floor and over the white bed sheets, bathing the room in warmth. The white-noise machine under the window dulled the beeping of the monitors next to the bed. The only other noise came from occasional footsteps in the hallway and a TV somewhere.

"Fire truck."

I hardly heard it, he said it so quietly. I wasn't even sure he was awake at first; his eyes barely opened, but he licked his lips.

"Fire truck," he said again, a little louder. "Strawberry, stop sign, ladybug, Kool-Aid, tomato, tulip. . . ."

He slowly raised his arm and reached out, feeling for the bedside table. "Glasses."

I had his glasses; they dangled off my right index finger. I gently took his hand and placed them in his palm. He fumbled with them for a moment before finally getting them straight on his face. He blinked a few times and stared at the ceiling.

"Am I dead?"

"Fortunately, no. I know you were pretty hell-bent on it, but it didn't really work out."

"What happened to the good dying young?" he said, his voice breaking. I smiled even though it felt like nails were being hammered into the left side of my face.

"We're not good, remember?"

He frowned and tried to sit up and fell back again, groaning.

"God . . . what happened?"

"You got beaten up and thrown down a flight of stairs. Want to explain what you were doing?"

"I don't really remember. I was upset. . . ."

"Yeah, I figured that much."

"It wasn't supposed to go that way. I provoked him." He looked around. Saw the other bed. "You're in this room, too?"

I nodded. "Someone likes us."

He carefully turned his head, wincing, to look at me. "Your face."

I smiled again; I was wondering when he'd notice.

"It's only the left side," I said. "The doctor got all the glass out. He said when the swelling and redness go down, I'll look basically the same as I used to. Just with a lot of scars."

Miles frowned. "Are you okay?"

"Great," I said. "Concussion, electrocution, scarring . . . nothing I can't handle, trust me. You should be more worried about yourself. I know how you like to keep people away, but after this I think you might have your own fan club."

"What are you talking about?" he asked, licking his lips again. "Is there any water in here?"

I reached for the glass of water the nurse had brought earlier. As he drank, I explained what had happened to Cleveland after he'd thrown Miles down the stairs.

"They got him. He was pissed. I guess he thought they were going to help him or something, because he told them exactly where he lived and what had happened. There was already an ambulance at your house, so they pieced it all together." I paused and curled my legs up underneath me. "Anyway, Cleveland's sitting in jail. They aren't going to hold the trial until their three star witnesses are ready to testify."

Miles opened his mouth to say something else, but

then smiled and shook his head. I searched for a word for what I was feeling, for this mix of relief and exultation and serenity, but I couldn't think of anything.

Words were his thing, not mine.

A few moments later the nurse came back to check Miles's bandages and ask him how he felt and if he needed anything.

"Well, I guess if you're feeling up to it, your friends can come on in," the nurse said.

"Who . . . ?"

"Did she zay come een?" Jetta poked her curly-haired head through the doorway and looked around. The rest of the club was visible over her shoulder.

"Don't be too rowdy." The nurse edged her way out the door as the club came spilling in.

"Hey, Boss!"

"Mein Chef!"

"You look like hell!"

Miles looked at all of them—Art, Jetta, and the triplets—gathered at the foot and side of his bed, and frowned.

"What are you all doing here?"

"We're your friends," Theo said slowly, like she was explaining some fundamental truth to a child. "We were worried about you."

"See?" I said. "They *do* like you."

"Who said anything about liking him?" Evan asked.

"Yeah, we never said we liked you," said Ian, smiling. "We just prefer that you don't die."

"Where would we be without our fearless leader?" Theo added.

"How'd you guys get out of school?" Miles asked.

"Skipped," said Art. "Wasn't hard."

"You two are, like, heroes," said Theo. "The story is in every paper. Have you seen all the presents you've been getting?" She motioned to the stacks of cards and flowers on the table by the window. They'd been arriving on an hourly basis since the story had gotten out.

"I still don't understand why they'd send gifts," Miles said sharply.

"It was your mom," Theo said. "She told us the story— why you did all that stuff in school, why you worked all the time."

"Why didn't you ever tell us?" Ian asked, but Miles didn't seem to hear him. He was looking past Jetta, toward the doorway.

"Mom."

June leaned through the door, clutching a large purse in both hands, looking like a deer in headlights. She took a few steps into the room. I wondered if this was the first time in years she'd really been outside of Crims—Woodlands. I wondered if she'd only been able to leave for Miles.

We all filed out past her.

I stopped outside the doorway and looked back in. June held Miles tightly, rocking back and forth. I couldn't see his face, but I could hear him laughing and crying and saying something muffled by June's shirt. A moment later, a smartly dressed woman walked past us into the room. I waited in the doorway long enough to hear her reassure them that everything would be better, then ducked out into the hall.

The triplets went down to get food while everyone else headed to the waiting room. I went with them; my parents were around somewhere, and I wanted to tell them what was going on.

I didn't even have to leave the floor to find them. They sat in a small, secluded little waiting room, alone except for my doctor and the Gravedigger. Their voices were strained and hard. Anxiety settled in my stomach. They hadn't seen me coming down the hallway, so I pressed my back to the wall and crept closer, positioning myself around the corner.

"I don't think we have any other option at this point." That was the Gravedigger, talking like she had any say in what happened to me.

"How could she have known that it was falling?" Mom asked. "Unless . . . ?"

"But they said the principal loosened the supports,"

Dad said. "He was trying to drop it on that girl. Lexi didn't have anything to do with it—she was just reacting."

"Still." Damn you, Gravedigger. Shut up. Shut the fuck up. "This incident can't have done her any good. She's unstable. I've noticed her getting worse all year."

"But we've seen her, too," Dad pushed. "Good things have happened, too. She's *coping*. She has friends. A boyfriend, even. I wouldn't feel right, taking that away from her."

"I think Leann may have a point, David," my mother said.

The Gravedigger jumped back in again. "In my professional opinion, this is a critical time, and she needs to be in a safe, monitored place where she can regain control. I don't mean to restrict her, and I'm glad she's added to her support structure. But that doesn't change the facts."

I couldn't listen to any more. I made my way back to my room, where the lawyer had left but Miles and June were still smiling and laughing.

"Alex, dear, there you are!" June motioned to me. "Come and sit over here for a while; we have so much to talk about!"

"I'm feeling a little tired. I think I'm going to sleep for a while," I said.

"You get all the rest you need." June smiled warmly.

"There will be plenty of time to talk afterward."

I pulled myself into the bed and yanked the sheets up, my face and side burning with pain. I wondered how much time I would actually have.

Because as much as I hated it, and hated this, and hated her, the Gravedigger was right.

Chapter Sixty

I woke up once in the middle of the night. Bloody Miles stood at the end of the bed, blue eyes wide and piercing, blood oozing from his freckles. Holding his hand was a girl with blood-red hair and a million cuts on the side of her face, her eyes as wide as his. They stood there for a long time, staring at me. Neither of them said a word, but they both smiled with bloodstained teeth.

Chapter
Sixty-one

I woke later. It was still night. Miles was writing in his notebook. He looked over when I rolled onto my back and sat up.

"Feeling any better?" he asked, smiling.

"No, not really."

He closed his notebook and set it in his lap. "Come here."

I tottered to the edge of his bed, pulled my legs up next to his, and leaned my head back against his shoulder. His arm wound around me.

The world was hollow. What had been the point of this year? Senior year, all the college applications . . . would it have been better just to go straight to the hospital after Hillpark? I was the one who said no. I said I could do it; I said I had it under control. The only thing my parents could be accused of was trusting me too much.

Miles waited patiently, pretending to be interested in brushing my hair back.

"My parents are sending me to Crimson—to that hospital. I heard them talking about it."

"But you're old enough—they can't decide that for you," he said quietly. "You don't have to go if you don't want to."

Then the tears came, spilling out before I could catch them, stinging my face on their way down. "I don't," I said. "But I think I need to. I can't tell the difference by myself. Not anymore."

I didn't know if he understood anything I said through my blubbering, but his arm tightened around me and he kissed the side of my forehead. He didn't say anything. Didn't try to persuade me otherwise.

He'd escaped the tank. I didn't know if I ever would.

Chapter Sixty-two

Later, when I'd calmed down, Miles leaned over the side of the bed and grabbed his backpack. He unzipped it and took out a few things.

"Can I look in your notebook?" I asked.

He quirked his eyebrow. "What for?"

"Just because."

He handed it over. Most of this notebook was in German, but there were still bits and pieces in English. June's name was scattered through the pages.

"Why'd you keep your mom's maiden name?" I asked.

"How'd you know?"

"When Tucker and I were looking up Scarlet in the library, June was mentioned in an article. She was the valedictorian."

"Oh. Yeah. We switched to her name when we went to Germany."

"Ah." He didn't need to give more explanation than that. I flipped through a few more pages of his notebook and said, "I have a confession—I've read this."

"What? When?"

"Um . . . when Erwin died and you gave me a ride home. You went in the building to turn in those papers, and I peeked."

"Why didn't you tell me?" he asked, but he didn't swipe the notebook away from me. I shrugged. Pain spiked my collarbone.

"Well, obviously I didn't want you to know that I looked. You didn't exactly seem like the most forgiving person." I flipped through a few more pages. "What are these German parts?"

"Journal entries," he said. "I didn't want other people to read them."

"Well, good job," I said. "I did see my name a few times in that other notebook, though."

"Ah, yeah," he said, laughing again. "Yeah, I was a little upset on the first day of school. I didn't think you were the right person. It was stupid, but I guess I didn't think it was you at first because you didn't act at all like I'd imagined you would."

"Hah, sorry. I thought that about you, too."

I turned to the last pages.

What you loved as a child, you will love forever.

"I think you're an improvement on my imagination," I said, flipping back through the pages.

"You, too," he said. "My imagination—well, what little imagination I have—doesn't quite live up to the real thing."

"Agreed," I said. "The real thing is much better."

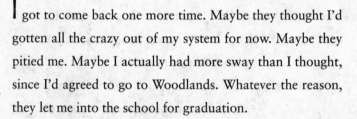

I got to come back one more time. Maybe they thought I'd gotten all the crazy out of my system for now. Maybe they pitied me. Maybe I actually had more sway than I thought, since I'd agreed to go to Woodlands. Whatever the reason, they let me into the school for graduation.

There were a few stipulations, of course. The first: I wasn't allowed into the ceremony, but I got to stand by the auditorium doors and watch. The second: I had to have a pair of Woodlands orderlies (read: thugs in scrubs) flanking me at all times. Sure, they were driving me up to Woodlands as soon as the ceremony was over, but did they have to look so menacing while they did it? The third was the worst: Because of the McCoy ordeal and the school board looking to avoid any further mishaps, I wasn't allowed out of the car without wrist restraints. At least they'd agreed to let me wear a sweatshirt to partially cover up the cuffs. The only reason I was going to the damn hospital was because I'd decided to—you'd think they'd be a little more lenient.

By the time we reached the auditorium, everyone else was already seated. Parents and other relatives took up the right and left sides of the auditorium stage. I noticed June because of the golden halo in her sandy hair. My classmates sat in the middle section. They all wore East Shoal graduation green.

The stage was bathed in bright light. It was Mr. Gunthrie who filled Mr. McCoy's vacated principal's seat; his gray suit made him look like a golem. I could definitely believe Mr. Gunthrie was animated by magic.

Next to him were the four senior student officers, most of them fidgeting. Tucker sat next to the class treasurer, glasses flashing in the light, wringing his speech mercilessly between his hands.

Miles was there, the valedictorian's golden cord slung over his shoulders. His hands were clasped in his lap, his eyes focused somewhere around the edge of the stage.

Mr. Gunthrie started the ceremony with his usual thunderous yell. The lights dimmed until I could no longer distinguish individual people in the auditorium.

The class president stood and gave his speech. The vice

president said a few short words, the band played the school song, and then Mr. Gunthrie began announcing names. The honors students went up first. I had to grind my teeth to keep from laughing when Miles shook Mr. Gunthrie's hand—even from where I stood, I could see the Cheshire cat grin that spread across Miles's face, and the stony frown Mr. Gunthrie gave him in return.

When my name should have been called, I rocked forward onto the balls of my feet, my insides aching. I'd worked so hard for that diploma . . . .

One of the orderlies grabbed my sweatshirt hood and gently tugged me back. I grunted, sitting back on my heels, and stood still while the rest of my classmates graduated. Evan and Ian pretended to get their diplomas mixed up, then tried to shake Mr. Gunthrie's hand at the same time. Theo looked like she was ready to go and pull the both of them offstage. Art made Mr. Gunthrie look like a large pebble when they stood next to each other. Then everyone took their seats except for Mr. Gunthrie.

"Before we end the ceremony, there are a few more parting words. The first are from your salutatorian, Tucker Beaumont." A round of lukewarm applause ran through the theater. Tucker, face red, moved to stand at the podium.

I felt a rush of pride. Mr. Soggy Potato Salad, who'd decided to break into McCoy's house, jumped into the brawl at Finnegan's, and helped bring Miles home. Who'd forgiven me for everything I'd done, and then some. I didn't know if I deserved a friend like him, but I was glad I had him.

He spent a moment adjusting the microphone and smoothing his twisted speech, then he cleared his throat and looked around at everyone.

"I guess I'll start with a bit of a cliché," he said. "We made it!" The auditorium erupted with shouts of excitement and victory.

Tucker smiled. "Okay, now that that's out of the way—I think we can all safely say that this was the craziest year of school any of us has ever experienced." He glanced back at Miles, who only quirked an eyebrow. "Even if you weren't there every moment, you heard about it. You were still a part of it. You survived it. And really, if you can survive pythons coming out of the woodwork, you can survive almost anything."

Laughter. Tucker repositioned his glasses and took a deep breath.

"People say teenagers think they're immortal, and I agree with that. But I think there's a difference between thinking you're immortal and knowing you can survive. Thinking you're immortal leads to arrogance, thinking you deserve the best. Surviving means having the worst thrown at you and being able to continue on despite that. It means striving for what you want most, even when it seems out of your reach, even when everything is working against you.

"And then, after you've survived, you get over it. And you live."

Tucker took another deep breath and leaned against the podium, looking around at everyone. He smiled.

"We're survivors. So now let's live."

The auditorium erupted again and Tucker could barely hide his grin as he walked back to his seat, twirling his silver salutatorian tassels. I couldn't help but smile, too. *Survivors.* What better word for people who made it out of this place alive?

Mr. Gunthrie waited for the applause and cheering to die down, and then said, "Ladies and gentlemen, your valedictorian, Miles Richter."

The sudden silence in the auditorium was even more pronounced because of the deafening noise that had preceded it. No one clapped. I couldn't tell if it was because they were scared, angry, or surprised.

Miles stood and looked around much like Tucker had, but he didn't fidget while he did it. His fingers rapped against the wooden top of the podium. *Tap, tap, tap, tap.* Mr. Gunthrie cleared his throat loudly, but Miles was silent.

Then Miles looked toward where I stood in the doorway. He smiled.

"I know that most of you don't want to hear anything I have to say," he began. "And I know the rest of you really do. And I also know that these two things mean that all of you are listening attentively. That's exactly what I want.

"James Baldwin said, 'The most dangerous creation of any society is the man who has nothing to lose.'" Miles sighed and swept the graduation cap off his head. He glared at it for a moment, then threw it to the side of the stage. Behind him, Mr. Gunthrie's face turned a mottled hue of purple.

"I always thought those things looked ridiculous," Miles grumbled into the microphone. A few hesitant chuckles came from the crowd, like they weren't sure if he was joking or not. Then he said, "For a long time, I had nothing to lose. *I* was that dangerous creation. I know most of you probably think I'm a jerk"—he glanced at me again—"and you're right, I am. Not the kind that vandalizes cars and kills pets, but I am an arrogant, pretentious jerk. I *do* think I'm better than all of you, because I'm smarter. I'm smarter and I'm more determined to do what I set out to do."

I wasn't sure what guidelines Miles had been given for his speech, but if the shade of Mr. Gunthrie's face was anything to go by, he had wildly ignored them.

"I used to think all of that, anyway," he continued. "I still do, kind of. I'm learning to . . . not to change, because in all honesty I like the way I am. Not what I do, but who I am. No, I'm learning to . . . keep it bottled up? Displace it? Control my frustration? Whatever it is, it's working. I don't feel like that dangerous creation anymore. I no longer have any motivation to do the things I did here.

"For anyone I've wronged—I'm sorry. Whatever I did and for whatever reason I did it, I'm sorry. *Meine Mutter*"—I pictured Cliff squirming in his seat—"always taught me that apologizing is the polite thing to do."

I could imagine the radiant smile stretching across June's face.

"I want to say a few more things. The first is to our wonderful salutatorian." He turned and addressed Tucker. "I didn't mean what I said to you. You were my best friend, and I screwed that up. You deserved better.

"The second is to the East Shoal High School Recreational Athletics Support Club. I think if it hadn't been for you, I would have killed myself a long time ago."

We were probably the only ones who realized how serious he was.

"The third is to all of you. I used to be scared of you all. It's true. I used to care what you thought and I used to care that you might try to hurt me. Well, not anymore. So, to the latter, see how far you get in a fistfight. And to the former, try this on for size—I am in love with Alexandra

Ridgemont, and I don't care what you think about it."

He looked up at me again, and the world solidified under my feet.

"I feel like there's something else, but I can't quite remember. . . ." His fingers tapped against the podium. He shrugged and began to walk back to his seat . . . then he clapped his hands together with an "Oh, right!" and whipped back around, yanking the microphone to his face in time to say, *"Fickt euch!"*

From somewhere in the middle of the sea of students, Jetta's hands shot into the air and she cried out a triumphant, *"Mein Chef!"*

I couldn't tell why everyone else began cheering—the realization that what Miles had said was probably very vulgar?—but their voices shook the floor.

Mr. Gunthrie stood, perhaps to haul Miles off the stage, but Miles slipped away at the last second and made his way down the aisle. My orderlies pulled me back, into the hallway. I heard the auditorium doors swing open again, but we were outside, standing in the crisp night air, before Miles caught up with us.

"Wait!"

"I just want to talk to him!" I said, glancing over my shoulder at Miles. "Please. I won't try anything."

The orderlies looked at each other, then at me. "Two

minutes," one of them said. "We have to leave before everyone else gets out here."

"Fine. Got it."

They let go of my arms. I turned and jogged the short distance back to Miles.

"I didn't think they'd let you come back," he said.

"I'm very persuasive."

He laughed, but the sound was hollow. "I've taught you well."

"Are you kidding? If I did things the way you do them, I would've been locked up a long time ago."

Miles didn't say anything to that, but reached up to touch my face—the raw, still mutilated side of my face. I grabbed his hand.

"When did you get so touchy-feely?" I asked. He wasn't listening. He stared at the soft cuffs, at the metal clasp that jangled between them. "They're a precaution," I said before he could ask. "I had to wear them so I could come here. Apparently the school was feeling sentimental enough to let me back, but not sentimental enough to risk a lawsuit."

"I don't like this," he said.

"Yeah, well, join the club."

"When are you going?"

"Tonight. Right now, actually. It was supposed to be

this morning, but since the school agreed to let me come here, they pushed it back . . ."

His frown deepened.

"It's not like I have anything to wait for."

"Fine. I'll come visit you tomorrow."

"At—at Woodlands?"

His eyebrow shot up. "What, did you think you were going to get rid of me that easily? You should know by now—I've got the tenacity of a cockroach."

I blinked at him. "Surely you've got better things to do."

He shrugged. "I've got a few pretty good ideas, but they can wait."

"We need to go!" one of the orderlies called. I waved my hands to show I understood, then turned back to Miles.

"So . . . I guess . . ." I took a quick step forward, hiding my face in his graduation robe. "Stop looking at me like that!"

He laughed—I could hear and feel it—and hugged me tightly. Soap and pastries. After a moment he pushed me away.

"Are you crying?"

"No," I said, sniffling. "My face hurts when I cry, so I don't do it."

"Right."

My face did hurt, now that I thought about it.

"I don't want to leave," I said.

Miles said nothing. There really wasn't anything he could say. Everything was over. There would be no more adventures for us. It was time to go.

He leaned down and kissed me. Then he hugged me again. I grabbed the front of his robe with both hands and pulled him down so I could whisper into his ear.

"*Ich liebe dich auch.*"

I made my way back to the orderlies waiting by the car, swung myself into the backseat, buckled myself up, and turned around. Miles stood alone on the dark sidewalk, his hand brushing the spot on his chest where my tears had stained his green robe. I waved halfheartedly, one hand dragging the other up by the wrist.

Miles raised his other hand, but it fell back down as if it were too heavy to hold up. I watched as he grew smaller and smaller, along with the sidewalk, the parking lot, the school, and the oversized stadium. Then we passed a row of trees and he was gone.

I turned back around in my seat and listened to the orderlies talking, "We Didn't Start the Fire" playing on the radio, and the steady thrum of the car's engine.

I rested my head against the car window, watching the warm night streak by outside, and smiled.

Epilogue

The Freeing of the Lobster

"So that's how it happened," I said.

"That was very detailed for such a long story." Lil trimmed off a little more of my hair and fluffed it out. It just hit my shoulders—my head felt light.

"Well, yeah, it's a lot to remember, but I wasn't going to forget bits and pieces of it, right? What kind of story would that be?"

"Mm-hmm."

Lil rarely believed the stories I told her. As far as she was concerned, East Shoal and everything that had happened was nothing but a figment of my imagination.

It didn't matter; I was getting out today.

"So what happened to Miles?" Lil asked.

"What do you mean, what happened to him? He comes

to visit me every weekend."

"He does?"

"If he came during the week, you would've seen him."

She stood in front of me, a tiny line forming between her eyebrows. She didn't think he was real. She never had.

Lil finished with my hair and helped me pack my suitcase. I'd started throwing things in this morning, when I didn't really care about space conservation. I found the mess charming. Lil looked disgusted.

The rest of my room was bare now. Everything was ready to go, except the chunk of Berlin Wall perched on my desk. I swiped it up, running my fingers over the rough surface. Some places were starting to wear smooth where I always stroked them with my thumb. More than once Lil had woken me up and scolded me for having slept with it hugged to my chest. I tried telling her I didn't take it to bed on purpose, that I must've woken up in the middle of the night to get it. She didn't believe that, either.

I waved goodbye to the other patients—my friends, as strange and as absurdly normal as that was—as we passed the rec room, the place where I'd spent every weekend for months with Miles. He seemed to find it perfectly obvious that he should come and visit so often, when it was so out of his way.

Now, finally, I got to go to him. All I had to do was sign

out at the front desk and walk the last long mile to the door. And I'd be free.

When I shouldered my way out of the building, blinking in the autumn sunlight, I looked down the walk and found a sky-blue pickup parked along the curb. Miles leaned against the truck's side, looking familiar in an old baseball shirt and bomber jacket. Something had changed in his face since graduation, though. Every time I saw him, he was a little brighter, a little happier, a little more excited about whatever the day had in store for him.

"*That* is Miles Richter," I said to Lil. "And he is not imaginary, thank you very much."

I took my suitcase, gave her a hug, and approached Miles.

I stopped in front of him, smiling. He smiled back and leaned down to kiss me. A feeling erupted in my stomach, like nothing would ever be the same again. Like good karma was catching up with me. Like someone had opened up the lid to my lobster tank and I was finally breathing in the shockingly fresh air.

"Ready to go?" His smile looked permanent. The tiniest German accent wrapped around his voice. "They're all waiting to see you." His fingers absentmindedly traced the scars on the left side of my face, but they were fading now, and didn't hurt anymore. I didn't try to stop him.

I climbed into the truck, breathing deep the smell of mint soap and pastries. He tossed my stuff in the truck bed.

"I bet they've made up stories," I said.

"Oh, they have." He glanced at me as he closed the passenger door. His impossible blue eyes sparkled in the sun. "They have, trust me. But they aren't as good as the real thing, of course." He slid into the driver's seat. The truck roared to life.

I glanced back only once as Miles pulled away from the curb. Wisps of violin music floated on the air. Tchaikovsky's *1812 Overture*.

I turned away and closed my eyes.

"They never are."

Acknowledgments

First and foremost I want to thank my editor, Virginia Duncan, for finding the truth in my mess of a story and dragging it, kicking and screaming, into the daylight. Without you, this book would have no backbone.

To Sylvie Le Floc'h, whose design work, both exterior and interior, absolutely stuns me every single time I see the book; to Tim Smith, for those sharp copyedits (and for appreciating my Norm Abram reference); and to Katie Heit and everyone else at Greenwillow and HarperCollins, for being such a welcoming family.

Thank you to my fantastic pit bull of an agent, Louise Fury, for taking a chance on this weird book (and my future weird book endeavors), and for knowing exactly when to rein me in and when to cut me loose. I honestly didn't believe in dream agents until you came along.

To Kristin Smith, for working so hard to make this book perfect, and for giving Alex her voice back. To the amazing Team Fury, for their unwavering support, and to the wonderful people at both the L. Perkins Agency and the Bent Agency.

A thousand thank-yous to Erica Chapman, whose belief in *Made You Up* started it all. (She'll try to be humble and deny this. I will ignore her.)

To all my critique partners who kept me going: Darci Cole, Marieke Nijkamp, Leigh Ann Kopans, Dahlia Adler, Caitlin Greer, Lyla Lee, Jamie Grey, Gina Ciocca, Megan Whitmer, Jenny Kaczorowski, and Angi Nicole Black. And thank you to Christina Bejjani, who keeps me sane in the little world of publishing. Also to the Class of 2K15, the Fearless Fifteeners, and We Are One Four debut groups. You made this journey so much easier.

Thank you to my friends who carried this book around high school in a three-inch binder so you could read it during class, and to everyone who ever asked to be mentioned in my acknowledgments, because you believed that one day I'd have acknowledgments to mention you in.

Thank you to Dominic and Andrea, for teaching me all the best ways to terrorize a younger sibling (I still haven't gotten over all those vile things you made me drink). And finally, thank you to my parents. They moaned and groaned every time I told them I was rewriting this book, but only because they knew it would be something when I finished.